WHERE HEROES ARE MADE

WHERE HEROES ARE MADE

Legendary GAA People and the Places That Made Them

JOHN SCALLY

Black&White

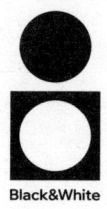

First published in the UK in 2025 by Black & White Publishing
An imprint of Bonnier Books UK
5th Floor, HYLO, 105 Bunhill Row,
London, EC1Y 8LZ

Copyright © John Scally 2025

All rights reserved.
No part of this publication may be reproduced,
stored or transmitted in any form by any means, electronic,
mechanical, photocopying or otherwise, without the
prior written permission of the publisher.

The right of John Scally to be identified as Author of this
work has been asserted by him in accordance with the
Copyright, Designs and Patents Act, 1988.

The publisher has made every reasonable effort to contact copyright holders of images in the picture section. Any errors are inadvertent and anyone who for any reason has not been contacted is invited to write to the publisher so that a full acknowledgement can be made in subsequent editions of this work.

Cover Images: Front cover: © Sportsfile / Piaras Ó Mídheach (Ailish O'Reilly & Corke Park); © INPHO / Andrew Paton (Cormac McAnallen); Donall Farmer (Jason Sherlock); © Adobe Stock (glow & grass); Back cover: © INPHO / Ryan Byrne

A CIP catalogue record for this book is available from the British Library.

ISBN: 978 1 78530 861 1

1 3 5 7 9 10 8 6 4 2

Typeset by IDSUK (Data Connection) Ltd
Printed and bound in Great Britain by Clays Ltd, Elcograf S.p.A.

The authorised representative in the EEA is
Bonnier Books UK (Ireland) Limited.
Registered office address: Floor 3, Block 3, Miesian Plaza,
Dublin 2, D02 Y754, Ireland
compliance@bonnierbooks.ie
www.bonnierbooks.co.uk

The GAA is where we all belong.
Jarlath Burns

Once an All-Ireland final is over, especially the last one of the year, it's like closing in something, but you're already looking forward to the resurrection. And like the flowers that grow after the flowers dying with the frost in the winter, the new ones will come if you're lucky enough to be around for them.
Mícheál Ó Muircheartaigh

John O'Mahony gave Leitrim the happiest day of our lives in 1994.
Mickey Quinn

In Clare, hurling is like our religion and Brian Lohan is like our God.
Tony Kelly

Jim McGuinness is the Rasputin of Gaelic football.
Joe Brolly

Armagh hate Down. Monaghan hate Cavan. They both hate Tyrone. But when it comes to each other, there's hardly a cross word between them.
Malachy Clerkin

To an exceptional group of heroes:

*Those who care for people with dementia or Alzheimer's –
and for all carers in their many forms.
David Bowie sang that we could be heroes just for one day.
They are heroes every single day.*

CONTENTS

Foreword By Michael Lyster — xi

Introduction: Home Truths — 1

1. The Jacks Are Back: The Hut — 5
2. The West's Awake: The NI7 — 35
3. Raising the Banner: Biddy Early's Lake — 46
4. Where Everyone Knows Your Name: The Club — 54
5. Giants of the Ash: The Village — 64
6. The Keys of the Kingdom: Castle Island — 70
7. The Boulevard of Broken Dreams: Round Towers Lusk — 86
8. Culture Club: Mauritius — 89
9. Bridges Not Walls: East Belfast — 95
10. Hair and There: The Barber Shop — 105
11. The Ties that Bind: The Family — 120
12. Hope and Tears: Ellis Island — 128

13.	Face the Music: Cúil Aodha	141
14.	Who Fears to Speak of 98?: Wexford	149
15.	The Torture Chamber: The Sand Dunes at Bettystown	155
16.	What It Says in the Papers: The Kildare Nationalist	161
17.	The Poet for all Seasons: Inniskeen	175
18.	Dunnes' Deal: Dunnes' Car Park Castlebar	178
19.	The Home of Hurling: Hayes Hotel	187
20.	Just a Lad of Eighteen Summers: The City of Brotherly Love	193
21.	Every Day Is Like Sunday: Croke Park	197
22.	Cavan's Fairytale in New York: The Polo Grounds	202
23.	Sing a Song for Ireland: Frognoch	206
24.	When David Beat Goliath: Mullinalaghta	219
25.	Seasons of Sundays: RTÉ	223
26.	Island in the Sun: Fiji	231
27.	The Lynch Mob: Bray	238
28.	The Master Storyteller: John B's Pub	245
29.	School of Thought: St Flannan's College	255
30.	Lion-Hearted: Trillick	266
31.	Giant of the Ash: The Limerick Leader	268
32.	King of the Kingdom: Waterville	271
33.	With a Little Help from Our Friends: Bansha	279

The Final Whistle   284

Acknowledgements   288

FOREWORD

Michael Lyster

For over thirty years I had the privilege of presenting *The Sunday Game*. More recently I have the pleasure of presenting my podcast *The Game on Sunday*. Both experiences have given me a front row seat in seeing how important the GAA is in Irish life.

Growing up in Galway I saw that at an early age. I attended school at the legendary football nursery St Jarlath's College. It gave us some of the immortals of the game like Seán Purcell and Enda Colleran.

As a boy I remember the great pride in the county when Galway won the three-in-a-row between 1964–6. I didn't think then we would have to wait another thirty-two years to see Sam Maguire returning to the West but when the late, great John O'Mahony guided a star-laden team to All-Irelands in 1998 and 2001, playing thrilling football, the pride in the county was plain for all to see.

Of course, few sporting occasions are remembered more affectionately than Galway's All-Ireland hurling triumph in 1980. Nobody captured the importance of place in the GAA more eloquently than Joe Connolly with his unforgettable speech in which he famously said: 'People of Galway, we love you.' And the late Joe McDonagh added to the strong sense of place with his unforgettable rendition of 'The West's Awake'.

At its core, the heart of the GAA is the strong sense of place and playing for the pride of the parish and county.

This book is a celebration of these great places and the people associated with them.

I hope you enjoy it.

INTRODUCTION

Home Truths

If you want one year of prosperity, grow grain.
If you want ten years of prosperity, grow trees.
If you want one hundred years of prosperity, grow people.
CHINESE PROVERB

Angels and demons dance within us.

Most of the things that we notice, we observe in passing, on our way to something else; then, every so often, something gives us reason to pause. Something catches our eye or draws our attention, and we're drawn for a moment to reflect on that which awakened us in this way. Without warning, we find ourselves falling into the abyss of a star-strewn sky or find our heart impaled by a child's laughter or the unexpected appearance of a beloved's face. Without warning we lose our footing in the silence broken and, in the breaking, deepened by the flittering of a butterfly we did not know was there. What is so extraordinary about such moments is that nothing beyond the ordinary is present. It is simply the primal stuff of life that has unexpectedly broken through the web of opinions and concerns that all too often hold us in their spell. It is life in the immediacy of the present moment before thought begins. These moments pass and the real question then for us is, 'What happens next?' From time to time what happens is that although the moment has passed, you reflect back upon it, and you realise that the subtle moment was a kind of homecoming. You settled, with a sense like *I belong here*.

Deep down I am very deep. However, I can sum up the meaning of the GAA for me in just one word in the meadow of delight.

Home.

Our love of our games shows itself in subtle ways. Like the Sligo fan who went into the Xtra-vision shop in 1997 intending to rent the Tom Cruise classic *Jerry Maguire* but instead asked for 'Jimmy Magee'.

Sometimes it manifests itself in a love of a native son. Witness Donegal native Tommy Martin's sheer joy when Michael Murphy made his return to competitive action for Donegal last February: 'It was as if an immortal had just stepped off the pages of mythology.'

For those who had been hibernating during the dark winter months Easter Sunday 2025 was a resurrection experience for hurling fans with two pulsating draws between Cork and Clare, followed by Tipperary and Limerick. It was like a double Spring miracle.

I hope Ryanair CEO Michael O'Leary was not talking of works like this when he spoke of 'books that are bullsh*t and generally written by wankers'.

This volume celebrates the great places associated with the GAA and the people associated with them. In the earth of the heart, these unique theatres of the real, meaninglessness is filled with meaning. They are the places that steer us home because they are our home. They give us our bearings, our compass.

INTRODUCTION

We live in an era when a new American president, memorably described by economist David McWilliams as 'a cross between Julius Caesar and Mattress Mick', has brought huge uncertainty to our political and economic systems. In troubled times these places are touchstones of hope and comfort. The sense of community thrives here like a flower growing in the crack of a pavement.

Everyone will have many of the same reference points for places that are central to the GAA such as Croke Park. New locations are emerging each year like Los San Patricios GAA Club in Mexico City.

Happily, I can still roll out of bed in the morning. What kills me though is picking myself up off the floor.

I have a strict regime going to the gym. I always walk past it. Hence my exposure to these venues has been as a spectator. Each of us has our personal places which we associate with the GAA so some of my choices are personal ones. I am very conscious that not everybody will agree with my selections, but I learned so much from my past mistakes that I decided I was going to make a few more. One of the biggest changes in the GAA in my lifetime is that it has become a global phenomenon and it is important to reflect that in this volume.

These are places that have the capacity to open our eyes to innocence: as if we can see the world again for the first time. Here there are no strangers, only friends we haven't met. They are locations that manage to be welcoming even on the dullest day.

Níl aon tinteán mar do thinteán féin
There's no place like home.
Home is where we give all of our heart to.
That is the real home truth.
Of course what makes home special is the people.
This book is like a magic carpet.
It will take you to many enchanting places.

1

THE JACKS ARE BACK

The Hut

Well . . . the Jacks are back all right and the way they are playing right now, the Galway backs are jacked.
MICHEÁL O'HEHIR'S COMMENTARY DURING THE 1974
ALL-IRELAND FINAL.

We need big gates not small hinges.

We sat in silence: him because of grief, me by knowing there were no words.

Despite our physical proximity he stood alone – as if on some small island in a vast ocean, no mainland in sight.

He shook his head.

Lost in the past.

As he squeezed his eyes shut I felt a sharp thrust into my own heart. I said what I knew were empty words. But I had to offer him something.

I feared, though, I would leave him more devastated than I found him.

He let out a long breath.

WHERE HEROES ARE MADE

Last year's Olympic Opening Ceremony in Paris concluded with Celine Dion singing evocatively 'l'Hymne à l'Amour' (Hymn to Love).

The last line of the song is a heartfelt prayer:

'Dieu réunit ceux qui s'aiment.' 'God reunites those who love each other.'

This sentiment has a particular resonance for legendary Dublin footballer David Hickey.

He has made Elizabeth Barrett Browning's lines his own:

How do I love thee? Let me count the ways.
I love thee to the depth and breadth and height
My soul can reach, when feeling out of sight
For the ends of being and ideal grace.

'How Do I Love Thee?' or 'Sonnet 43' is one of Barrett Browning's most famous poems. She was a renowned Victorian poet who managed to achieve acclaim in her lifetime. Her poems came to the attention of another famous poet of the time, Robert Browning.

The two poets eventually married but were forced to wed secretly because of Barrett Browning's father. He found out about the nuptials and disinherited his daughter. The romantic in Hickey approves of that kind of commitment regardless of what others think.

He experienced a grief so great it threatened to swallow him – the tragic death of his beloved wife, Yami, in a drowning accident in her native Cuba.

WHEN ALL IS RUIN ONCE AGAIN

Grief left him facing countless nights as if they were never going to end: a cycle of staring up into the darkness, of extreme exhaustion that made sleep almost impossible. It was as if he had entered some parallel universe in which everything was turned on its head, everything good in his life had been taken away and he wanted more than anything to step back through the looking glass of his old life – like the perfect penitent kneeling at an abundant altar.

Perhaps the simplest and most inclusive definition of grief is 'unfinished hurt'. It feels like a demon spinning around inside of us and it hurts too much, so we immediately look for someone else to blame. In the ghost of loss we have to learn to remain open to our grief, to wait in patient expectation for what it has to teach us. When we close in too tightly around our sadness or grief, when we try to fix it, control it, or understand it, we only deny ourselves its lessons.

The human instinct is to block suffering and pain. This is especially true in the West where we have been influenced by the rationalism of the Enlightenment. As anyone who has experienced grief can attest, it isn't rational. We really don't know how to hurt. We simply don't know what to do with our pain.

At night you have to believe in the light.

Like everybody locked in a nightmare, Hickey wishes he could wind back the clock.

A broken heart will never end.

A true love will never end.

THE WHOLE TOOTH AND NOTHING BUT THE TOOTH

Trying to write about Hickey is like an excavation site – the challenge is to sift through so much to find the pieces which represent each stage of his life and then try to weave them seamlessly together to tell his story. He has not been able to eat a meal for six years because of a twenty-year battle with cancer. To an outsider his life appears stable, ordered, without drama, but, beneath his calm, controlled exterior, there is a sense of fear and quiet trepidation, a low-level dread caused by the diagnosis. He manages to keep these threatening forces at bay, but only just. At any given moment, the ground might give.

The cancer which has leaked into his life, offers brief glimpses of clarity, too; moments of consciousness. Afterwards, of course, the veil falls back down again, and ordinary life resumes in all its mundanity. He is a forceful advocate for regular dental check-ups to ensure people at risk get the benefits of early intervention.

Back in his childhood, life and death were different. A woman accompanied an undertaker in the hearse taking the remains of her aunt from Dublin to her home place in the country. This was a common practice in Ireland. A son sat in the hearse when a father's coffin was taken to the church and graveyard. As regards his cancer journey, he doesn't consciously think of its metaphorical meaning. Nonetheless, the intensity and the claustrophobic feeling of two people trapped together in the confined space of a car or, in this case, a hearse resonates powerfully for him. Everything is condensed. That terrain is as much a psychological space as a physical one. In that sense, it's very fertile ground for tangled thoughts.

The mind that is stretched by new experience can never go back to its old dimensions. Tragedy brings out the better angels of our nature. A huge element of Hickey's energy is channelled now into his campaigning work. There is something of the dissident in him believing that injustice in one place is a threat to justice everywhere.

This is evident in his choice of causes, such as Cuba and Palestine, as one of his core convictions is that there may be moments when we are powerless to prevent injustice, but there must never be a day when we fail to protest. Tyranny is not easily conquered. The manner in which he reanimates himself daily is one of his most appealing attributes.

His convictions impinge into all areas and awaken a sense of duty. A cinema buff, one of the actors he most admired was the late Donald Sutherland because of 'how active he was against the Vietnam war with Jane Fonda'.

He believes that evil is unspectacular and always human and shares our beds and lunches at our own tables. When the subject of American foreign policy crops up it is best not to mention a trumped-up presidency. He is from the Jimmy Carter school: 'A strong nation, like a strong person, can afford to be gentle, firm, thoughtful, and restrained. It can afford to extend a helping hand to others. It is a weak nation, like a weak person, that must behave with bluster and boasting and rashness and other signs of insecurity.'

He speaks for those who can't speak for themselves. Although he is not particularly religious, he has embraced the biblical imperative: 'Learn to do right; seek justice. Defend the oppressed.'

Of course, there are other Hickeys at work: a sharp laconic wit and a satiric touch that Jonathan Swift would have admired have long been part of his arsenal.

He sometimes uses a crisp, pared-down language to great effect – one that is a model of clarity and always mellifluous. He can move from the here and now to the mystical. His words like silent raindrops fall. One of his great strengths is his directness. There is a deceptive ease to his style.

NUMBER ONE

With autumn starting to nip around Dublin Bay Hickey is engulfed by memories of warm and pleasant evenings – when shadows were distancing themselves from the goalposts and players, elongating and straining away. The light was winning

WHERE HEROES ARE MADE

decisively. The memories flow not to the great days in Croke Park but to 'the Hut' (known to others as 'the Shack') – the lantern that lit the Dubs' path.

At Paddy Cullen's funeral in 2025, stories of his role were retold with nothing less than love.

After Seamus Darby's sensational last-minute winner for Offaly against Kerry in 1982, Mikey Sheehy's goal in 1978 is the most famous ever scored in an All-Ireland final. Paddy Cullen's frantic effort to keep the ball out was memorably described afterwards by the legendary Con Houlihan, who wrote that it was like 'a woman who smells a cake burning'.

The goal spawned two riddles:

Q: What's the difference between Paddy Cullen and a turnstile?
A: A turnstile only lets in one at a time.
Kerry fan after Cullen conceded five goals in the 1978 All-Ireland final.
Q: What's the difference between Paddy Cullen and Cinderella?
A: At least Cinderella got to the ball.

Paddy's role as Dublin manager in the 1990s was also considered. It was the time when Meath and Dublin were drawing more often than Michelangelo – a four-game saga which enthralled the nation in the first round of the Leinster Championship in 1991. At a time when Ireland was going through soccer mania after Italia 90 and when the nation was under the spell of Jack Charlton, the series of games showed that reports of the GAA's demise were premature.

Despite their intensity the four-match saga did produce one moment of light relief. Paul Curran was dropped for the third game but came on in the second half and scored the equalising point. A few nights later, Dublin manager Paddy Cullen had a team meeting with the players and did some video analysis with them. Cullen was severely critical of the forwards' first half performance and turned to Curran and asked him: 'Where were you in the first half?' To the hilarity of his teammates Curran replied: 'Sitting beside you, as a sub on the bench Paddy!'

David Hickey will always remember his colleague with fondness:

'Paddy was a special fellow: kind, warm, funny and great company. A real loss.'

He elaborates:

'I have few memories of the 1974 final. I remember walking onto the field and being shocked at the condition of the pitch. It was like a ploughed field in parts. Some stupid motorbike show had taken place a few days before and they destroyed the pitch – so much for the GAA's priorities. I felt we were always in control on the day but, looking at the game since, I realise that was not the case. In fact, a number of great saves (not just the penalty) by Paddy Cullen, kept us in touch when the game was up for grabs. In the end, in an eighty-minute game, Heffernan's training regime ensured that if we were there or thereabouts at sixty-five minutes it was "game over" for any opposition.

'Who was Paddy Cullen? Greatest goalkeeper of all time before Cluxton, joker, funny guy, life and soul of the party, rapier wit, supremely confident? Yes, all of the above but, even more so, he was an outstanding human being.

'Paddy was an electrician but because of his fame he was made head of human resources at the place where he worked. As Paddy described it he didn't know what human resources was. He interpreted it as getting resources for the humans, which is precisely the opposite to what management's idea of it was. Their idea was to reduce all workers to a line on an excel spread sheet and make sure their "productivity" went up as their wages and entitlements went down. Increase shareholder profit – that was the responsibility of management and little else mattered. His first job was to fire Joe who had been late for work every morning for three weeks. This was Paddy's acid test. Paddy called Joe into his office for a serious chat, it turned out that Joe was late because his Honda 50 was finished. He had to drop a disabled sibling to a special school and then go to work. Without the Honda he had to get two buses to get to the school and then two to get to work and that's why he was late. Paddy solved the problem not by firing Joe but by getting him a new Honda! That was Paddy Cullen, the human being.

'When I first came onto the panel Paddy was already well established not only as Dublin's keeper, but also as Leinster's. He was the main man on the team in the late sixties and early seventies. My memory of him was playing as a sort of sweeper keeper, one minute making point-blank saves, the next minute winning a high ball on our twenty-one-yard line against the opposition full forward. As the training heated up in the spring of 1974, Paddy was the life and soul of those gruelling sessions. Around 8 p.m. every Tuesday and Thursday a westward bound 747 would fly over Parnell Park. Every Tuesday and Thursday Paddy would look up and say, "That's us next year, lads, on our way to the USA." As All-Ireland Champions. Paddy had been there earlier in the year with the All Stars and was smitten by the place but before we had won our first game he actually believed we were going to win the All-Ireland that year. He kept that going all year and eventually we started to believe it too. He was a huge player for us always but particularly that year. He should have been awarded player of the year in 1974 but Heffo was given it and accepted it!

THE JACKS ARE BACK

'Jimmy Keaveney and Paddy were hilarious when they were together. "Paddy was the only goalie in the world who became a millionaire on the back of a goal he let in", was Jimmy's verdict on Mikey Sheehy's controversial goal in 1978. Paddy went on to manage the team to the 1992 final which they lost to Donegal. I watched that game at 8 a.m. in Chicago having driven over from Madison Wisconsin where I was working at the time. I was the only Dublin supporter in the hall that morning (just like McGettigans in Dubai in 2018 when Dublin hammered Tyrone). They threw that match away, but what I remember about that year is a story about "Doers" Paddy Dwane. Halfway through the second half Paddy told Doers to warm up. Doers took off his tracksuit and started to "warm up". The match was very tense and Paddy forgot about Doers until, after ten minutes of warming up, Doers shouts at Paddy Cullen: "For f**k's sake Paddy how hot do you want me?"'

SWEET DREAMS ARE MADE OF THIS

In that hut Hickey's team's ideas were dreamed and danced as well as thought. They made their own music and were in tune with themselves. The Hut has the power to whisper stories in his ear, transcending melodies to unravel sagas filled with love, heartache, and the pursuit of something greater. It offers a captivating tale that captures not only the ears but also the very emotional core. In this haven voices intertwined like old friends sharing secrets, and words were more than just sounds – but experiences that echoed through time.

It has become the accepted wisdom that the 1990s were 'the revolution years' in hurling because from 1994 to 1998 Offaly, Clare and Wexford deprived the three traditional superpowers of hurling – Kilkenny, Cork and Tipperary – of the All-Ireland crown. However, the idea of the revolutionary era is undermined

WHERE HEROES ARE MADE

by the fact that after their five years away from the top table the three traditional powers won every All-Ireland between 1999 and 2012. Could it be that the real 'revolution years' were in the 1970s when Hickey's Dublin team turned Gaelic football into an urban Ireland obsession as much as a rural Ireland one and when their rivalry with the late Mick O'Dwyer's Kerry team enthralled the sporting nation?

On narrow streets of cobblestone David Hickey has no doubts about the achievements of the Dubs in the 1970s:

'The Dublin team had a huge sociological impact on life in the city and county. We achieved this because we were not just a group of footballers. By accident of circumstances, we filled a huge void in the spiritual life of the county and city. We gave the local population something to feel good about, something that was theirs, something they could touch and feel part of. Characters like Jimmy Keaveney and Paddy Cullen replaced the English soccer player in the hearts and minds of Dublin youth and saved the GAA in Dublin and also in Ireland.'

WHITE BOOTS AND DODGY JERSEYS

Hickey begins in delight and ends in wisdom. He recalls his early years in the Dublin jersey with wry amusement:

'We played in Roscommon in the league in 1972 in awful weather and lost the match. My only memory of the game was that our full-back Mick Jones from Skerries was, I think, the first Gaelic footballer to wear white boots. If ever a man should have had a low profile it was Mick. All I still remember is this pair of white boots chasing the Roscommon full-forward before he planted the ball in our net. Twice! It was Mick's last game for Dublin. He set back the arrival of the white boot in football by years – don't know what happened to the boots!'

Further personal disappointment lay in store for Hickey:

'After the match I asked Mick Leahy, one of the backroom boys, if I could keep my jersey as a souvenir of my four years' service to the team. Mick said, "That jersey is very muddy, let me give you a clean one." He gave me a lovely unused jersey in a plastic bag. I thanked him profusely and put the jersey in my bag. On the bus home I remember sitting beside Tony Hanahoe. He gave me this advice: "Dave," he said, "never retire from anything." I took his advice, got the rugby thing out of my system and was back two years later for the wild ride that was the Dublin team of the seventies. And today we are both working, as neither of us ever retired from anything.

'When I got home that night and took out my souvenir jersey it had no number on the back and the crest had been hacked off the front. Probably Jim King's idea rather Mick's. That was part of Dublin in the rare old times too!

'I got my own back a few years later. It was in Carlow before a Leinster championship match on the usual stifling June day. We had asked the county board to get us short-sleeved jerseys for the summer. In the dressing room we were handed long-sleeved jerseys by Mick. I was pi**ed off, we didn't ask for much, and the little we asked for was ignored. We had no idea of how powerful we were. I took my jersey and asked Mick, who kinda was the logistics man to give me the "team" scissors. I then proceeded to neatly cut the sleeves off my jersey to Mick's disgust and surprise. We won that game and we won the All-Ireland that year with short sleeves, probably a first in GAA history.

'Mick's other great line (he had some good ones) was in Croke Park after the 1974 final. He came into the dressing room flustered and asked us if anyone had a spare pair of trousers with them. Amid the hilarity expressed at the idea that someone would go to an All-Ireland final with a spare pair of trousers,

WHERE HEROES ARE MADE

Mick explained that some great supporter had torn the arse out of his trousers trying to get over the wire at the Hill, as he tried to get onto the pitch. And he needed a pair of trousers.'

THE MAGIC FACTORY

Hickey immediately bats away any compliments about his career: 'Reputation is what other people think you are!'

He believes the seeds of the Dublin success were sown in a hut:

'Parnell Park is in Donnycarney, not a very accessible place, yet every Tuesday, Thursday and Saturday for seven or eight years twenty-seven or thirty guys made the pilgrimage to that Holy of Holies known to us then simply as "the Hut". Georgie Wilson and Stephen Rooney thumbed lifts, in from and home to Balbriggan, I got the bus from Portmarnock and walked the two miles from Killester to Parnell Park, Kevin Moran arrived on his Honda 60, Jim and Bernard Brogan arrived on a motorbike, TH (Tony Hanahoe) arrived in his Mercedes, Brian Mullins in a bambino. The car park was small but it was more than big enough as many used public transport to and from training.

'But it was like the Camino de Santiago de Compostela, a trail of believers inching their ways towards the Holy Grail, which was the next match (we never looked beyond that), and inherently, unconsciously, understanding that it was the journey not the destination that was the reward. Tony Hanahoe always emphasised: "Guys this won't last forever, and you will remember these days as the best." Tony had insight, and he was right.'

In this heady environment the ethos was very unambiguous. They believed that what they obtained too cheaply, they esteemed too lightly:

'Bernard Brogan, after a poor run of less than his usual stellar performances, when asked what he thought the problem was, came out with the suggestion, "Kevin I think the problem is I'm just not enjoying my football at the moment." You could hear a pin drop in the Hut. "What the f**k has inter-county football got to do with enjoyment Bernard?" thundered Heffo. "Hickey, are you enjoying your football?" he demanded giving me the evil eye. "Of course not, Kevin," I spluttered out, dropping Bernard in it.

'Actually, it was true that the enjoyment was the training, the comradery, the craic, and the retrospective enjoyment, not the actual playing. I could honestly say enjoyment is not a word that springs immediately to mind when thinking of the actual games.

'We sacrificed our youth, our hearts and souls to those football days. Seven of the best years of our lives where everything played second fiddle to our team, and the realities of life could wait. It was an addiction. I personally lived for those evenings in Parnell, year in, year out. In those days the National Leagues started two weeks after the All-Ireland final which meant that for seven years we played year-round with no break for summer holidays, no working abroad for the summer, also practically no social life.

'Year in and year out I trudged up Collins Avenue from Killester having got the 6 p.m. bus from Portmarnock. We togged out in the shed which the county board called the dressing rooms, trained pretty hard for two hours, back to the shed for the Marietta biscuits and cup of tea and the Hut for a session, then home with Jimmy Keaveney. I did this from my seventeenth till my twenty-ninth year and it was the centre of my existence. Everything else was secondary – study, girlfriends and friends.'

Hickey points to their recipe for glory:

'Why were we so successful? There are many elements involved, obviously, but above all we were a "Band of

WHERE HEROES ARE MADE

Brothers" – a group who bought into the enterprise, who sublimated personal goals for the collective, and who above all enjoyed (and still do) one another's company.

> *We few, we lucky few.*
> *We Band of Brothers.*
>
> (HENRY V ACT IV) – WILLIAM SHAKESPEARE

'Our Parnell Park experiences are the treasure of our lives, and the reward is that that group are still together, available at the drop of a hat, if one of us is in trouble, to answer the call, and once again battle for another Tuesday.'

Yet his nostalgia is tempered by the unsentimental:

'We togged out in what were grandly called the dressing rooms. If the Department of Health ever visited this cesspit they would have closed it down as a community health hazard. It was a green building with a reddish corrugated iron roof, the kind of kip you see in outback Australia. I don't know when it was built but it was well past its sell-by date when we were there.

'There were actually two changing rooms, and we used the one on the left for training. It was fairly cramped for twenty-six or twenty-seven players. In the centre of the room was the treatment table where Lorcan Redmond gave you the "treatment". Lorcan, a really lovely and great, kind man, was selector, physio, masseur, holder of the "magic sponge" and nutritionist. He also was our psychologist, which essentially meant telling you that you were better than you actually were.

'The floor was made of splintering wood that was well worn by fifty years or so of muddy boots when football boots were really boots. There were two showers between the twenty-seven of us, winter and summer, with variable quantities of water, but we often didn't bother and went home covered in muck and cleaned up there.

'The floor of the showers was covered with a thick layer of slime, a combination of muck, wintergreen, sweat and Jeyes Fluid. Paddy Gogarty described it thus: "The good thing about the showers . . . is that the floor was so dirty you knew no virus, bacteria, or fungus would ever survive there." He may have been onto something there because I never developed a verruca and can't remember any of the others having a problem either.

'Between the two changing rooms was a tearoom where twenty bottles of milk and the Marietta biscuits were dished out by Christy Thompson with the grace of a capo at Auschwitz.

'My God, I still can't believe how fu**ing mean spirited our county board were to a team that was the golden-egg-laying goose for them and the GAA in general. And yet the joy and camaraderie that was indigenous to that group made us oblivious to that contemptible treatment. Jimmy Gray tried to build new dressing rooms in Parnell Park in 1976 but Jim King managed to squash the idea.'

Two people did stand full square behind the team though:

'Summer and winter in all kinds of weather Christy "Sweets" Downes was there. Christy would kick back all the footballs that flew out of the training area. He would run up and down that bank behind the goals to retrieve the balls. He travelled everywhere with us and he always brought a large bag of Fox's Glacier Mints which he doled out to us after training sessions.

'Christy was a single man and the team were his family, and he was part of the team. He was the only person who ever did anything for the team out of his own pocket! In the end the Dublin County Board got tired of him and wouldn't let him travel on the team bus. This was after our team had dispersed and there was nobody to stand up for him.'

TOP CHEF

Hickey also feels a debt of gratitude to Ireland's answer to Nigella Lawson:

'Seán Kinsella, owner of the Mirabeau restaurant, was our other great supporter. Seán was Ireland's first celebrity chef. We had a brilliant night in his restaurant in 1976. He closed the Mirabeau for the night and we mingled with stars like Alma Carroll, ate food the like of which none of us, with the exception of TH (Tony Hanahoe), would ever have seen. Jimmy Keaveney asked for a spear rather than a fork for his New Zealand prawns. We drank jeroboams or was it methuselahs of champagne. Alma Carroll and Ray Treacy sang with us. Raymond Smyth told stories.

'I think it was the best night we had together as a team. It certainly put our tacky, post-All-Ireland dinners to shame. I also remember occasions when the Rolls Royce would arrive in Parnell Park with amazing food for us, and we were raised on fish and chips! Seán was always kind and self-effacing and a genuine fellow and one of the few who did anything for us.

'Heffernan didn't like it and put a stop to it. He felt Mariettas and milk were good enough for us, a kinda no pain, no gain mentality. Or an "in my day" attitude. Seán never used us in any way. All these outings were private and never publicised. I'm sorry that when he hit hard times, I didn't think of doing anything useful to help him. Again, I regret my lack of insight. He was ahead of his time as a person and truly loved our team, and really was the only person that ever did anything for that team. All the other events had payback for our benefactors.'

BAND OF BROTHERS

For Hickey it was all about the brotherhood of the players connected by an invisible thread, but there was a hierarchy:

THE JACKS ARE BACK

'On 17 September 2022 I was driving in the September sunshine south, retracing the journey undertaken a million times in the past towards Parnell Park. This time I would travel past Parnell down towards the hospice in Raheny. The hospice is built on the grounds of what was The Oval – the former home of St Vincent's football and hurling club. I was visiting Brian Mullins maybe for the last time. On the drive down my mind wandered and wondered back to what we like to see as the Rare Auld Times.

'It was a long time ago but as I pilgrimed to Brian's bedside on this third week of September 2022, I was transported back to 1974 and realised (not for the first time) that none of it would have happened without Brian Mullins.

'I think of the Cork game, 4 August 1974, the day Mullins and our team arrived from nowhere with a loud bang. His penalty that day ended the game and announced our arrival! It was quintessential Mullins. Confident, arrogant and extremely competent. There had been no pre-match plan, we had never practised penos. Mullins just picked up the ball, coolly side footed it to the net and launched a football revolution. That Dublin team was a great TEAM. We had twenty players who all played for the team. We were not the best twenty footballers in Dublin, but we were the "best twenty". To paraphrase Notre Dame's Lou Holtz: "I play my best fifteen not my fifteen best". However, Brian was the exception. Physically, mentally, *tactically* and technically he had it all. He was in my opinion the best footballer of all time. We would have won nothing without him as his absence in the 1977 League final and the 1980 Leinster final proved.

'I think one of the great survival stories in sport is Brian's recovery from a catastrophic car crash just before the Leinster final in 1980. I remember seeing the car on the Clontarf Road the following day. It was concertinaed against a lamppost with the driver's side completely crushed into the front passenger seat. How he survived was a miracle. He spent four months in hospital and ended up with one leg two inches shorter than the other. He didn't play again for two years. He returned to win the All-Ireland in 1983 and his performance in the semi-final against Cork was heroic. He was an absolute monster that day, owning midfield and scoring, yes, a penalty that sent Dublin on their way.

'Brian was also a great rugby player and played on the Leinster under-19 team with my brother Mike. Coming back from Ravenhill in 1973, Mike and (former Irish captain who toured with the Lions in 1980) Johnny Robbie spent the time trying to convince Mullins to stick to rugby as he would surely play for Ireland if he continued. He dismissed this idea off hand. Playing for Dublin was far more important for him. Mike tells how, during a match for the Leinster 19s in London, Mullins made a break for the Home Counties line. On the 22 there was just the full-back blocking Mullins' way to the try. Mike was outside him for the shoo-in try and screaming for the ball. Mullins sold the full-back a dummy (he was more than glad to buy the dummy) and sailed in between the posts with a smile for Mike.

'In real life Brian was a much-loved head teacher in the biggest school in Ireland in Carndonagh in Donegal before becoming head of sports in University College Dublin (UCD). He was also involved in setting up the UCD access programme to help young people back into education. In fact, Brian's contribution to life in Ireland far transcends his achievements on the field of play.

'Brian's great quality was his humanness. He had great ideas, a lot of experience, and the generosity of spirit to offer his support to people who were struggling. It was the last of his many, to quote Wordsworth, "little, nameless, unremembered, acts of kindness and of love". But not unremembered in my case.'

Hamlet says to Ophelia: 'God hath given you one face and you make yourselves another.' He is hinting at the distinction between who we are and who we pretend to be. Part of the appeal of Brian Mullins for David Hickey was that he only had one face:

'In this age of celebrity and celebrity worship, where real achievement is undervalued, Brian Mullins was a hero. He was a man of substance who through his hard, generous work and time freely given enhanced the lives of countless people in Ireland.

'American historian Daniel J. Boorstin puts it well: "The hero was distinguished by his achievements, the celebrity by his image or trademark. The hero created himself, the celebrity is created by the media. The hero was a big man, the celebrity a big name."

'He adds: "We lose sight of the men and women who do not simply seem great because they are famous BUT ARE FAMOUS BECAUSE THEY ARE GREAT."

'That was the essential Brian. He was a very private guy in an age when we are daily regaled by celebrities "opening up" on their huge trials and tribulations. Brian's private life was his private life! Brian was authentic.

He was a big man. A man of dignity. A man who cared:

'Typical of Mullins who did not do interviews: "No comment . . . and you can't quote me on that!"'

UNITED WE STAND

The Hut spawned a new superstar:

'He turned up out of nowhere (Good Counsel) and was togging out beside me in the dressing room before some sort of "friendly" against Kerry in Tralee in February or March 1976. He stood out immediately for his confident, friendly, outgoing personality. I was a bit fazed to be honest by his lack of awe. But once I saw him in action, I was completely won over.

'Kevin Moran was a force of nature, incredibly strong mentally and physically. He was only with us for two years but in that whirlwind tour he had a phenomenal impact on the spirit and the competitiveness of the Dublin team. He became instantly one of the lads off the field, and his contribution on the field was seismic. The opening minute of the 1976 All Ireland final was my greatest memory of Kevin on the field.'

In the canon of GAA mythology one moment encapsulates Moran's glittering career:

'We won both league and championship that year, playing the best football we ever played. It was seventy minutes of single-minded commitment to the team's goal: win the next ball every time. I think our approach was epitomised by Kevin Moran's bursting run in the first move of the game, not just Kevin's run but the surge of energy that emitted from the whole team movement around that great statement.

'That confident, swashbuckling style set down a marker for Kerry and for us, his teammates, that this was our day. If he had scored that goal it would probably be marked down as the greatest of all time from a Dublin perspective. It would have been right up there with Kevin Mac's 2011 one.

'However, in retrospect, I think not scoring was even more important. It set the tone of the game and it hardened our resolve. We got no tangible reward like a goal for that great move which impressed on us that this had to be repeated over and over for the seventy minutes, and that fairytales don't happen, they have to be worked for. As a result of Kevin's run we were galvanised as a group. Looking at that opening it wasn't just

Kev but a wave of Dublin players that swept through the Kerry team defence. That opening tempo was maintained for the entire game and it was our best-ever performance as a team, no doubt! Kevin's abandon framed the context of that game; his approach epitomised the mantra of that team on that day.'

PARTY GAMES
Like his teammates, Moran knew how to enjoy himself:

'1977 started with a US tour as All Ireland winners. It was the usual stuff, lots of hospitality, lots of drinking, lousy matches and then more drinking. Our base was the Richelieu (pronounced Richy Loo) situated on Geary and Van Ness. It was a real kip. After a few days a group of us – Mike, Kevin Moran and Tommy Drumm, Martin Noctor and myself – hired a car and took a trip down Highway 101 to Monterey, a pretty beautiful drive. Monterey I wanted to see, because of the John Steinbeck connection. We stayed at a Holiday Inn on the beach, visited Cannery Row and played golf at Pebble Beach near Carmel. Then we stopped off at the beautiful sounding Half Moon Bay only to find out that it was "The Artichoke Capital of the World" and home of the "Biggest Pumpkin Festival in the World". We drove through!

'On our way back to San Francisco, I suggested a detour to see the Big Sur, "the longest and most scenic stretch of undeveloped coastline in the USA" or "one of the most beautiful coastlines anywhere in the world" depending on the guide you read – anyway, sounded like a great idea. I made the suggestion as I was the driver and was met with "Big Sur my bollix, Davy. We could have been in the Richelieu for the last three days having a great time. No way". The speaker was Kevin Moran but I got the feeling there was pretty much universal agreement in the car. Back to the Richy Loo and I never got to see the Big Sur.'

Hickey was surprised when a rare opportunity came knocking on the door for Moran:

'I have a photo of the two of us walking out to training on the Saturday morning in March 1978 when he told us he was leaving for . . . Manchester United. It was a true shock-and-awe situation in the literal sense of that phrase. We were devastated to lose our young friend after such a short association. But to a man we accepted it. Kevin Moran gave everything to the cause in his two years and although we hated the thought of losing him, we knew in our hearts that this was the chance of a lifetime for Kevin. Nonetheless, there was a certain uneasy feeling in my bones that this was the beginning of Götterdämmerung – the Twilight of the Gods.

'When Kevin went to Manchester, Tony Hanahoe and Kevin Heffernan went over with him to meet David Sexton who was the manager at the time. I remember Hanahoe telling me after of what happened at that meeting. Kevin addressed the two Dublin men as Tony and Kevin and he referred to Sexton as Boss. Welcome to professional sport!

'A few months after leaving, Kevin came back to visit us and a meeting was held in the Hut. Tony had invited Heffo along out of courtesy. Tony made a speech, a few of the lads said a few words, then Tony said, "I would like Kevin now to say a few words." Immediately Heffo got up and Hanahoe had to say: "No, Kevin, I meant the other Kevin." You could hear a pin drop!'

For a time, Moran tried to ride two horses:

'Kevin played for us in the All-Ireland final of 1978. Dave Sexton allowed Kevin a week off to come over and prepare for the final. Kevin explained to them that we were his mates, it was an amateur game, and there would be no problem. The Monday after the final Kevin showed up at training in Manchester on crutches (torn hamstring), nine stitches in a head wound and with a hangover. Some amateur game! He was never released by Manchester again. Kevin Moran: primus inter pares (first among equals).

'Kevin moved on to achieve great things with Manchester and was central to Ireland's great days when Jack Charlton's team almost won the World Cup. He never lost touch with us and invariably turns up for our annual golf trips and funerals. For us he has lost none of the qualities that made an instant hit with the entire team. He was only with us for two years but I actually hardly think of our team either before or after he left. It seems he was always part of it. I remember the first day he arrived in Parnell Park with an old anorak, on a Honda 60 (Kevin wouldn't be seen dead on a Honda 50) and despite all his success he is the same Kevin – the Kevin of the Hut.'

THE BLUE PANTHER

Few indulge in self-reflection at the level at which Hickey has become a master. He still grieves for another star of that team, Anton O'Toole, though the depth of their connection is a crumb of comfort to him. The late legend is not simply a memory for Hickey but a real presence – a presence he can feel more than see, a comforting reassurance that eases the hurt into a deeply filled sadness, yet that same sadness as it becomes reflective, lifts him. He draws on a depth of emotion that is raw and honest:

'It is still impossible to reconcile the fact that he is gone. I am looking at a photo taken in 2019 of Yami and Anton at our home in Balbriggan. It was essentially Tooler's wake. I didn't realise it was also my darling Yami's wake. Six months later they were both dead, and I am still part of that race known as the "living dead" and probably will be for the rest of my life. My friends have tried to "turn my nights to days" but the loss of Yami in my life has gutted me. Anton's loss is much less acute, but he also visits me often and I must say it always brings a smile to my spirit.

'That day in April, actually we had three consecutive days of glorious sunshine and great craic, were de facto Anton's last break from the palliative care unit in St James Hospital. All the "lads" turned up, along with Anton's family, and Tooler regaled us with anecdotes and stories for most of the day speaking Ex Cathedra from his motorised wheelchair as if he was going to live forever. He had that sort of "Zorba" quality about him and, yes, men like him should live a thousand years.

'We all loved him and it was typical Tooler easy humour, style and grace. We all – me, Mullins, Drummer (Tommy Drumm), (Alan) Larkin, Doyler (Bobby Doyle), (Stephen) Rooney, Georgie (George Wilson), the Rile (Paddy Reilly) and Macker (John McCarthy) – were transported back to the rare old times and amid laughter and repressed tears slowly began to realise we were witnessing the twilight of a God.

'Another photo from 2018 has Alan Larkin, Bobby Doyle, Paddy Reilly and John McCarthy waiting with Anton for the final word in the radiology department in Beaumont Hospital. These brothers in arms waited with him, which was like waiting for the verdict of a rigged trial with a "hanging judge" in Alabama in the thirties. After that, Anton had salvage surgery and a few good months (on the surface) for him, and a few sad but great months for the rest of us. Those precious months were in a large way gifted to us by Professor Donncha O'Brien, neurosurgeon and former Glen Rovers and Cork hurler. His skill, attention and kindness to Tooler was way above and beyond the call of duty, and very much appreciated by us all.

'Anton's funeral was a genuine celebration of his multifaceted life. People from all walks of life were there; his racing friends, his music friends (Mary Black sang) his friends in the press, all his old comrades of the seventies and all the current Dublin team. What was unique about Anton was that his old "enemies", Mikey Sheehy, Ger Power, Seán Walsh, and many of that great team, showed up, confirming how much Tooler was loved and how great a group of guys that Kerry team was. The Galway lads were there in force too; T.J. Gilmore, Johnny Hughes, Mick Judge, all there because they loved the guy.'

FOREVER FRIENDS

Hickey and O'Toole shared a long history:

'Anton came into my life after a hard match at under-16 level in O'Toole Park (of all places) in the spring of 1968. I asked Brendan Lee after the game who was that guy at midfield for Synge Street with the big rugby boots who had played a blinder. "That's Anton O'Toole" Brendan answered, kinda amazed that I didn't know who it was. He didn't make the minor team that year or the next and that stupidity probably cost us All-Ireland. The next time I met him was three years later (1971) when we lined out together for the under 21s against Meath in Drogheda. We lost that game and I didn't see Tooler again until March 1974.

'UCD rugby were beaten in the semi-final of the Leinster Cup in March 1974 by Bective and that evening Kevin Heffernan called home and asked me to come to training next Tuesday. I had nothing planned for the summer so I said yes. My expectations were one, maybe two championship games then back to UCD rugby in August. As it happened, it was six years before I played rugby seriously again as a twenty-eight-year-old, first with Clontarf and then in La Rochelle.

'The next six years, the great days, were spent with that "Band of Brothers" the Dublin seventies team of which Anton

O'Toole was a key figure. Tooler had been a member of the Junior All-Ireland-winning team the year before and had been on the team when they lost the final of the Division 2 National League in March 1974. He told me afterwards (after the final in 1974) his thoughts as I strolled into training that Tuesday. They went something like this: "They're wheeling these f**kers back out again, that's the end of my championship." Thankfully it didn't work out that way.'

MASTERPIECE
Hickey felt that O'Toole had no peers on and off the pitch:

'He was physically and spiritually a "once off", absolutely. My brother Michael describes him best as being like a Picasso painting: individually the parts made no sense, but the big picture was a masterpiece!

'That's Tooler, Anton, the Blue Panther, the first of the 1974 All-Ireland-winning team to die. From his weird-shaped size thirteen feet to his enormous size nine hands to his beautiful compassionate smile, Anton was almost a new type of human being. It all came together both on and off the pitch. Anton O'Toole was our life saver on many an occasion on the field of play, and even more occasions as an example of how to treat people. I have never met a soul that had an unkind word to say about him, and I would say he taught me by example far more than I ever learned about empathy and compassion from any medical school professor.

'As a footballer I have no idea how it worked, but that guy when he got going was unstoppable and the 1977 semi-final was one of the great one-man shows of all time. The "greatest" game of all time was his greatest day. In his day he was unmarkable and not only because of his skill, but also because of his mental and physical toughness.'

O'Toole brought effortless grace to the task:

'Playing against him must have been like playing on an octopus. A friend of mine, Willie Downey, describes Micheál O'Hehir doing a Dublin match on the radio. His abiding memory are the words "... Anton O'Toole is on the ball for Dublin, Anton pretends to go left ... and goes left." I'm sure Ger Power can vouch for that description. The only other player that had a similar type of movement was the Colombian and Parma soccer player Faustino Asprilla, also known as the octopus.

'I'm not going to dwell on Anton's football achievements, they are more than adequately documented elsewhere, but we were connected football wise one last time in 1983. I was back in Dublin and got invited by Kevin Heffernan to play in a friendly in Parnell in March of that year. I was in good shape having worked in Waterford for the previous year and played rugby with Waterpark and football with Killure. I was doing well till I went over on my knee and tore a cartilage and my anterior cruciate ligament. The "renowned" surgeon in Jervis Street told me after his arthroscopic evaluation that I should face the fact that my playing football days were behind me. He was wrong of course but I was out for most of that year.

'I always told Anton he got my place but what is the truth is that without him Dublin would not have won that All-Ireland. So, I guess it was a lucky injury!

'Anton was much more than a footballer and I think it's a great pity that he never had a family – a few more Toolers certainly would have made the world a better place. He was kindness personified, he had time for everyone no matter who you were or what you did. I remember during the "hay days" a group of three girls used to travel from Naas, no matter what the weather, to bring their friend O, who had special needs, to see us train.

'Anton, after every training session, as we all raced to get the milk and biscuits (God, the county board really treated us like sh*t), before they were all gone, would spend fifteen minutes chatting to these great, kind, human girls. That was Tooler; he treated everyone the same, he was one hundred per cent authentic and interested in them and their opinions. This was his approach to everyone and we all loved him for it.'

Hickey and O'Toole were kindred spirits – not least in their penchant for straight talking:

'He also had the courage of his convictions and would let Heffernan know in no uncertain terms if and when he was talking sh*te.

'Anton passed away in the hospice in Harold's Cross in May 2019. He actually loved the place and spoke of it in glowing terms. He was never alone. Tommy Drumm describes dropping in one evening and finding Tony Hanahoe, a bottle of Dom Perignon (true Tony) and Tooler laughing their heads off with Anton's brother Pedro and Geraldine his sister-in-law. Paddy Reilly and John McCarthy even slept over in his room some nights to give both the family and Tooler a break!

'We all miss him so much. With misty eyes the great realisation comes to me that Yami and Tooler may be gone but are with us para siempre – forever.

'We would never have won anything without "the Blue Panther".'

HOME THOUGHTS FROM ABROAD
Time has not dimmed Hickey's bittersweet memories of 'the Hut'. If his memories were put to a song it would be 'Bob Dylan's Dream' where he wishes in vain that they might sit

simply in that room again – a small fortune he would pay if their lives could be like that:

'We would never have won anything without those special days in the Hut. We were children of the Hut.

'It was a kip. It was a small shack where "everything" could be discussed and "what happened and was said in the Hut (like Vegas) stayed in the Hut". JFK, it is said, when he expected twenty at a rally, he booked a room for fifteen so that when the meeting was reported in the press it would always state there was "standing room only". The Hut was a similar kind of experience. Thirty freshly showered (well, showered at least) fellows crammed into this tiny space wondering whether to offer a platitudinous comment or risk everything by saying something important. The atmosphere was usually quite tense, however it's the "funny incidents" I remember now.

'Before the 1979 All-Ireland Final when Heffernan asked if anyone needed a sleeping tablet prior to the game, nobody put up their hand (we were all cool, tough guys). Eventually Mick Holden RIP put up his hand. Kevin was taken aback because Mick was the most laid-back of the group. When he expressed surprise that Mick of all people needed a sleeping tablet, Mick answered: "Well, Kevin, it's not for me, it's for me mother. She can never sleep before a big match."

'Bernard Donovan at the start of the season stated: "Every year at this time we have a new panel of players, but the only thing that changes is the subs who never get a chance to show if we are any good. There was some truth in that statement. In an effort to advance his claim at a subsequent training match, Bernard slammed me into the fence at Parnell Park leaving me with a three-inch gash in my right arm, the scar I can see now. It was a week before the first round of the 1976 Championship – I can still see Heffernan's face!

'John McCarthy, after the group presented him with a wedding present in 1974, said: "I'm not inviting ye to the wedding but ye can come to the christening next Saturday after training." That, in the Ireland of 1974 with its strict Catholic mores, was some statement!'

In July another of the band of brothers was lost with the death of Seán 'the Doc' Doherty. For David Hickey part of his legacy will always be the decisive intervention against Kerry 'in the greatest game of all time': 'That catch is a highlight of GAA folklore. It was a real leap of faith and won 1977 for us.'

2

THE WEST'S AWAKE

The N17

There are times when fate makes a decision and isn't for turning.
MICK O'DWYER

He is the man who lives by his own lyric: Maroon and White Forever.

As a passionate fan of Gaelic football in particular, Leo Moran is proud that his band The Saw Doctors have become part of the furniture of the GAA. In 2009 the GAA began its 125th year celebration with a *Late Late Show* special devoted entirely to the association's history. The opening of the show was The Saw Doctors' rousing rendition of 'N17'. That famous road, the GAA and The Saw Doctors are now part of a holy Trinity.

It helps that Moran was born into football:

'My father, (Jimmy), played for Galway at minor and junior level. Sadly, he never passed those genes to me! He refereed a county final at twenty-four and was chairman of the Galway County board at twenty-eight which Jim Carney tells me would have been very unusual for such a young man back in the day.'

WHERE HEROES ARE MADE

SAME OLD TOWN

Football was part of the fabric of Tuam life:

'In the 1970s we had less colour in our lives; it was pre-band, pre-Macnas, pre-boomtime economy, pre-Boomtown Rats. But we had something to interest, amuse and stir our passions. Football. Playing, watching and hearing the stories of legendary feats. The Master, Seán Purcell, and Frank Stockwell were the heroes of the town. Their legacy and that of other great footballers inspired and thrilled us. They had won the All-Ireland in 1956 and the "three-in-a-row" team were more recent, but still a long time ago to a six-year-old.'

Leo was reared on a diet of disappointment:

'In 1971, my father, a long time GAA sufferer, county player and administrator, brought me to my first All-Ireland final. We were up against Offaly. I sat on his knee in the Hogan Stand: it rained and we lost. I remember Tony McTague doing the damage, and Willie Bryan. I recall the journey up on the train from Tuam with the colour pages in the Sunday papers and I remember the endless journey home of delays, drunkenness and the smell of spilt beer.

'Our house is no more than 200 yards from Tuam Stadium, the traditional centre of Galway football. In those days of the early 1970s, we, the local kids, served as ball-boys and ball-girls to our heroes, Tommy Joe Gilmore in particular and Brendan Colleran who was always very kind to us. Three nights a week kicking the ball back in from the concrete seats. We loved it. And every night, as darkness enveloped the scene, we'd go out on the playing surface and have a few kicks with our heroes. It was sheer heaven.

'In 1973, Galway met Cork in the final. I sat on my father's knee again. I recall the nineteen-year-old Morgan Hughes coming into the team at the last minute: Galway were good, but not good enough. It was Jimmy-Barry's day. Aside from the wonderful inspiring point that Tommy Joe Gilmore scored, I can remember very little else.

'The following year we made it to the final once more against Dublin. Heffo's Army. Croke Park was an arena of intimidation. The Dublin fans had an air of English soccer fans. Urbanised. The Jackeens versus the Culchies. Liam Sammon had a penalty saved by Paddy Cullen. Guess what? We lost again.

'It felt like I would never get to see the maroon and white celebrating on the pitch after the final whistle. My heroes were brave and skilful, but not winners. If the All-Ireland was over at half-time, Galway would have won a load of half All-Irelands, especially the hurlers.'

Leo experienced a famous rivalry in Tuam:

'I went to school in the CBS and we played everything Gaelic – football, soccer and basketball – but of course Jarlath's (Saint Jarlaths College) were our big rivals. Every year we'd head up to the back of the stand and every year we'd lose to them but I remember going on to Athlone as well to cheer on Jarlath's. Then when I was in Inter Cert, I think it was 1980, didn't we finally beat them. Eddie Steede of Corofin was on the team. It was the first time we beat them in fifty years, I think. We were flying flags for months. We beat them twice that year, in the Connacht final on St Patrick's Day as well, but then lost to Maghera in the semis in Sligo.'

RE-JOYCE

Laughter punctuated our chat when we recalled the late Billy Joyce. Once, before he played a big match in Croke Park, Billy took his Galway colleagues by surprise by asking: 'Did ye ring the airport?' Brian Talty asked him why would they ring the airport. He replied: 'To tell them not to have airplanes flying over Croke Park. I'm going to be jumping so high I don't want to be in collision with them.'

Billy was not a man to take prisoners. When Galway were getting beaten in midfield by a particular player, Joyce would turn and say: 'Time to take the chopper out.' The next ball that came their way a thud and a sigh of pain was heard. Galway were playing Roscommon in Pearse Stadium on an atrocious wet day in the 1978 Connacht final. Before the throw-in his opponent Marty McDermott turned to Billy: 'Tis an awful day for football.' Joyce looked at him and said, 'You don't have to worry about it. You won't be out in it very long.'

He was right!

THANK YOU FOR THE MUSIC

In pursuit of glory Leo found himself answering the call to music. Where did the band's iconic name come from?

'The story goes that someone who worked at the local sawmill was very lazy, so the boss decided that some motivation was required and presented him with a white coat – from that day onwards he was known as "The Saw Doctor". Mind you, the person who originally told me that tale later denied it. Of course there was Guinness involved in the telling!'

In 1991 The Saw Doctors released their legendary debut album, *If This Is Rock and Roll, I Want My Old Job Back*, with smash hits 'I Useta Lover' and 'N17' and other enduring songs like 'Red Cortina', 'Presentation Boarder', and 'I Hope You Meet Again', rocketing the band to stardom.

The band, with its two core members of Davy Carton and Leo Moran, have carved a unique niche in the Irish cultural landscape. Thirty years later, Tolü Makay's version of 'N17', with the RTÉ Concert Orchestra, was a phenomenal success, with over 500,000 streams on Spotify. It highlighted that The

THE WEST'S AWAKE

Saw Doctors' songs still speak powerfully to a contemporary audience.

In April 2025 the band went viral again courtesy of a haunting version of their classic 'Same Oul' Town' with the forty-five-piece RTÉ Concert Orchestra to end an episode of *The Tommy Tiernan Show*. Within thirty-six hours the video of the performance had already been viewed over half a million times and quickly rocketed up the charts. 'It turned out even better than we could have imagined. Some privilege to play with the orchestra,' Leo said.

NEVER MIND THE STRANGERS

'N17' was inspired by the fact that so many Irish people were emigrating in the 1980s. Not surprisingly, the band have a big audience abroad:

'Irish Americans were our natural seed audience . . . They were the only people who knew we existed when we went over first – but after many trips we fit into a lot of different areas now. I would say that in Britain the more north you go the more boisterous the show! We don't try and be too serious – it doesn't seem to suit us! We've always had songs taking the subject matter more seriously like 'I Hope You Meet Again', because it shows another side of us.'

By 1998 The Saw Doctors were on the crest of a wave. Then came the most magical of days:

'Sunday, 27 September 1998. Galway won their first All-Ireland in thirty-two years. It was exhilaration and ecstasy. It was so magical after going through all the years of defeat. It was nearly worth losing all those games because we felt such sheer elation. I was delighted for the players when they won again in 2001 because they needed to win a second All-Ireland to be considered a great team. As a fan in 2001 I felt satisfaction when we won but nothing like the joy of 1998.

WHERE HEROES ARE MADE

'I loved Michael Donnellan. He invented a new way of playing. Of course, I also loved Ja Fallon our local hero in Tuam.'

The Saw Doctors found themselves immersed in the celebrations in 1998:

'Along with the exhilaration of the game itself, the excitement of the championship campaign and the universal praise of the young Galwaymen's style of football, we got to play our songs at an open-air concert on College Green the night before the game.

'We were also honoured to be asked to perform at the team's victory celebrations in the Burlington Hotel after the match. We got permission from the band who were booked to play a few songs. They made us pay a deposit in case there was any damage to the equipment on the stage. I couldn't understand why they needed one but they said there would be people getting up on the stage. I told them they were crazy because nobody would be coming up to join us on the stage. We were thirty seconds into our set when half the Galway team were on the stage with us.

'Then came the homecoming in Tuam. Standing room only. Forty, maybe fifty thousand people awaited the victorious Galway team's homecoming in the Abbey Trinity car park. At last! The dream was now reality and it had come about unexpectedly. A young team, confident, mostly coached into the ways of success at St Jarlath's College, had managed to cross the bridge in Athlone in possession of the Sam Maguire Cup. It was brilliant, wonderful . . . and chaotic.

'On 12 October that year we performed the finale to our 1998 tour-end gig at London's Royal Albert Hall. As the show reached the climax, some of the victorious Galway football team trooped onto the stage, hoisting the Sam Maguire Cup aloft, and there was such an explosion of noise. I will never forget that moment.'

THE WEST'S AWAKE

In 2024 Galway looked to be on the edge of glory after they sent Dublin crashing out of the championship. It led to a famous piece of commentary. Ollie Turner of Galway Bay FM declared:

'Galway have won! It's the greatest day Galway football has seen in over two decades. And every man, woman and child stands to applaud Pádraic Joyce and his gallant Galway men. Sweet mother of Jesus they have pulled off the unthinkable! Forget about Taylor Swift. Shake it off at the Aviva and come over here to Croke Park because you are witnessing the West awake. Gaillimh Abú!'

THE GREEN AND RED OF MAYO
Despite being a proud Tuam band, The Saw Doctors, have a huge bond with neighbouring Mayo:

'When I was growing up, basketball was huge in Tuam, and Ballina also had a huge basketball culture, so there was a big connection. People used to go and play against each other and stay in each other's houses. We had loads of the Ballina lads staying in our house when I was a kid. At the time, Liam McHale was the best basketball player in Ireland and he was the best basketball player Ireland had ever produced, he possibly still is. So, there was always that great connection between Tuam and Ballina.

'Of course, there's a huge connection between Tuam and Mayo in general because of the boarding schools at the time. You had people coming to board in the Mercy (Convent School), the Pres (Presentation Sisters Convent School) and Jarlath's. I went to Tuam CBS, so I had no direct connection with those people but I knew of them.

'In later years, when you got independent and began doing a bit of travelling, Mayo was the place to go. I didn't have a car myself till I was thirty, but I'd stay in Galway with Joe Wall of

WHERE HEROES ARE MADE

The Stunning, and he'd get the loan of his mother's car, and we used to head off to Westport. I found that when you go there or anywhere else on the western seaboard, you always bump into people that told you, "I went to school in Tuam."'

Galway and Mayo's famous football rivalry cemented that connection stronger:

'Mayo people were coming to Tuam for decades for the matches. Tuam loved seeing the Mayo people coming and staying; there was always great sociability between the two. Really, when you think about it, it's an imaginary line between Milltown and Ballindine, and it's a system imposed by the British on us and it's a system we've taken to heart. It's funny how we think we're different but we're much the same.'

The anthemic 'Green and Red of Mayo' was inspired by one of Leo's many visits 'across the border':

'In 1990, when The Saw Doctors were just up and running, 'I Useta Lover' had just been released and Paul Cunniffe was home for the first time since 1981. There happened to be a gig on Clare Island. The Maimin Cajun Band were playing, and we knew them from being around Galway. Paul had a car, so we headed off to Clare Island and we hadn't a clue where we were going. That was our first time going there and it was a magical weekend, it was just beautiful out there.

'The gig didn't start till 2.30 in the morning, and we loved it, and we were coming back in on the boat and we wrote the words for the 'Green and Red of Mayo', with Gerry Mulholland, who prefers to go by his Muslim name, Jarir Al-Majar. We wrote that coming on the boat back in, looking across at Croagh Patrick and the hills beside it. We saw the green grass and the red heather and we said sure it's no wonder their county colours are green and red. We wrote it first as a poem and then Davy came up with a melody and it became a song. It was released in 1992 and we never looked back after that. We had a solid connection with Mayo, which we always had before, but this solidified it. It's lovely to hear it at the matches. It's a great buzz. It is brilliant to think that people like the song.

'It was pure natural for us. We were great fans of Mayo even before Galway won the All-Ireland in 1998. In 1989, 1996 and 1997 we were well behind Mayo. I actually went to the 1996 final, the drawn game, that was awful disappointing. I remember that match being over and it was worse than a loss for some reason. There was no result at all, but you knew the result was ominous.

'We would have loved to have seen a Connacht team win. The rivalry is at its highest at the border areas – Milltown/Ballindine, Clonbur/Cong and Ballinrobe, Caherlistrane and Headford/Shrule. I had lived back in Clonbur for a while, and the rivalry is very strong there. I went to the All-Ireland semi-final when Galway played Derry in 1998, and I was standing on the platform waiting to get on the train home and there were a few Clonbur lads that I knew, young lads, standing beside me. I heard one of them saying, "Well, at least we're as good as Mayo now!" I didn't think about it like that but that's the way the lads on the border think about it.

'I tell Mayo people we wrote a trilogy for them: 'The Green and Red of Mayo'; 'Clare Island' and . . . 'To Win Just Once'!'

In 2023 on his visit to Ballina President Joe Biden remarked:

'And I can tell you what: That song speaks to me.' He continued, 'It goes like: "Oh, the feeling [that came] over me to stay . . . forever more, forever more. Stay forever more. The Green and Red of Mayo, oh the Green and Red of Mayo, oh the Green and Red of Mayo."'

Although Leo is best known for his songwriting and as Ireland's answer to Johnny Marr on the guitar, he also brings his vocal talents to 'Hay Wrap' which is an ode to Willie Joe Padden. His truth was on the march and nothing could stop it:

'To me Willie Joe is *the* icon of Mayo football. I really enjoy his company. He was interviewed once on Mid-West radio and the interviewer said: "The Saw Doctors made you famous." Quick as a flash he answered: "No. I made The Saw Doctors famous."'

A CLASSIC QUIP

Leo Moran has a nice line in self-deprecation. When I asked him what he would like as the band's obituary, his response was: 'They weren't too bad.'

As Mike Tyson put it everyone has a plan until they get punched in the face. Leo Moran's plans have occasionally gone awry. With the solemnity of a man making the sign of the cross he confesses he has a unique claim to fame. For a few minutes he wished to have Padre Pio's glove to rub on some venerable joints:

'I nearly killed Seán Purcell! In 1991 we had a famous concert in Tuam Stadium called *The West's Awake*. It generated a lot of attention and the next day Jim Fahy was interviewing me in the town square for the RTÉ news. Out of the corner of his eye Jim saw Seán walking nearby and called him over to ask him what he thought. There was a ball around us and Jim decided it would be a great idea for his report if he filmed Seán catching a ball as he did so often in his glory days. The problem was that the ball was a bit high for Seán and he overreached and fell over and smashed his head on the pavement. There was blood flowing like a river. Seán was not moving and I was full sure he was dead.

'I remember thinking: *Jaysus I've killed The Master*. It was a very strange feeling to have killed Galway's greatest-ever footballer! I was in a state of shock but tried to revive him by opening his tie and then Seán began to stir a little bit and opened his eyes again. I blurted out: "Seán, you're not dead." He looked up and, considering he was literally just out of a concussion and had blood all over his shirt, came back immediately with this most incredible quip: "Ah, sure I often got worse when we played Annaghdown."'

3

RAISING THE BANNER

Biddy Early's Lake

On your way to greatness, you will fall, but like a Phoenix rising from the ashes, you too shall rise again.

MICHAEL BASSEY JOHNSON — *NIGHT OF A THOUSAND THOUGHTS*

The dead ask the best questions.

We are answerable for them.

In 1995 Clare ended a sixty-three-year wait for a Munster Championship triumph and eighty-one years without an All-Ireland title, culminating in a 1–13 to 2–8 victory over Offaly in the All-Ireland final, consigning to the dustbin of history 'The Curse of Biddy Early'.

Biddy, a healer, used herbal medicine and was accused of witchcraft. Her legend passed down through the generations and a hex became inextricably linked with the chalice of torture the Clare hurlers drank from in their barren years. One claim was that all of the Clare players who acquired Munster medals in 1932 (a full fifty-eight years after Early went to her eternal reward) would have to pass away before Clare would go on to land another title.

RAISING THE BANNER

There were a few Clare fans who thought the curse of Biddy Early returned in 1998 as the hurling team became mired in an extraordinary series of controversies, notably the 'Colin Lynch saga' and when the late Jimmy Cooney blew the final whistle early in the All-Ireland semi-final replay with Clare leading Offaly and attacking. Their captain that day Anthony Daly does not accept the excuse:

'It's just life that some people would blame Jimmy for costing us that title, but, honestly, I really don't think any genuine Clare fans ever held it against Jimmy. I know for a fact that none of the players or management did. Yeah, it was a pity but that's one of those things. Life goes on. Unfortunately for Jimmy and his family, that great life is over now. So we should be remembering what Jimmy did, and the legacy he left, rather than a genuine mistake that, unfortunately, Jimmy had to carry to his final day.'

Legend has it that 'the witch of Feakle' put a curse on the hurlers of Clare. Over a hundred years later the wizard from Feagle would finally undo her curse. It's a nice story but it would be more plausible if Biddy Early hadn't died ten years before the GAA was founded.

THE STUFF OF LEGEND

To walk with Ger Loughnane to the lake in Kilbarron is to travel into the irreversible, irresistible rhythm of ancient times. There is no posturing: when he feels the need to, his attacks are full-blooded as he assails Ireland's sacred cows with a vengeance. Equally, his laugh is a deep rich rumbling sound that fills the space with genuine amusement.

 He explained that one of Biddy's powers was said to be her capacity to prevent the fury of the fairies. Patrons would visit her who had been bewitched by the 'little people'. One example was Frankin the farmer who had his entire herd of cattle cursed by the fairies and they all became seriously sick. After looking into her bottle, Biddy identified the problem. He had planted a whitethorn bush along a fairy path in his field. She told him to go home and get rid of the bush. Once this was done, his full herd immediately returned to health. Legend has it that even 'the great Liberator' himself, Daniel O'Connell, paid her a visit.

Loughnane has no time for the dark art of banality. He explained that many believed that Biddy's bottle lay in the lake after her death. His tone was clipped and cold, tight with suppressed anger as if I was a favourite son, who had disappointed him when I asked him if even a small part of him had ever believed in the curse. His eyes slid coldly over me as he said ruefully, 'That nonsense was just an excuse for the failures of the past. When I took over the Clare team we were not looking back we were only looking forward.'

Poker players have a saying: 'I am all in.' In every role he took on Loughnane was all in. I learned quickly that he is not a man to mince his words. After the first meal I cooked for him he assured me that I am uniquely talented in the kitchen. As I glowed with pride he clarified that my special talent is to turn lasagna into 'las-agony'.

I told him, 'We would have less arguments if you weren't so pedantic.'

He replied, 'I think you mean: fewer.'

He brought his sharpness to his punditry. Witness his reaction to Davy Fitzgerald's appointment for the second time as Waterford manager:

'He'll present his plan as one only a rocket scientist could devise. He'll have eight different ways of playing. One with a sweeper, two with a sweeper, up as far as eight – with a sweeper.

'And, after some deep thought, he will declare that these are the best players he's ever worked with and, while everyone else has written them off, they might surprise a few people.'

However, he is anxious to correct one report. It is not true that after the birth of one of his younger siblings he asked his mother: 'Was another baby really necessary?'

It is also fake news that he once greeted a new priest to Feakle: 'You're very welcome Father. I hope you'll be very happy here but if you're any good you won't be here long.'

WOOD YOU BELIEVE?

Hurling managers can be tough and leave no place for sentiment. One of the images John Kiely uses of himself is that of a spear. While normally he treats his players with a velvet glove – when necessary he applies the pressure in a very pointed way.

My enduring memory of meeting Kilkenny legend Richie Hogan is of his personal warmth. However, I was also taken by the nuance in the way he spoke about Brian Cody – including his recollection of Brian Cody roaring at him at half-time in an All-Ireland quarter-final against Limerick to 'shut the f**k up and sit the f**k down'. He went on to ask Hogan: 'When the f**k are you going to start living up to the potential that you have?'

When he needed to as Clare manager, Loughnane was like a thorn looking for a side. If it was easy everybody would do it. Duty has no sweetheart. He applied kitchen rules to his players: 'The last day to complain was yesterday.'

BRINGING IT ALL BACK HOME

The best way to unlock the secrets of Loughnane the man is to walk with him, in the softness of the western mist, through the fields in Feakle bequeathed to him by his late father. A hint of a frown is replaced by a boyish smile and he seems to shed years in an instant.

Without understanding the pride and passion Loughnane feels about Feakle it is impossible to understand how excruciatingly painful two choices were for him. Disappointment is etched all over his face as he speaks about them many years on. Like any advance, Clare's march to glory did not arrive without unintended entangled complications. At various times he needed to be calibrated, complicated, coldhearted. He was not afraid to give up the good to arrive at the great as he took the job at a time when his strong faith in Clare hurling seemed like a single candle burning in an empty Church:

'In my first year as manager I was faced with two very tough decisions. I had to let two of my former teammates from Feakle off the panel. I had played with Tommy Guilfoyle for Clare. In the 1986 Munster final he was marvellous and he was the one who had kept Clare in the game. He started training with us in the autumn of 1994 but he had a problem with his hip and wasn't up to the pace and I reluctantly had to let him go. That cost, and continues to cost, me a friend or two in Feakle.

'To have to release one friend, neighbour and teammate is bad enough but I had to let go a second one as well. Worst of all, he was a huge hero in Feakle.

'Val Donnellan had been on the panel for all the league games in 1994–5 and he had trained really, really hard all through the winter. I always thought that he'd be ideal for Croke Park because it was a smaller pitch and although he hadn't great pace he had fantastic skill. I always had it in my mind that if we needed a goal in Croke Park he could come on and get it for us, and that would be the day we would use him.

'There was one game which brought matters to a head. We didn't bring him on for the last league match in Cork. A few days later I got a letter from Val. I never opened it. I knew straight away that it was telling me that he was pulling out of the panel. I gave it to Tony Considine to read and when he did, he said, "Isn't that terrible?" I never asked him what was in the letter but Val was off the panel. That was it. These were two men who had won a county championship with me in 1988 but they had to go. We needed people who were going to give themselves completely to what we decided. They had to have faith in what we did.'

One of the sweetest moments in Loughnane's career came in the wake of the Munster final in 1995:

'The highlight for me was when we brought the Cup to Feakle. My home place had supplied a number of players to the Clare team down the years. Dermot Sheedy had played in the Munster final in 1954 when Clare were hot favourites but were well beaten. We had Séamus Durack, myself, Val Donnellan and Tommy Guilfoyle, who had all played in Munster finals but had lost. To bring back the Cup was so satisfying. Everybody was there. All the older generation who had followed Clare all their lives were there. There is something really special about the GAA, that feeling of community it generates. People are interested in other sports but there is no other sport that produces a local pride like that.'

Where we love is home – that place that our feet may leave, but not our hearts.

CHANCING HIS ARM

Some managers seem to have the strategic capacity of a kitten in a washing machine. In contrast, Loughnane believed that idealism was impotent without realism. He was a great man for clever ploys. After his famous interview on Clare FM in 1998 at the height of the Colin Lynch controversy, as Billy Keane colourfully put it, he 'got more stick than a lazy donkey during the turf-cutting season.'

If you know your enemy and you know yourself you can win any battle. For all the intensity of his passion and desire to win he nonetheless could stay calm and focused during a match which enabled him to offer a penetrating analysis of the team's performance at half-time. Never was this talent more needed than the 1995 Munster Championship when Clare trailed Cork by four points and faced the wind in the second half. Loughnane defiantly told his team, 'The ship has sprung a leak but we are not going down!'

'The show looked really over, especially as we had been beaten badly in the League final. I was praying for half-time. It couldn't come quick enough and I clearly remember as I spoke, Mike O'Halloran, who was as mentally tough as anyone on the team, looked at me for the first time straight in the eye. He knew immediately it wasn't the normal half-time speech of the "Come on now, lads" variety. It struck a chord even though we went seven points down in the second half. It was as if something magic had occurred – even though we were playing against the wind and Seánie McMahon broke his shoulder.

'The half-time speech was central to our revival but, important as it was, going in on the pitch to drive them on was equally crucial. That was the first time the players ever saw me doing that. I can still see the look of surprise on Liam Doyle's face when he saw me coming on. I could almost see him thinking, *Christ, there's something big going on here.*

'I was up and down and across the field, talking to players, encouraging them, telling them the tide had turned and that we were going to win even though we were seven points down. This set the scene not alone for a marvellous victory but established the pattern for the years ahead.'

His main worry going into the 1995 Munster final was an injury to one of his most trusted generals. Given the absolute centrality of Seánie McMahon to the Clare team, Loughnane resorted to unusual tactics to conceal his injury:

'In the week leading up to the game there was a debate about whether Seánie should play after his shoulder injury. Opinion in our group was divided. Their job was to advise me. My job was to make the decision. I decided that we'd do something I never did which was to have a match between backs and forwards for five minutes. Nobody was trying too hard but Seánie seemed fine.

'The problem was that we knew that the first thing that would happen was that Limerick were going to hit him on the shoulder. We decided to strap him up on the wrong shoulder. Practically the first thing that happened was that a Limerick forward crashed into Seánie's shoulder. There was a terrific outcry from the crowd but it was the wrong shoulder! Seánie was outstanding in the Munster final.

'There are men, then there are men. Then there's Seánie McMahon.'

4

WHERE EVERYONE KNOWS YOUR NAME

The Club

What comes easy won't last long, and what lasts long won't come easy.

ANONYMOUS

In the GAA it's not ultimately about who holds the power. It's about where the power is held.

If fans are its lifeblood, the heart of the GAA is the club.

The club is the gift that no Gaelic games fan can renounce. It is the unbroken chain in the association's ageless passing of wisdom.

As a boy my twin ambition was to become a star player for both Saint Brigid's and Roscommon. Sadly, neither materialised for me. My underage career with Saint Brigid's was distinguished. It was distinguished by how undistinguished it was. In search for insight I went to somebody who has left a more significant imprint on my club than I did. Although he is deeply immersed in the club today, he was born a long way from it.

WHERE EVERYONE KNOWS YOUR NAME

BOOM SHAKALAKA

He has become a national institution. He is to basketball in Ireland what Ted Walsh is to racing and just as Ted has shaped the national vernacular with phrases like: 'I rode her mother' (a reference to a horse lest there be any confusion) Timmy McCarthy has carved a unique mark onto the national consciousness with the immortal: 'Boom shakalaka!'

'When I began out working on television, I was given the same advice by the late great Jimmy Magee and Ger Canning – "be yourself". I'm not trying to copy anyone, this is my style, you can only be yourself. The phrases that I use like "downtown" or "coast to coast" would be normal basketball lingo. But I don't know where Boom Shakalaka came from. I was commentating on one game, and it just came out. Then it became a phrase that I used. No idea where I heard it if I heard it anywhere.'

RTÉ sports presenters are encouraged to be their authentic selves. In April we lost Ian Corr, former head of Radio Sport. Ian once tore strips out of a presenter (in very colourful language) for changing his accent on air. Ian's punchline was that, if he wanted someone with a mid-Atlantic accent, he had any amount of them around the corner in 2FM!

Timmy has stretched his wings to cover a Ryder Cup for RTÉ, and even those who stay hale and hearty listening to Marty enjoyed his appearances on *The Sunday Game*. There he showcased his linguistic brilliance with gems like: 'John Mullane: he shakes, he bakes, he scores!' For years he was Ger Canning's stats man during his commentaries of big games.

McCarthy played over one hundred times for Ireland at basketball – both captaining and coaching his country. In 2023 he was inducted into the Basketball Ireland Hall of Fame.

WHERE HE SPORTED AND PLAYED

He is a native of Cork where he left school at fifteen:

'On the northside we're very clear where we're from. We're working class, so we're very prepared to help each other and support each other. When I was growing up, my mother and the neighbours would help each other out; they all knew each other's kids, they'd all help out with feeding them and looking after them. When I later moved to the southside, it wasn't like that.

'On the northside, we didn't have much – but we had so much. We didn't have the trappings of wealth or luxury but we had the gift of love and affection and friendship and camaraderie. I see that in someone like Roy Keane. He got that from his parents and community.'

McCarthy, like his grandmother, has a philosophical streak of his own:

'None of my generation went to college so it was a very, very simple background. It taught me about the importance of doing your best with whatever you're given – and you're not better than anybody else, but you're not worse than them, either.'

He left school at fifteen to work on the yoghurt production line of the CMP Dairies where his father was a supervisor. Although to the outside world he was the personification of self-assurance, for years the lack of a third level qualification undermined his confidence. As he worked a different shift than his Dad, he had to walk an hour to get to work, then another hour back home where at the end of the week he handed half his salary to his mum.

After another job making wheel moulds for articulated lorries, he landed a job a few years later as a sales rep for New Ireland Assurance:

'I can still remember coming home to tell my parents, God rest their souls, the news and seeing the pride and smile of my mother: that her son had got a job on the South Mall and would now be wearing a suit.

'The people of the northside were incredibly good to me. They paid their insurance because they now had Maggie Kelly's son collecting it; they didn't want to be in arrears with Maggie Kelly's son and leave her and him stuck. And they bought a lot of insurance from me. I was a Norrie. And they were going to do their best to support one of their own.

'I always talk about the northside of Cork being like Munster rugby in its golden period. Leinster were more nonchalant and classier and probably more skilful but Munster rugby was about heart, leaving it all on the field.'

In Cork his links with the GAA intensified:

'Back in 1988, Ger Cunningham asked me to train the St Finbarr's hurlers. The philosophy then was that you'd go off and run laps around the pitch. I had them use the hurley and sliotar in everything they did. It was an incredible time, amazing people at the club on and off the pitch. We won the Cork Senior Championship, which was a big deal.

'A few years ago, David Power – who took Tipperary to the Munster football title in 2020 – became the Wexford manager. He asked me if I'd come in as part of his coaching team. Looking back, we lost by a point to Kildare in Leinster. We weren't that far away. And we were the highest goal scorers across all four divisions and had the best disciplinary record.'

SETBACK

In life, sport and business all was going well for Timmy McCarthy and then in the presence of his devoted wife Anne all his certainties suddenly crumbled:

WHERE HEROES ARE MADE

'It was 28 February 2018, during a vicious snowstorm. It was 11.01 a.m. I remember the date, I remember the time, I remember where I was sitting when I was told I had cancer. I was devastated and burst into tears when the doctor told me. I was crying with fear, crying with anxiety. Your mortality is right in front of you, you think you're going to die. That was the first thing I asked the doctor – "am I going to die?"'

The previous year he had found he was going to the bathroom at an alarming frequency. A visit to his GP led to consultations with some specialists for a range of check-ups and scans that showed up nothing of concern, but a consultant urologist, suggested he undergo a biopsy, "just to be sure to be sure to be sure".

'I have bad news for you,' he said. 'I'm really sorry to have to tell you this but you have prostate cancer.'

After being told that he had the most aggressive form of prostate cancer there is, McCarthy tried to apply some of the advice he regularly dispensed to chief executives in his work as the CEO of McCarthy Consultancy: control the controllables.

The first challenge was to inform his children of his news. The test run was Karen, his daughter, who had just beaten the snow and managed to get back home from college in Limerick where she was studying physiotherapy:

'It was the hardest thing I've ever had to tell anyone. Because Karen is my princess; I've always called her Princess, ever since she was a child, and I still call her that even though she's now an adult. And this was the first time in her life that her dad couldn't fix something for her. I couldn't fix this cancer. I had to depend on other people to fix this disease. So, we just held each other for the longest time in the hallway in our house.'

Then he rang his sons, Brian and David, snowed in in their houses in Ferbane and Moate respectively:

'I wanted to keep on this planet as long as I could and do everything I could do to enjoy time with my family. I was very clear on that. I'd get bad thoughts but once they came in, I kicked them out. I was going to do everything I could to get through this.'

The following week he faced surgery. So aggressive was the cancer in his prostate – ninety-five per cent of it was covered with a tumour – the surgery lasted three times longer than the average prostate procedure:

'First, my mortality had been challenged; then my humanity was. I was incontinent. I remember being helped out of the bed by the physiotherapist and I saw I was wearing nappies and so I had all these emotions.'

There followed eighteen weeks of chemotherapy. It brought unpleasant side effects including diarrhoea, persistent fatigue, loss of taste of his food and pins and needles in his fingers and toes.

HOMEWARD BOUND

As his recovery took hold St Brigid's came knocking on the door. Over twenty years earlier the call of work had brought McCarthy to Kiltoom on the Roscommon side of Athlone. Through an accident of geography he became a 'Brigid's man'.

For a generation Saint Brigid's had been a sleeping giant of Roscommon football, after the retirement of their most iconic player Gerry O'Malley. Then in 1996 club stalwart Sean Kilbride persuaded his former Mayo teammate John O'Mahony to coach and manage the side. O'Mahony had just stepped down from managing Leitrim, where he enjoyed great success, notably the never to be forgotten Connacht final triumph in 1994.

Ní hé lá na gaoithe lá na scolb: A windy day is not a day for thatching. O'Mahony instilled a new culture of proper preparation into the squad. His Midas touch would work its magic for St Brigid's and he led them to a county title in 1997. Galway, though, came calling for O'Mahony and he led the Tribesmen to All-Irelands in 1998 and 2001. It would not be until 2013 that St Brigid's climbed the summit to become the first Roscommon side to claim a Senior All-Ireland club title at the high altar of Croke Park.

Seven years later the star players from that side like Karol Mannion, Frankie Dolan and Shane Curran had left the stage. New manager Benny O'Brien invited McCarthy to be coach. It was a marriage made in heaven. McCarthy was good for Brigid's and they were good for him as he made his recovery. The strong ties with his new home were cemented when the side won the county championship.

It was the GAA's most difficult year as Covid wreaked havoc on the nation. However, the GAA rose to the occasion as countless volunteers all around the country brought meals, food parcels and good cheer to many vulnerable people isolated in their communities. It showed how we could come together as a nation while staying apart.

As a man of deep faith McCarthy was deeply attuned to the spiritual significance:

'I was very conscious of minding myself because of Covid, but it was a great experience. We had a team that was exceptionally young. There were seventeen- and eighteen-year-olds with a combination of some experience. We got better and better with every game. We played football, they used their talents to express themselves in a footballing sense and we won the Championship. We won and I healed.

'When we won the county final Ben O'Carroll, who has since become a star with Roscommon but who was only seventeen years at the time, came up to me and said: "Thank you so much for all you have done for the team." It really struck me that for such a young man he had such maturity. These are the small things that are really big things when you give so much time and effort to coaching a club. They are in their own way more important than any trophy or medal.'

They joined a company of local legends like Louis Feeley who died in March. He went to work in Kilkenny with the Office of Public Works and he was known for his diligence in everything he did. The Main Guard in Clonmel is a glowing example of his attention to detail – never hurried, but always high quality work under his supervision. It was his last major project before retirement.

WE CAN BE HEROES

McCarthy has met luminaries like Bill Clinton, Tiger Woods and Michael Jordan but two other people stand head and shoulders above all the others for him:

'The two most inspirational people I have ever met were my parents. They had such remarkable generosity. Even though they had very little they gave everything they had. Indeed, when they had nothing they were the sort of people who would go to money lenders to borrow money to help people in greater need than them. The popular perception is that community is only really strong in rural areas but in the working-class areas of northside Cork the bonds of community could not have been stronger. But I would say the bonds of community are very strong today in rural Ireland as I have discovered here in the last twenty-five years.'

There was a third person who also had a deep influence:

'When I was in my teens a friend of mine who was a similar age to me died very unexpectedly and I was finding it very hard at the time to handle it. And my grandmother, God rest her soul, was very philosophical, and she said to me, "Life is this wheel and you don't know how long you have on it until you step off it and die, but all you're asked to do is leave the wheel just a little bit better off. I think *just* is an important word. I would like to hope that when my time is up I will have left Saint Brigid's just a little better than I found it. Every day I meet people in Kiltoom who have the same mindset, and it is that ethos which drives not just Saint Brigid's but all the clubs around the country. That is what makes the GAA great and why the future is so bright.'

CHEERS

When McCarthy came to Kiltoom and got involved in Saint Brigid's the sense of community he rediscovered was like what he experienced as a child. He saw there a mirror to the values he had been brought up with. When he got involved with Brigid's – he immediately was made to feel at home and everybody was welcoming – they realised that his talents as a basketball player and coach could be applied to coaching football. He graduated from initially coaching the club's underage teams to eventually coaching the senior team. This involvement embedded him into the community and got him to know many people in the parish and make many great friends.

He credits the club for two reasons; the sense of purpose he got from coaching teams and the overwhelming support he got from people when he was ill. As a young man he watched the TV series *Cheers* but in St Brigid's the words of the theme song took on a new significance. Like Ted Danson on the small screen, he discovered in real life that you've got to go 'where everybody knows your name'.

His journey back to health was an eloquent statement of what the GAA is all about. In times of crisis St Brigid's demonstrated that the struggle of one is the wound of all. These moments illustrated the power of the club to be the ties that bind and heralded a horizon of hope in the darkest chapters of Timmy McCarthy's history. A deep personal crisis put humanity front and centre and the dark clouds were pushed to the margins:

'Before I got involved with coaching the team people knew me but definitely after my involvement people saw me differently and people reached out to me in a whole new way. When I became ill so many people approached me and said if I ever needed a lift to the hospital for chemo or whatever I shouldn't hesitate to contact them. I see that type of support replicated so often in the club in times of bereavement or personal crisis.'

It was a virtuous circle. He gave and he received.

Ernest Hemingway claimed that the world breaks everyone and afterwards many are stronger in the broken places. St Brigid's helped Timmy McCarthy come through his crisis stronger in the broken places.

In the immortal words of The Cure, it felt just like heaven.

If the GAA is the flower, the club is the fruit – a nurturing place where values are cultivated, harmony is practised (though sometimes tested!) and mutual respect grows.

5

GIANTS OF THE ASH

The Village

As a young footballer, Michael (Murphy) was so good it was cartoonish. Here was a real life Hotshot Hamish, fetching impossible high balls and driving them to the net like Tony Yeboah. A Glenswilly game became a must-see event. We went, we laughed, we cheered, we talked about him for days afterwards.

JOE BROLLY

There are no secrets in life – only truths hidden below the surface.

It has been said that Charles Kickham rose like Slievenamon (he wrote 'Slievenamon', the song most synonymous with Co Tipperary) about the men of his time. As result of an accident in his youth, he had impaired eyesight and was almost totally deaf – yet he wrote *Knocknagow*, the most popular Irish novel up to the mid-twentieth century, running to twenty-eight editions between 1873 and 1944. Fellow Fenian John O'Leary wrote of him: 'He knew the Irish people thoroughly . . . and from thoroughness of knowledge came thoroughness of sympathy . . .

and, anyway, what merits or demerits they might have, they were his people.'

Judge William Keogh sentenced him to fourteen years of penal servitude, at least to some extent in retaliation for the articles he had written in the *Irish People* about the 'hanging judge', who sentenced the McCormack brothers to be executed unjustly for the murder of a land steward. *Knocknagow* has provided the anthem for clubs in the GAA. Matt the Thresher's cri de coeur 'for the credit of the little village' continues to resonate deeply in the GAA. As John McGahern with typical insight observed: 'The local and the individual were more powerful than any national identity.'

A brilliant illustration of this came in 2023 when newly crowned Cork senior hurling champions Sarsfields, who defeated Midleton to lift their seventh Cork senior crown, took the decision to turn their pitch into a flood plain to limit the damage to the Glanmire area from Storm Babet. At the time Cork was being ravaged by extensive flooding in Midleton, Glanmire and Blackpool. Properties were flooded and roads deemed impassable in towns across the county. It was said that a 'month's worth of rain' had fallen in the town in those twenty-four hours. Sarsfields took the decision to sacrifice their pitch in an attempt to spare the wider community and nearby businesses.

In a statement the club said: 'We will be forever proud of our senior team on Sunday and today Sars Hurling Club experienced heroism in the form of our pitch committee and volunteers. Although we wanted to ensure we could limit the damage to the clubhouse we made the decision to open the two large gates (behind the bar area and at the end of the pitch). As a result, our main pitch essentially became a flood plain in order to relieve the flooding to the immediate Riverstown area, Orchard Manor and surrounding businesses. We won a county, lost a pitch but hopefully saved a part of the Glanmire community.'

DAN THE MAN
Another champion of the centrality of the local place is Waterford legend Dan Shanahan. Although he lit up venues like Semple Stadium with his goal-scoring feats in the county jersey, his happiest days were in a more intimate setting:

'If there were only one place in the world where I could be for the rest of my life, it would have to be Lismore, the place, the community, and the parish where I grew up and got to know what place, community and parish mean to so many people throughout the country. It is the place where I feel most at home, the community in which I learned about life and which gave me a special identity as a player representing my parish.

'When the Lismore club developed a hurling pitch near my home it brought lads together from all parts of the town and we got to know people whom we would never have known otherwise. The matches we played there as children led on to greater things with the club and Lismore CBS and our "Munster finals" were always thrilling and well contested, a herald of things to come as adult players wearing the blue and white of Waterford.

'The great strength of the GAA is that players are heroes in their own community: they live and work in their own villages and towns and are available and accessible to everyone. I cannot remember a time when I did not have a hurley in my hand when I was outside my house. It seemed as if it was an extension of my arm! The first games I remember playing in were a five-a-side at school and a Dick Ahern league in the local field. I must have made some progress as by the time I was eleven years old I was selected to play in Croke Park in the Cumann na mBunscol mini-games at the 1998 All-Ireland semi-finals between Tipperary and Galway, and Offaly and Antrim.

'That was a wonderful moment: being out on the hallowed turf, looking up at the enormous stands, playing in front of thousands of fans, our parents cheering us on, and wondering if we would ever play there again.

'I developed further in the next five years, and I know I did, because I was called into the Lismore senior team in 1993 when I was only sixteen years old. I came on as a sub in the county semi-final against Roanmore for whom my Uncle Tom was playing in the forwards. We won that game and defeated Passage in the final.

'This place means everything to me. When I think of those generous souls who coached us as children, the mentors who put us right when we were not able to read the flow of a game and the people who ferried us to matches all over the county I cannot but respect them and the effort they made to develop our skills and nurture our love of hurling.'

In his lowest moments in hurling it was the people of Lismore who lifted Shanahan up again:

'When Waterford lost heavily to Kilkenny in the 2008 All-Ireland final we were gutted. But the fans rallied us and as we travelled through the streets of Dublin after the game we knew by the way they clapped and cheered that they appreciated the effort we had put in over the year; and I am always grateful for that.

'It is a wonderful feeling to play in Semple Stadium, Páirc Uí Chaoimh or Croke Park and to represent the Déise in Munster or All-Ireland finals. We are there because of the time, effort and dedication of the legions of volunteers who give unselfishly of their time to help us bring glory to our county, our club, our parish, our community and our family.

'I knew I represented the community when I pulled on the club or county jersey, but I am one of the community as well. I can be seen in the local shops, I might be talking with young people, coaching children to play the game or just being available to give a word of encouragement to anyone who might need a listening ear.

'Inter-county players are not removed from their local village or town: they do not live in large mansions out of sight of the public and they do the ordinary things that everybody else does in the community. They have a great pride in and love of their place, their community and their parish as expressed through their club. And they will go to their maker with dreams of bringing that pride and love with them and, maybe, playing in county, Munster and All-Ireland finals in the next world.'

LET IT SNOW

A lovely snapshot of a hurler's commitment to his community came in the midst of an intense snow blizzard in January 2025. Former Limerick hurler, Garda Mike Fitzgerald, and his colleague, Garda John Clifford, swapped out their patrol car for a red Zetor tractor to bring much needed medication to two pensioners snowed in in Doon. When he learned about the couple's predicament the tractor-owning former Limerick hurler braved the snow in his tractor to ensure the essential supplies reached those in need.

A very poignant example of the power of the link between club and community came just a few weeks later with the waves of emotion triggered by the last-minute penalty from Conor Loftus which won the All-Ireland Intermediate football final for Crossmolina Deel. The Crossmolina players surrounded Loftus at the final whistle, having come from behind to thwart the Derry champions Ballinderry. Tragically Loftus' twenty-eight-year-old fiancée Róisín Cryan had died a fortnight previously and the whole community mourned with him. Team captain Mikie Loftus dedicated his triumph to Róisín with a poignant speech on the steps of the Hogan Stand in Croke Park:

'This victory is obviously bittersweet. Róisín Cryan was an amazing person and we as a team are lucky to have known her. I know she's looking down on us smiling today. Crossmolina is a small, proud town and it's been overwhelming to see how the community can come together in the good times and the bad times.'

Then just a few weeks later former Galway All Star hurler Michael Coleman, died in an accident on Friday evening clearing up storm damage near his home in Crumlin, Ballyglunin. As Anthony Daly incisively observed: 'He was a guy who looked unbreakable, untouchable, but, in this life, nobody is.'

Tipperary's shock victory over Cork in the 2025 All-Ireland was a reminder of why they are 'the Premier County'. It was apt that a fallen hero was celebrated afterwards. Tipperary captain Ronan Maher, in his speech, singled out, 'one player who's no longer with us, but is so much a part of what we are, Dillon Quirke. We carried your spirit with us every step of the way. You were in the dressing room, you were on the field of play, you were in our hearts.'

6

THE KEYS OF THE KINGDOM

Castle Island

There was never a night or a problem that could defeat sunrise or hope.

BERNARD WILLIAMS

He was to journalism and the GAA what Kate Bush is to music – a true original.

His voice still lingers over me and engulfs me like a warm blanket on a cold January morning. It was like brandy, full of subtleties and depth – beautiful in a strange kind of way because of its tonality and richness.

His passing left a hole in my heart.

I fear, though, that he would have struggled in today's landscape where the truth can become a lie and a lie can become the truth.

He once told me that he didn't like the term original sin because he believed that there was nothing original in the evil that people do. He was put on this earth to party not to lament. He had a mind as sharp as a steel trap. He believed fully in E.M. Forster's assertion that life is easy to chronicle but bewildering to practise.

THE KEYS OF THE KINGDOM

As a boy the first publication that captivated my attention was *The Evening Press*: because of both Joe Sherwood's regular feature 'In the Soup' and the column written by the peerless Con Houlihan. Con's articles hit home every time. His words lit up the page and evoked a deep nostalgia for lovelier, simpler things. I loved his work, his capacity to write in so many styles and genres on such wide and varied topics, entertaining, informing, calming us down and waking us up. The English language danced for him. My only problem is that I made such slow progress reading him, arrested as I always was by an image, a choice of word, a turn of phrase – genius word crafting, creating a beauty and magic I did not know existed. I often re-read his articles because they have that wistfulness that as an adult you appreciate more and more.

DUNNE DEAL

When reacting poetically to the death of W.B. Yeats in 1939, W.H. Auden claimed 'he became his readers'. Con achieved that level of connection with his audience.

Yet he was a very shy man. Eileen Dunne tells a story which captures his essence. She was sitting at the Kerry table during an All-Stars banquet and Con and his partner Harriet were sitting beside her. Eileen mentioned that she happened to be down in Houlihan's home place in Castle Island (the correct spelling in Con's view) a few days previously. Con bent down and put his hand over his face and turned to Harriet rather than Eileen and said: 'Ask her what she was down there for?'

DOWN MEMORY LANE

Last night I came across a piece he wrote in 1982 after the Five Nations Championship in which Ireland won the title and claimed their first Triple Crown in thirty-three years, only the fifth in its history and the first ever in Lansdowne Road. Ireland were denied a Grand Slam after losing 22-9 to France in their last game but Ollie Campbell's play that year inspired Con to write a piece on that Triple Crown win entitled 'Ollie Campbell was a conductor who could bring glorious music from a scratch band'.

He was born on 6 December 1925 into a very different Ireland – a time when Patrick Kavanagh had begun writing *Tarry Flynn*. The book describes a young farmer's struggle to rise above the burden of family, Catholicism, farm work and lust, all set in 1930s rural Ireland. In this more censorious era, the novel was banned. Irish writers censored in Ireland were 'the best banned in the land', claimed Kavanagh's bête noire Brendan Behan. The attitude of some to our nearest neighbours was: 'Burn everything English but their coal.'

As a young student I shared a cheap bedsit in Rathmines which was less than salubrious. The walls were so paper-thin that not only could I hear the man snoring in the room beside me, I could hear his most intimate inner thoughts. The only thing in its favour was that it was very close to a hostelry favoured by Con Houlihan.

One evening I almost literally bumped into him. I was in awe but in the following months we had a few great chats. John Travolta's character, Tony Manero, in the 1977 movie *Saturday Night Fever*, sat in front of the mirror making sure that there wasn't a single hair on his head out of place before he went out for the evening. It is fair to say Con was not cast in a similar mould. His voice was softer than I expected, making him seem younger than his appearance suggested.

He was not a man to roll over. Once when a theatre company complained about his snoring during a stage production, he replied that it was a shame the audience was required to stay awake for it.

COUNTY PRIDE

I listened spellbound as he told me about the wonders of Kerry:

'As you come from Limerick into Kerry, the road starts to rise at Headley's Bridge. After about three miles you reach the summit of the road in the townland of Gleannsharoon. Now you are looking down at a great valley ringed all around with hills and mountains. Geographers call it The Castle Island Gap: sensible people call it The Heart of The Kingdom.

'In the middle of the valley you can see an old town sloping from East to West. In the days when the Gaelic language prevailed, it was known as Oileán Chiarraigh, The Island of Kerry. The island was a great outcropping of rock surrounded by marsh. Eventually the marshland was drained for grazing and tillage. The Normans came and built a castle in the western end of the outcropping of rock. Trade followed the flag. Houses were created from the rock – and on both sides of it a town began to grow. It was an ideal location for fairs and markets: all around were small farmers and plot holders and labourers.'

Con was a very well-read man and drew on that treasure trove of knowledge in all his descriptions:

'Thomas Wolfe, the brilliant half-forgotten novelist, used to say that the most evocative of all American sounds was the whistle of a distant train. For my generation in rural Ireland the most evocative of all sounds was the lowing of cattle being driven to the fair in what Thomas Hardy called the non-human hours. Rounding up those same cattle was not quite as romantic as in the novels and the films about The Old West. The cowboys had horses and lassoes; we had our voices and wattles. Some cattle can spot a gap in a fence as quickly as Paddy MacEntee can see a flaw in the case for the prosecution. And if you think that we enjoyed a full Irish breakfast, it wasn't so. I don't remember all that honey and soda farls, whatever they are. I remember mugs of tea and slices of bread and butter.

'Nor were there sloe-eyed colleens fingering a harp and singing 'The Coolin' or 'The Derry Air' or 'She Moved Through the Fair'. It was more than likely that someone of the womenfolk would be giving out "Hurry up or the fair will be over before you get there".

'The fair had its own rough charm: it was essentially a battle of wits between yourself and the jobbers. You could bargain and bargain and bargain and refuse to sell, knowing that if you had a good animal or animals, your opponent would come back. In the cattle mart you have only a few minutes to make up your mind. Like most of the changes brought about by the European Union, it is not friendly to the small man. Will we ever hear a sloe-eyed colleen singing "She moved through the Mart"?

'The Fountain was the centre of our town, even though it is away down at the bottom of the street. It isn't really a fountain: it is an ornamental pump with flat slabs at its base. For the time being it is not flowing; for generations it supplied all the people who had no indoor water. Most came from a collection of little houses called Pound Road, houses made from stone and mud and wood and corrugated iron and thatch. I used to envy the women who sat around by the base of the fountain waiting for their buckets to fill. Most of them worked for the better-off people: they knew life upstairs and downstairs and no-stairs. I envied them because I felt they knew more about life than Freud or Adler or Jung.'

Con was a marvellous chronicler of the Ireland of yesteryear:

'The people of Pound Road were proud and honest – above all they were survivors. The most famous citizen of that settlement was a man called Mikey Conway. He was the town bell man – he would be called a town crier in England. He performed many useful functions, such as announcing when the water would be cut off. He was born with weak sight and was barely able to read. Thus you could hear: "Tonight in the Carnegie Hall you can see the famous Greek play Oedipus the Wreck". Like many people with little education, he was marvellously articulate.

'One of his sons, Georgie, was in The Eighth Army when Montgomery and Rommel were head-to-head in the Battle of El Alamein. It was a battle of enormous importance: the wirelesses were blazing out news of it every few minutes. One night in the street corner parliament at The Market House there was enormous speculation as the battle appeared to be reaching its climax.

'When Mikey arrived, someone said to him: "You must be very worried about Georgie in the middle of all that fighting..." Mikey said: "He's well able to look after himself. Before he went to England he spent three years working with the farmers."

'The battle ended, Georgie came home on furlough. That night Mikey was down at the parliament. He said: "Our Georgie is a humble lad. All we had today for our dinner was spuds and mutton and turnips – he never complained – and last week he had his legs under Montgomery's table."

'I would love to see a memorial to Mikey – a plaque perhaps on The Market House. It was people such as he who gave our town its flavour. Mikey contributed to the world far more than he got back.'

Con followed the Kerry seanchaí tradition championed by Eamon Kelly. One of his favourite stories was about a Kerry pensioner who travelled by pony and trap to Cahersiveen on Christmas Eve. After finishing his shopping duty demanded he visit the pub. As he did not want his relatives in the town to know he was there, he sat in the snug (the small room that pubs provided for those who wanted to drink privately). Having drunk very generously, he headed for home, stopping at the Daniel O'Connell Memorial Church for Confession. There was as usual a huge crowd awaiting absolution. By the time it was his turn to enter the Confession box, he was very drowsy. In the box he fell fast asleep, as the priest tended to the penitent on the other side of the curtain for a long time. Awakened from his slumber by the pulling back of the curtain, bewildered by where he was, the man blurted out: 'The same again, and turn on the blady lights in the snug.'

ODD SHAPED BALLS

Today Kerry is synonymous with Gaelic football. However, Con was fascinated that in the early years of the GAA, rugby rivalled Gaelic football as Kerry's pre-eminent sport. The ancient game of caid had been enjoyed by the Kerry population for countless generations. Rugby's spread into Kerry was facilitated by the characteristics it shared with caid. Both involved a group of men seeking possession of the ball before passing to faster players on the wings, who ran with the ball in hand. The similarities with both games would see ten players line out both for Killorglin rugby club in February 1888 and for Laune Rangers Gaelic football team in the 1890 county championship.

Con was also intrigued by the sociology of Kerry sport such as how rugby got its tentacles into the larger towns of the Kingdom. An example was Tralee Rugby Club, founded in 1882 which competed in the inaugural Munster Senior Cup in 1886. Their star fly-half Dr John Hayes was introduced to rugby as a student in Trinity College. In common with the experience in Britain, university graduates, once they moved home, brought their passion for the game to their local area. A further catalyst in the spread of the sport was the influence of 'foreign' companies, like the Anglo-American Cable Company, in areas like Valentia from the 1860s onwards. British employees familiar with rugby introduced it to the islanders to form their own club.

Con's love for Kerry was only matched by his great love for his native town:

'Castle Island was once described as a street amidst the fields – that was fair enough. It is a remarkable street: when all the outcropping stone had been quarried, a huge space remained. And so the citizens could boast that their town had the widest street in Ireland. The famous street is as wide as ever but now there are trees down the middle – small birds are delighted.'

It was here that Con's love of the GAA was nurtured. However, he was not an uncritical fan. In particular, he disliked the growing backroom teams behind football teams. Witness his feeling of sympathy for a referee 'as he tried to chase away the bottle-carriers and the counsellors and the bone-setters and the physiologists and the next of kin and the sympathisers and the motivators'. And, as for sports psychologists? He looked askance at their endless talk of 'motivation', and wondered: 'Would you need to motivate a man running from a bull?'

His articles were triumphs of emotional storytelling, bracing and brave. He was strident in his opposition to the GAA's ban on 'foreign games' and contended that 'not alone are the values embodied in the ban insane, but the proscribed games aren't in any sense "foreign".' In 1974 his condemnation of IRA bombings in the UK prompted threats to blow up *The Kerryman*'s office (where he was a contributor), and the paper had a police guard for weeks afterwards.

A bronze bust was unveiled in Castle Island in 2004, with an inscription penned by Con: 'Fisherman, Turf-cutter, Rugby Player and Teacher'.

WHERE HEROES ARE MADE

In the book of unpunished love we will never see Con's like again to give praise to Kerry's contribution to the GAA. After his death in 2010 his ashes were spread in Castle Island for him to forever rest in peace in the Kingdom.

In an age when the real is no longer real, where misinformation and disinformation have led to a decline in trust in traditional sources of authority, people like Con are needed more than ever. He was a comic genius, a social realist who had the power to take down the fatuous with a well-aimed dagger of a sentence.

When I heard of the passing of Paddy Cullen in February I recalled immediately Con's capacity to 'nail it' with his take on the first modern goalkeeper: 'He guards not only the goal but its forecourt.'

THE GIFT

Every encounter with Con was memorable and educational. It was him who explained to me that 'dystopia' means 'bad place' and it was the opposite to 'utopia' which means 'good place'. He told me that the first person to use the term was the philosopher John Stuart Mill in 1868 as he described British land policy to Ireland at the time.

He was embarrassed when I, in my days as a poor student, bought him a double brandy one Christmas. He asked me what I wanted in return. Two weeks later he granted my request. It remains an abiding memory of Con. He read for me his match report of the 1981 All-Ireland hurling final:

> *Since the All-Ireland became a purely inter-county competition sixty years ago, only eight names have appeared on the trophy.*
>
> *And the latest new name was in 1955 when Wexford at last reaped a harvest. But it wasn't their first attempt in a final – they had lost narrowly to Cork the year before.*

THE KEYS OF THE KINGDOM

And Galway last year had ended a long drought after they too had suffered defeat in the previous final.

And so Offaly yesterday found themselves facing not only the reigning champions: there was also the old husbands' tale that before being summoned to the round table you must already have been rebuffed at least once.

And the 'traditionalists' – those amusing mystics who believe that it takes several generations to produce a hurler – looked on as Offaly's presence in the final as aficionados of the bullring might look on an Irish matador.

Galway were hoping to make history too – if on a lesser stage. They had never won the minor title – they were the only members of the round table not to have done so.

It was Offaly's first time being in Croke Park in a Hurling final of any kind. They won the junior title in 1929 – but the final was played in Birr. It was on a December Sunday – and only about five hundred watched. It was hardly a glamorous setting – but Mick Digan remembered it well. He played on the winning team on that near-Christmas Day long ago – when a pint of stout was eight old pence and a labourer was expected to survive on a little over a pound a week.

Mick, needless to say, is loyal to his generation – and reckons the Hurling was far better in his day. Players now, he says, cannot pull on the overhead ball.

And what does he think of men who like to run with the ball on the hurley?

'They're like a woman feeding hens,' he says. So now . . .

Mick lives snugly in his thatched cottage and didn't travel to Croke Park yesterday; he watched the battle on television. And he surely reflected on the great changes that have taken place in Hurling and in Ireland since that winter day long ago when he won his place in the folk gallery.

Another man with cause to reflect on change yesterday was Tom Donoghue, Offaly's full-back. A year ago he stood on Hill 16 – and watched his native county wash away the bitterness and sadness of two generations.

Tom had played for Galway when they won their Under21 All-Ireland – but now he was nearing thirty, had drifted away from Hurling into Rugby, and in his wildest daydreams didn't see himself ever again playing in Croke Park on a final day.

Yet yesterday he was little more than an hour from the highest honour – and it wouldn't be a whit diminished if earned with his adopted county. His involvement made even more piquant the meeting of these Shannon-divided neighbours.

Another piquant aspect was that while the Offaly players spent Saturday night in their own beds, a big advance guard of their supporters invaded Dublin on the eve of the battle. It was as if they felt their early presence might be a blow in the psychological welfare, a little source of unease to Galway and their followers, who came as usual on the Saturday.

And by noon yesterday there were so many Offaly people in Dublin that you hoped no cow in the Faithful County would slip into a drain or no ass wander into a bog-hole.

And you feared that if the Martians landed there, not even the gallant Mick Digan would be able to do much about it.

The county of Galway was just as vulnerable: by half past one when their minors came out to do battle with Kilkenny, the Maroon-and-White was blossoming all over Croke Park. Seldom can the headquarters have been so well populated so early. Even then there were big queues outside the Canal Terrace, an almost-forgotten sight at a Hurling final.

And the Maroon-and-White forest waved in the very first minute as a flashing goal gave Galway the kind of start that helped their seniors topple Cork in that unforgettable semi-final of 1975.

But Kilkenny showed the coolness that seems part of their heritage – and it was soon clear that this was to be a struggle that would continue all the way into the home straight.

THE KEYS OF THE KINGDOM

Galway seemed the better in the first half – but the light wind blowing into the Canal goal was probably a factor in their apparent superiority. The teams were level going into the last quarter – and for about six minutes there was a fierce battle of nerves as both strove to pull clear.

Galway were the more dashing – but Kilkenny the more crafty. And in the last furlong they stole away in the fashion long associated with the Black and Amber. It was the old Kilkenny formula: look for the points and let the goals look for themselves.

The points came in a little stream – and you felt that `Flow on Lovely River' could be equally applied to Hurling. At the end it was 1-20 to 3-9 – and Galway were still without a minor title.

The setback didn't seem to worry their huge following and there was a carnival air as the champions ran out a few minutes before three. The biggest Maroon-and-White banner at the Canal End said with mock politeness, `We're Offaly Sorry'.

The banter in the crowd was friendly – and there was about as much danger of violence on the terraces as of a shower of snow. Despite the wind, the terrace crowds were sweltering and the ice-cream vendors would have been set up for life if only they could devise a method of delivering their merchandise from overhead.

The green pitch looked like an oasis – and you envied the players their freedom of movement. It is doubtful if many of them looked up to see the colour of the sky: it was dry-blue and the sun shone brightly into the eyes of those behind the Railway goal.

The march provoked such an orgy of flags and banners that you feared a clothing shortage; the National Anthem was guillotined by a hurricane of sound.

It came as a blessed relief when Frank Murphy loosed the ball – at last the mill of the mind could grind on something substantial. It eased the tension in the crowd – but the men on the field were obviously not as confident as their followers.

WHERE HEROES ARE MADE

And there was thirty seconds of stuttering and stammering before Ger Coughlan uttered the first long sentence. It led to a free for his side – and Pat Delaney rifled over an eighty-yard point with the coolness of William Tell.

Michael Conneely's puck-out indicated the help given by the wind – and brought a Galway surge and a low shot from Joe Connolly. Damian Martin held it cleanly – but then went on a too-ambitious run that brought Galway a free. Joe Connolly lofted it over – the battle was truly on.

As the players settled, the Hurling began to glow – and now we saw Offaly's fierce determination and Galway's menacing fluency.

In that trying time for Offaly as they faced the champions and the wind, their hero was Ger Coughlan. The little left half-back was playing as if he had the power of seeing the future: time and again he put his hurley in the hole in the dyke-wall.

His namesake Eugene at full-back was doing well too and even though the corner-backs, Tom Donoghue and Pat Fleury, were struggling, they were giving little away.

But outfield, Galway were playing majestically – as if determined not only to win but to silence forever those who doubted their standing. Seldom has Croke Park seen such magnificent points as flowed over the Canal goal. Whenever a Galway man shot, the ball seemed like a homing pigeon.

Only one thing marred this great first half: you had to pity the referee as he tried to chase away the bottle-carriers and the counsellors and the bone-setters and the physiologists and the next of kin and the sympathisers and the motivators.

There was a major hold-up in the tenth minute – and when play restarted, Johnny Flaherty made a little run and set up Pat Carroll for a great drive from thirty yards that went to the net off an upright. Offaly now led 1-2 to 0-3. By the mid-point of the half, the westerners were back in front, 0-6 to 1-2. And Steve Mahon was growing to such stature that Offaly were almost eclipsed in midfield. In the eighteenth minute he decorated his work with a mighty point.

In the twentieth minute Finbarr Gantley rattled the bar above Damian Martin's head; the ball flew wide. The puck-out was returned – Joe Connolly was playing superbly and sent over another glorious point. Two minutes later John Connolly set the western crowd roaring as he went charging through. As he came into the small rectangle, he collided with Damian Martin. The ball ended up in the net – but a freeout was signalled. It hardly seemed to matter at the time – Galway were rampant. But it figured large in the pub enquiry.

Pat Delaney eased Offaly's pain with another great point from a free. Michael Connolly answered with an even better point from play. In the twenty-seventh minute Liam Currums at last showed a flash of his talent with a lovely lift-and-strike that brought a point. Noel Lane made a darting run and replied. Galway seemed to abound in confidence – and Joe Connolly especially looked infallible. At the other end of the field Niall McInerney was cleaning up like a sheriff in an outrageously romantic western.

Galway's half-time lead – 0-13 to 1-4 – seemed no more than their due. And if anyone tells you he foresaw the second half, he is either a liar or a prophet. It is true that the wind was a factor – but it hardly accounts for the change that came over Galway. If this had happened in the days of the Borgias, you would have suspected that someone had interfered with their interval drink. But in the third quarter – with Mahon still outstanding they won as much of the ball as before. But now the homing pigeons behaved as if a cat was in the loft. They stayed out – and as Galway's forwards lost their touch, they attempted to take the ball close in and go for goals.

At the other end Paddy Horan showed more sense. Despite Galway's big lead, he was content to take a point from a twenty-one-yard free.

WHERE HEROES ARE MADE

Yet Galway seemed in no great danger – and at the mid-point of the half led 0-15 to 1-8. And their followers awaited the killing surge. It never came. Galway, in fact, had got their last score. The shots for points continued to go wide – and the few that were accurate and low brought out the best in Damian Martin. But Offaly's attackers were doing little better. The ball was not running kindly for Paddy Horan and Johnny Flaherty – and Pat Carroll was the most likely rainmaker.

But in looking back you could clearly see the part played by Offaly's half-forwards. Pat Kirwan and Brendan Birmingham and Mark Corrigan were not spectacular but they held down Galway's great half-back line. And now in the final quarter Joachim Kelly and Liam Currams began to flower in midfield. Behind them was the lion-hearted Delaney. Joe Connelly had inflicted a harrowing first half on him – and he had been glad of the cover given by Aidan Fogarty and Ger Coughlan. But he never lost head or heart – and his resurgence was a symbol of Offaly's sheer grit. In the twenty-fifth minute he scored a lovely point from play – it seemed to give Offaly the scent of victory. Then Iggy Clarke wided a seventy. Galway seemed becalmed. And then at last we saw a drop of the purest Flaherty – a sweet point made the score 0-15 to 1-10. Five minutes remained.

And there was more Flaherty to come. Less than two minutes later Delaney, Kelly and Birmingham combined to put the Offaly rover through. And from the razor's edge of the small rectangle he served up a triple-drop by palming to the net. All heaven broke loose – and its colours were green, white and gold.

Then Danny Owens – who like Brendan Keeshan came on as a second-half sub – hit a thundering point. Offaly were two up. Both subs excelled. Then Horan from a free made the final score 2-12 to 0-15. But I doubt if most of the Offaly crowd knew it exactly – they were gone out of their delighted minds. And Tom Donoghue was marvelling at how his fortune had changed since a year ago he paid £2 into the Hill.

And a deputation from Kinnitty were holding down Johnny Flaherty lest he be taken away into the heavens in a fiery chariot.

And back at home in his snug thatched cottage Mick Digan was saying to himself that the fire he had fomented was now a blazing beacon.

Con's words will live on forever.
As he once said to me: 'Our heroes are gifted to us.'

THE HOMES OF DONEGAL

Con would have been amused watching Jim McGuinness in 2025. Dick Clerkin claimed that the 'main narrative from Donegal and Jim McGuinness is one of grievance'.

The Donegal manager was incensed after his side got a six-day turnaround for their All-Ireland quarter-final. The Ulster champions faced into a third Championship game against Monaghan in fourteen days. The Donegal manager had already been fiercely frustrated with the decision to play their All-Ireland round-robin game against Mayo in Roscommon. In the words of American politician Newt Gingrich he seemed to go through cycles 'finding a scapegoat, eliminating the scapegoat, and relaxing until we find the next scandal'.

Donegal's own Tommy Martin observed: 'Just because you are Cinderella doesn't mean all your sisters aren't ugly. Sorry, starting to sound like Conspiracy Jim there.'

7

THE BOULEVARD OF BROKEN DREAMS

Round Towers Lusk

Never give in . . . Never give in, except to convictions of honour and good sense.

WINSTON CHURCHILL

I could have been a contender.

Marlon Brando's cri de coeur from *On the Waterfront* is one of the most famous lines in the history of cinema. The GAA is full of hard luck stories. Nobody knows this better than Round Towers Lusk's Emma Dennis. Here is Emma's story in her own words:

'I had originally been a full-forward. Number 14 was my pride and joy. The more goals, the better. I plucked up like a turkey. However, to my surprise and also due to the longevity of my years left in the game, my coach asked me if I would play in goal. I had never been one to shy away from a challenge, so I grabbed the opportunity with both hands. I was naively anticipating a straightforward experience. I was not anticipating the looping shoots over my head while the umpire indicated that it was not a point but a goal.

THE BOULEVARD OF BROKEN DREAMS

'However, I worked hard and learned the art of goalkeeping. This all led me to try out for the position of goalkeeper on the *Underdogs* TG4 show. I stuck out like a sore thumb as I wore a scrum cap! (Due to previous brain surgery.) It was a real wake-up call. The standard of goalkeepers was immense and I felt quite humbled in the presence of keepers who had been plying their trade for over fifteen years compared to my six-month stint of trial and error between the posts. Most of these girls were ten years my junior but to my amazement, my name was called out by Mickey Ned O'Sullivan, and I was invited back to the final round of trials. I was in the top eight goalkeepers chosen that day. This would finally be whittled down to four. A fifty-fifty chance was a good one. I came away that day feeling like I had won the Lotto!

'The final trial occurred three weeks later in the national training center in Abbotstown. I was the first to arrive. I had practised hard in that three weeks . . . holes had been dented on my shed wall as I kicked the ball so many times against it and then dived down for a save. The drills were the same as the previous trial, but this time I WAS READY! I was doing much better than the last day and saving as many shots as the best of the best. I was full of confidence. I could feel I was going to make it through . . . I was doing great, and my confidence was sky-high. I even asked the coaches if I could take penalty shots while the next keeper was in (to show off the old full-forward skills that may strengthen my position)! They agreed and were impressed by some curlers to the top left-hand corner.

'The selectors told us that all that was left to do now was to play fifteen minutes each in a game, and then the decision would be made. I was convinced I was through. All that was required was a good fifteen minutes and my dream would come true. It began well . . . no mistakes. I was on the red team ... we were HAMMERING the blues. With about six minutes left on the clock, the blues came up the field, but my mind was already on that TV show. They got a solitary point. As I went for the kick-out, I looked up and passed it to the BLUE! A perfect thirty-yard curler into her hand. Exact specifications and skill. EXCEPT I was on the red team! I play with Round Towers Lusk who wear blue and a complete lapse of concentration caused me to make an unforgivable error! The girl on the opposition looked perplexed and ran the thirty yards towards me and SMASHED the ball into my bottom right-hand corner! In my confusion, I immediately ran to the net to pick it out before the next kick-out and ONCE AGAIN aimed a precision pass into the hands of ANOTHER blue player. Bang! Another goal. Two goals in less than ninety seconds!

'I looked at the selectors. They were just as stunned and perplexed as me! The referee blew the whistle, and my shot at the Underdogs was gone! Ninety seconds was all it took to take away all I had worked and hoped for.

'A valuable lesson was learned by me that day. Don't count your chickens before they hatch! Maintain concentration and finish the job. I will not make this mistake again.'

In the words of that great GAA man Ronan Keating: life is a rollercoaster.

8

CULTURE CLUB

Mauritius

When the Gods come out to play they play hurling.
MÍCHEÁL Ó MUIRCHEARTAIGH

He was a man of sharp intellect and a sincere desire to understand the mysteries of the cosmos and our place in it.

One of my most cherished possessions is a little note I got from him after the first time we met. I told him our encounter was my most joyous occasion since I made my confirmation. The note read simply: *Thanks John. Stay confirmed.*

Years later, as the relationship developed further, on a bright, cloudless morning he sent me another note which contained the poem 'The Point' by Seamus Heaney:

> *Those were the days –*
> *booting a leather football*
> *truer and farther*
> *than you ever expected!*
> *It went rattling*
> *hard and fast*

> *over daisies and benweeds,*
> *it thumped*
> *but it sang too,*
> *a kind of dry, ringing*
> *foreclosure of sound.*

The inscription on Seamus Heaney's headstone is a line from one of his own poems 'The Gravel Walks', which he used in his 1995 Nobel Prize acceptance speech. It reads: 'Walk on air against your better judgement.' It is an exhortation to be confident.

Hurling can be confident it will captivate generations to come.

THE GAA'S FIRST MIRACLE

Hurling goes back to when God's bicycle had training wheels. *Tales of the Elders of Ireland* is the first complete translation of the late Middle Irish *Acallam na Senorach*, the largest literary text surviving from twelfth-century Ireland. It contains the earliest and most comprehensive collection of Fenian stories and poetry, intermingling the contemporary Christian world of Saint Patrick. One of the accounts is of Patrick visiting Roscommon to spread the Gospel in Connacht. A tent is set up near Lough Croan where Muiredach Mór mac Finnachta, the king of Connacht, and his noble brethren pay homage to him. After the meeting the gathering celebrated with a game of a form of hurling. So fierce were the exchanges that the king's son was killed playing the match. Then comes the earliest great hurling tale of the unexpected. The very first GAA miracle takes place when Patrick invokes the ruah (breath) of God and raises the slain hurler from the dead.

One of the reasons to be confident about hurling and camogie was provided by the United Nations Educational, Scientific and

Cultural Organisation. It is a specialised agency of the United Nations aimed at promoting world peace and security through international cooperation in education, arts, sciences and culture.

At a meeting in Mauritius in 2018, UNESCO agreed to inscribe camogie and hurling on the Representative List of the Intangible Cultural Heritage of Humanity. The committee inscribed six new elements on the list, which 'seeks to enhance visibility for the traditions and know-how of communities without recognising standards of excellence or exclusivity'. The GAA, which worked with the Department of Culture, Heritage and the Gaeltacht on the application to UNESCO, said it proudly welcomed the decision to grant the national sports of hurling and camogie the prestigious status. It marked a global acknowledgement of the unique cultural significance of this part of our national culture, and of the important role Gaelic games play in Irish society. Moreover, it was a significant endorsement of the Gaelic sports associations and that these two games which form a central plank of our cultural heritage are worth protecting and celebrating. They are national treasures; ancient traditions that connect us to our Celtic past and a part of our DNA.

Ireland ratified the UNESCO Convention for the Safeguarding of the Intangible Cultural Heritage in 2015. Intangible cultural heritage, or living heritage, includes customs, traditions, crafts, games, and practices that are part of people's lives and identities both individually and as part of wider communities, and that are passed on from generation to generation. Ireland's first nomination, uilleann piping, was officially inscribed in 2017.

In its citation UNESCO observed:

'Hurling, or Camogie (a form of Hurling played by women), is a field game played by two teams which dates back 2,000 years and features strongly in Irish mythology, most notably in the epic saga of Cú Chulainn. It is played throughout the island of Ireland, particularly in more fertile agricultural areas, as well as overseas. Traditionally, the number of players in the game was unregulated and games were played across open fields. Nowadays, there are fifteen players on adult teams and the game is played on a clearly marked pitch. Players use a wooden stick (hurley), similar to a hockey stick but with a flat end, and a small ball (sliotar), with the aim being to use the hurley to strike the sliotar and hit it between the opposing team's goalposts. The primary bearers and practitioners are the players, known as 'hurlers' (male) and 'camógs' (female). Hurling is considered as an intrinsic part of Irish culture and plays a central role in promoting health and wellbeing, inclusiveness and team spirit. Today, the skills are promoted and transmitted through coaching and games in schools and clubs. As the custodians of Hurling, the Gaelic Athletic Association and the Camogie Association, both volunteer-led organisations, play a central role in transmitting the skills and values associated with hurling.'

W.B. Yeats was fond of invoking the mythic, muscular figure of Cú Chulainn as an exemplar for an independent, traditional Irish heroism.

OUT OF AFRICA
As if to confirm the global appeal of hurling in recent years a GAA club in Uganda has been established to advance the clash of the ash under African skies because a number of local children embraced hurling. Uganda GAA was founded by friends Moses Amanyire and Robert Bakaza after coming across videos of the sport on TikTok and YouTube. Mr Amanyire, explains: 'After seeing the videos, we had to establish ourselves if hurling was indeed the fastest sport on the grass.' It was unlike any other sport they had ever seen and it grew from there as word got around of how the kids got such great enjoyment from playing.

There was no Irish involvement at all for a few years until they got in touch with the GAA. They made hurls themselves recognising that hurling is the drumbeat of the soul.

We are all equals in the republic of hurling.

The central place of hurling in the community was wonderfully captured by Tony Kelly after accepting the Liam MacCarthy Cup in 2024:

'In Clare, hurling is like a religion and Brian Lohan is like our God.'

When Feakle won the Clare county title for the first time in thirty-six years that same year their manager Ger Conway captured the importance of the game to the area: 'In Feakle if you are not hurling you are not living.'

The soul selects its own society. In January 2025 GAA President Jarlath Burns stepped aside from presenting the All-Ireland Club Hurling trophy to Na Fianna as he let former GAA President John Horan present the trophy to captain Donal Burke. Horan is a member of Na Fianna and served as GAA President from 2018 to 2021. Due to his links with the club, Burns let Horan present the trophy. Burns' gesture is a parable of the feeling of togetherness and community of the hurling fraternity at its best.

THE PIGSKIN

There are those who believe that hurling takes second place to Gaelic football. In his book *Over the Bar*, Breandán Ó hEithir tackles this unconscious bias in an ingenious way by describing a meeting between Samuel Beckett, and Brendan Behan in Paris.

A couple of Irish priests recognised Beckett on the street, and one rushed up and asked him if he went home often.

'Rarely, but I have been invited to Dublin in September.'

'September? What time in September?'

'The middle of the month.'

'Ah, not so bad. You'll miss the hurling, but you'll be there for the football.'

In 2024 Gaelic football and ladies' Gaelic football received State recognition as cultural practices that are part of Ireland's living cultural heritage. In the wake of a recommendation from an expert advisory committee, the sports joined thirty-eight other cultural practices on Ireland's National Inventory of Intangible Cultural Heritage. The national inventory is maintained in line with a 2003 UNESCO convention for safeguarding intangible cultural heritage, which Ireland adopted in 2015.

In 2025, a Munster final for the ages and Dublin's shock win over Limerick offered conclusive confirmation of hurling's unique power to thrill the senses and lift the soul.

9

BRIDGES NOT WALLS

East Belfast

Nothing is impossible; the word itself says 'I'm possible'!
AUDREY HEPBURN

What you heard is not what I meant.

This sentiment captures much of our troubled history on our shared island.

In Belfast since 1969 many have tumbled into the mist and darkness of night because their children fell at the hands of those unburdened by the constraints of morality and conscience. The doors of these inconsolable parents, breathing desolation and grief, can seem locked to the grace of heaven.

These years saw both the worst of society and the best of humanity. In the darkest days of the Troubles it was difficult to be able to reimagine Belfast – as a city based on freedom, justice and peace.

2026 will mark the fifty-fifth anniversary of the introduction of internment without trial, called Operation Demetrius.

The move caused massive hostility among the Catholic and nationalist community from the unionist state and also was a brilliant recruitment weapon for the IRA, in the same way as Bloody Sunday would be six months later.

Behind the statistics were real flesh and blood stories. I once spent a wet Saturday afternoon close to Croke Park in the company of Joe Brolly and his late father, Francie. Pointing to his dad, Joe recalled:

'We were raided, turfed out of bed. Night-time was scary and there were a lot of very serious things going on. My father was interned. One morning they came and took him. He was taken away for three years. We saw him a few times during that time period.

'A knock came on our door one day and it was the shopkeeper next door saying, "you have to go and pick him up." He came home in triumph and it was never mentioned again.'

DIFFERENT TIMES

Today in one corner there is a sanctuary of civility and hospitality where the malevolent inflections that often rode into polite conversation on the backs of reasonable words during the Troubles are firmly banished – not by decree but by culture.

Visual symbols and symbolic actions have a mysterious power and they reverberate in the memory: tearful, joyful citizens dismantling the Berlin wall block by block; a student kneeling in front of an advancing tank in Tiananmen Square; the red ribbons of AIDS concern and the white ribbons of peace worn in Ireland during the IRA ceasefire; the broad smile on the face of Nelson Mandela as he walked the long walk to freedom; a million people in the streets of Spanish cities mourning the murder of a young politician by ETA.

Symbols define the community and its understanding of itself, its identity. Symbols give us our identity, self-image, our way of explaining ourselves to ourselves and to others. Symbols determine the kind of history we tell and retell.

Irish history testifies to the power of symbols; witness the bowler hats and insignia of the loyalist Orange marchers. In many towns and villages in Northern Ireland the very stones of the street were painted in loyalist or nationalist colours. Huge murals, with their massive images of the 'armed struggle', towered over the street corners in towns on both sides of the sectarian divide. Most of the predominant symbols in Northern Ireland were sectarian: they stressed difference, separateness, hostility, violence and above all they demonised the 'other side'. Often the mindset is that described by W.H. Auden: 'We would rather be ruined than changed.'

One of Seamus Heaney's most powerful poems is 'Punishment'. It was published in 1975 and focuses specifically on a body that has been buried in a peat bog for around 2,000 years. When Heaney wrote the piece, the body – known as the Windeby Girl, dug up in 1952 in Germany – was believed to have been ritually killed. Her hair had been shaved, a band covered her eyes and a halter (rope) was tight around her neck. In the lines, the speaker refers to the bog body as an 'adulteress' who was killed for breaking the tribal law. Heaney was taken by the idea that a young person from the Iron Age, preserved wonderfully in peat, was the victim of a tribal ritual, for the breach of an unwritten law.

In each page Heaney ripped away the parchment paper that so often covered depictions of Irish life, and offered authenticity frequently denied elsewhere. He employed the bog in a metaphorical sense and parallels the death of the bog girl with the punishments handed out to girls by the IRA during the Troubles in Northern Ireland. These girls were shaved, stripped, covered in tar and feathers and tied to railings for being perceived as friendly to British troops. It was a brutal illustration of the 'them' and 'us' mindset that bedevilled Northern Ireland for centuries. Heaney has incisively exposed the way in which sport, religion, race and politics were inextricably twined together in the Northern Ireland of his youth: the way in which walking through a street on Ash Wednesday with a forehead badged with the mortal dust enforced a sense of caste created by the sectarian circumstances; the way in which Pioneers were referred to as 'the strawberry brigade' and the manner in which the green chestnut tree that flourished at the entrance to the GAA grounds was more abundantly green from being the eminence where the tricolour was flown illegally at Easter. For the GAA faithful, though, football was central to their identity and an essential element of the fabric of their lives.

Bellaghy Wolfe Tones won the All-Ireland club championship in 1972, the year of Bloody Sunday. Bellaghy is also famous as the home of Seamus Heaney.

I shocked Seamus once when I described him as a rowboat. He was bemused by the analogy. I explained that it meant he moved forward while looking back. After a moment's reflection he smiled and nodded in agreement.

Then he caught me by surprise when he told me that in many ways he lived like a monk. When I rose my eyebrows in surprise he explained that in his work as a poet he 'was bowed to the desk like some monk bowed over his prie-dieu, some dutiful contemplative pivoting his understanding in an attempt to bear his portion of the weight of the world, knowing himself incapable of heroic virtue or redemptive effect, but constrained by his obedience to his rule to repeat the effort and the posture'.

One monk in particular held a fascination with him as is evident in his famous poem 'St Kevin and the Blackbird'. The poem is based on the time St Kevin was said to be kneeling with his arms stretched out in the form of a cross in Glendalough, a monastic site not too far from where Heaney himself once lived in County Wicklow, 'a place which to this day is one of the most wooded and watery retreats in the whole of the country'. While Kevin knelt and prayed, a blackbird mistook his outstretched hand for some form of roost and swooped down upon it, laid a clutch of eggs in it and began to nest in it as if it were the branch of a tree. Then, arising out of his great compassion and constrained by his faith to love the life in all creatures meek and tall, Kevin stayed immobile for hours and days and nights and weeks, holding out his hand until the eggs hatched and the fledglings grew wings. He explained that it was 'true to life if subversive of common sense, at the intersection of natural process and the glimpsed ideal, at one and the same time a signpost and a reminder.'

According to Heaney at that moment Kevin was, 'linked into the network of eternal life.' As the environmental crisis has accelerated I find myself often thinking of Seamus. In his poem on St Kevin he is pointing to an ecological spirituality that is furiously tender to the earth. It is as if he is speaking with the earth's voice and asking us all to paraphrase Yeats 'to tread softly on the earth because we tread on the earth's dreams'.

However, I know what troubled him with a more pressing urgency was the sectarian conflict which claimed among so many others his cousin Colum McCartney, who was the subject of his poem, 'The Strand at Lough Beg'. In 1972 the twenty-two-year-old was murdered at a bogus checkpoint as he returned from an All-Ireland semi-final between Derry and Dublin.

In 2022 to mark their fiftieth anniversary commemoration of the 1972 success, Bellaghy Wolfe Tones chose Heaney's poem 'Markings', ostensibly about children playing summer football. It opens with Heaney and his friends marking the pitch: four jackets for four goalposts, that was all. The match continued long after dark when the ball is no more than a shadow. The poem is an ode to the power of imagination and today a new generation in Northern Ireland are daring to imagine new possibilities.

THE PIPES OF PEACE
In the north there is often great kindness and accommodation. But even over twenty-five years after the Good Friday Agreement there can also be, in some quarters, great suspicions – on both 'sides' as though the place is encrusted with its own history. As Éamon Phoenix incisively observed: 'We have a common history, but not a common memory.' Many with blood on their hands were slow to learn that the most complete form of revenge is forgiveness.

Against this backdrop, in May 2020, just two months into Covid, two friends from East Belfast, a predominantly Protestant part of the city, were chatting. David McGreevy and Richard Maguire reflected on the lack of a GAA club in their neighbourhood and, curious to explore the possibilities, put out the following tweet: 'A new GAA club for East Belfast, if you're interested in playing, coaching or admin (More than likely all 3!) All ages, genders and backgrounds welcome. Please email EastBelfastGAA@gmail.com to register.'

Tweet it and they come. Hundreds of people showed up from around the county, and from outside it, to play football, hurling, and camogie. Many were wearing their county jerseys: so this was East Belfast's version of Nelson Mandela's rainbow nation.

The club cleverly used symbols not associated with nationalism or unionism. The club's crest features the iconic Harland & Wolff cranes, a sunrise, the Red Hand of Ulster, a shamrock and a thistle and the word 'Together' written in English, Irish and Ulster-Scots.

A County Down man who played for London for seven years, David McGreevy and co-founder Richard Maguire are both married to women from East Belfast. For McGreevy the early signs were promising:

'I remember the first night up training with the women. We partnered people up with someone who had played and someone who hadn't. I showed them the basics but I walked about and let them talk; there was a good feeling about the place where people were making friends and that's just continued.'

Irish language activist Linda Ervine, sister-in-law of the late Progressive Unionist Party (PUP) leader David Ervine, was among those who took notice. Raised in East Belfast but describing her mother's family as unionist she became honorary president of the GAA club.

Within two years East Belfast GAA club had more than 650 members on its books – including 200 children – and had become among the biggest clubs in Ulster.

It has not all been plain sailing. One evening as the ladies' team was packing up and heading home after training, the men's team still on the pitch, the PSNI received a call letting them know that explosive devices had been left on the grounds. The men's team were sent home. No one was hurt. The police got involved and did a sweep. A fifty-four-year-old man was later arrested on suspicion of making and possessing explosives. It emerged that he was posting on numerous social media platforms appealing for loyalists to show up in numbers to prevent the team from training at the Henry Jones playing fields. But these protests never materialised, and so he had taken matters into his own hands.

WHERE HEROES ARE MADE

THROUGH THE BARRICADES

In George Eliot's *Daniel Deronda* Gwendolen Harleth married the revolting Grandcourt in order to provide money for her family. She hoped she would dominate him with the strength of her personality, but when she was unsuccessful she came to hate him. One day she was with him, sailing in a small boat, while harbouring murderous thoughts against him, when he was swept overboard. Although she tried to save him, he was drowned. He died while she was wishing death on him, so she felt that she was in a sense an accomplice to murder. She carried a deep sense of guilt around with her and felt she could never be forgiven.

In the turmoil she approached her friend Deronda and shared her feelings of guilt: 'I did kill him in my thoughts . . . It can never be altered.'

Deronda handled the situation exceptionally well. He did not attempt to tell her she was wrong to condemn herself; he did not seek to take her pain away from her; he did not try to replace her flood of grief and accusation with soothing clichés of comfort. It would not be in Gwendolen's interests not to take seriously the wrong she felt she had been guilty of. However, he was aware that in the hour of darkness she had come, for the first time, to that point of self-knowledge when the 'worst' side of her nature has been absorbed and that she would not grow unless she was allowed to have the pain of knowledge.

While she did not cause her husband's death, it was accompanied by her own murderous thoughts. Hers was a sin of the heart. Neither event can be undone: her husband would remain dead, and she could not change what she felt towards him, but from Deronda's perspective, these terrible events could alter other things, i.e. how she lived the rest of her life. Deronda initiated the process of healing by taking seriously the struggle within Gwendolen as, for the first time, she was confronted with the truth of her nature. In this way the events of the past could alter the future since something new has been introduced into Gwendolen's experience. The tyranny of the past could be broken; the sin of the past could be healed in the future – not by minimising the seriousness of the past, but by putting the past in the perspective of a different future.

In May when Joe Duffy announced that he was retiring from RTÉ he spoke about his hatred of violence, recalling his interviews with families affected by The Troubles. 'The bullets that killed my James haven't stopped travelling,' he quoted one father as saying. 'If you put a bullet through a kid's kneecap, that bullet will not stop travelling for the rest of your life. Bullets don't stop travelling. We have to be much stronger as a country in rejecting violence,' Duffy argued.

Most of the GAA community understand that we need to break free from the tyranny of the past and try to put our difficult past in the perspective of a better future for our troubled island. For too long we have been like prisoners in cells. We must break free and end the 'them and us' mentality that was anathema to Seamus Heaney. They understand that we have to change our attitudes and our mindsets. It is not about negotiating convictions but about walking a path together. This aspiration is brought to life in East Belfast GAA club – binding people together: players; coaches; families and even communities. Here both traditions can live together, not always in complete agreement – both have suffered and lost too much to be completely at peace – but at least show deep respect and affection. There is a recognition of the need to respect the past but also let it go.

For years this was a space where darkness roared.

The country had changed in ways visible and subtle. Today there is dawn and radiance and a call for reconciliation and coexistence, rather than for more cycles of bloodshed and revenge – where good people were routinely killed by bad people. This can be heartwarming and revealing – because all we get constantly looking back is a stiff neck.

David McGreevy is emphatic:

'Some people looking on from the south see East Belfast in negative terms. They see the murals, but they don't see the people. It suits certain politics and interests that sectarianism and that divide remains, but you do not see it on the ground or in most of the population.

'We've got segregation in our education systems, segregation in our housing. With all that in mind, why do we have segregation in sport? It is not just the case of the two different traditions any more it is also a story of migrants as is the case of GAA clubs across the country.

'Our goal is twofold: building relationships through sport – and winning games. We are proud of the numbers of people who have been introduced to Gaelic games for the first time and the numbers who have come back to the games and the new fans we have created for the Down teams. Bringing people together is at the heart of what we do and we have weddings and babies because of the club.

'We are not the agent of the change but we reflect the change. Society has changed since the Good Friday Agreement and we shine a light into what is happening at the grassroots.'

They continue to play their part changing a great tomorrow into a great today.

10

HAIR AND THERE

The Barber Shop

Weak men wait for opportunities; strong men make them.
                                    ORISON SWETT MARDEN

They who have no charity deserve no mercy.

Despite my huge admiration for Charles Dickens my favourite Christmas story is a true story of the Wren Boys Day.

YULE LIKE THIS
Good friends are like stars. You don't aways see them, but you know they're always there. My good friend Paddy Joe Burke is a local legend because of his devotion to the Roscommon football team. He was not born with a silver spoon. When he was just a young boy his father died leaving a large family of hungry mouths to feed. It was the best of times. It was the worst of times. The family were poor materially but in terms of love and affection they were millionaires. Friday, though, was the most important day of the week for the household because it was the day the widow's pension was distributed. When he was eight Paddy Joe went 'on the Wren' on Saint Stephen's Day and made

a fortune by his standards – of six shillings and eleven pence. That evening he stored it in his version of a safe. He put all the money in an old sock and wrapped it up and hid it in the hen house. That night he could barely sleep with the excitement, thinking of all the terrific treats that his windfall would allow him to buy in the coming year.

His mother always tried to put on a brave face but the next morning she was uncharacteristically subdued. It was a Tuesday morning and nobody knew what was wrong. Suddenly she got up from her chair and burst into tears. It was three full days until Friday and she had no money for food for the family after trying to make it a good Christmas for all the children. Immediately Paddy Joe rushed out to the hen house and raced back with the sock full of money. His mother's eyes lit up like a Christmas tree. Paddy Joe had saved the day and the family would have enough to get through until Friday. Within a few minutes his oldest brother was sent off on his bicycle with the sock in one hand to buy a loaf of bread and some other essentials. When he came home with this 'feast' his mother never looked as happy. Paddy Joe has accomplished a lot in his life but he considers his greatest achievement to be the smile he put on his mother's face that Christmas.

To me he personifies the magic of the GAA – where we all understand that if all we think of is number one we are not going to add to very much. A wise man, he is a gift to very many, not so much of gold, frankincense and myrrh, but of kindness, spirit and humanity. In his own words: 'Kindness is like sugar. It makes life taste a little sweeter.'

YOUNG AT HEART
This book is dedicated to those who care for people with dementia or Alzheimer's – and for all carers in their many forms.

HAIR AND THERE

The Alzheimer Society of Ireland's National Helpline Service is open six days a week. Call 1800 341 341 or email helpline@alzheimer.ie. The Alzheimer Society of Ireland's National Helpline is a confidential information and support service for people with dementia and their families, carers, anyone concerned about their memory and those working or studying in the field. The Helpline service aims to provide accurate, up-to-date, accessible and relevant information and emotional support to service users.

The Alzheimer Society of Ireland Sporting Memories is an awareness and support programme which aims to tackle isolation, depression, and loneliness through safe, friendly sessions. The initiative is led by people with a passion for sport and a desire to help people stay engaged or re-engage in their communities.

Sporting Memories aims to empower communities to help improve the health and well-being of people with dementia and older people in general. Sporting Memories is for everyone, particularly people with dementia – the programme helps those with the condition to re-engage in the community which once played a huge role in their lives. Reminiscence is particularly important for people with dementia, as remembering can instil a sense of competence and confidence, boosting empowerment and connection. The programme strives to help create communities that actively embrace and include those living with dementia and their families.

An ambassador for the elderly every Wednesday evening, Paddy Joe visits an old person and brings them an apple tart. His reasoning is: 'It is better for me to bring an apple tart to the living rather than flowers for the dead.'

His professional life has given him a unique insight into our emotional fragilities:

'One of the saddest things that happened to me in my career came in the first week in January. A man in his seventies came into the shop and he told me that he hadn't talked to anybody for a few days so he was calling in for a chat not a haircut. Then he burst into tears because he hadn't got a single Christmas card. We are all big babies in nappies really. Wouldn't it be great if we could bring a little light into the dark shadows of loneliness?'

FOUR-MILE-HOUSE

Paddy Joe grew up in Kinnity, Four-Mile-House, one of the six children of Thomas and Jane. To this day he still feels a void because of the loss of his father when he should be so young.

'Recently, I saw a father and his son walking into a Roscommon match and I spoke to them. It dawned on me again that I never knew what it was like to have a dad when I was growing up. I never got to go to a game with him. I was told that my father was mad into football.'

He was extremely close to his mother, whom he adored. At 10.28 on 14 September 1999 when he was in the middle of a haircut he got a phone call. His mother had died suddenly. He was engulfed with grief:

'I owe a great debt of gratitude to Mam. She was a mother and father to me. I have dyslexia. The school curriculum passed me by. I remember once – I would have been eleven or twelve at the time – I asked Mum: how will I get a job when I grow up? She gave me some advice. She said to always have manners, to live my life by common sense, to always make eye contact when I meet someone, and to say hello to them and smile. My whole ethos for life is based on that.'

When he started out as a barber, there was further important loving support from his mother too. Having completed an apprenticeship, he opened his own barber's at just seventeen

HAIR AND THERE

years of age, renting Mrs Cahill's shop in Abbey Street (where Roscommon Credit Union is now).

'The rent was six pounds a week but I was only taking in three pounds. Every week my Mam collected her widow's pension and gave me the three pounds I needed. Eventually I was able to meet the rent and began to make a few bob for myself.'

A man called Paddy Coyle had been running a very successful barber shop in Church Street since around 1935. Paddy died in late 1973, and Paddy Joe moved into his premises in 1974. It was to be the making of him business-wise, as he 'inherited' Paddy Coyle's customers. Most were local farmers. Paddy Joe, being 'a farmer's son' had an immediate affinity with them:

'The farmer who was at the mart and wanted to pop in for a quick haircut became my typical customer. An English woman came in one day. She said, "Every time I pass this door I hear laughter . . . I had to come in and find out for myself!"'

Having given up alcohol himself in 1988, he is familiar with drink-related issues, and able to identify with the struggles faced by people dealing with addiction.

COME ON THE ROSSIES

In 2011 I made a radio documentary about Paddy Joe's passion for football. The plan was to attend all the Roscommon games that Championship season with him. Our season began in New York. The problem was that while I was at the game in the Big Apple he was at home in Roscommon. He booked his ticket for the following weekend!

Paddy Joe is one of the few people to have made his mark on the English language. He was sitting at home watching the 1982 World Cup on TV when he had a lightbulb moment. He mused that if Italy striker Paolo Rossi was from Roscommon, his family would be Rossis from Roscommon. The next time he went to a

WHERE HEROES ARE MADE

Roscommon match he started shouting 'Up the Rossies!' The phrase caught on and has entered the vernacular as the name for Roscommon supporters.

He loves the fretting – the fear that he's going to miss the start of the game – but he never does. He loves arriving at the turnstiles, when he has to keep his manners and remain calm, but he's only dying to get into the ground. He loves checking the programme once he gets in – especially the subs' bench – and by the time the players run out on to the pitch he knows exactly what number each sub is wearing. He gets 'goose-pimples at the soles of my shoes' when he hears the national anthem. And then the roars of support for his team: 'Come on the Rossies!'

Coming up to midnight on the night of 31 December 1999, Paddy Joe went to Dr Hyde Park. He brought a candle, a football and a radio with him. He brought a candle so he could 'shine a light into the next millennium'. He brought a football so he could become the first person in the new millennium to score a goal and a point at Hyde Park. And the radio was just to make sure he had the right time.

Paddy Joe is Roscommon's unofficial brand ambassador. He even wears his Roscommon jersey to Mass. Every trophy won by Roscommon since 1972 made its way to the barber shop, with players and management too:

'Roscommon football keeps me awake at night. I can't sleep before a big game. I go to all the games.'

His favourite-ever match was Roscommon's 1980 All-Ireland semi-final win over Armagh: 'I froze the moment in my mind . . . I thought *this doesn't get any better. This is magic. We will be there on All-Ireland final day, behind the Artane Boys Band, Roscommon emerging from the tunnel.*

'We partied for a week. We came home on Thursday. I had travelled up as part of a full carload. The plan had been to stay

HAIR AND THERE

Sunday night, but when Roscommon won, that plan changed. We borrowed a few bob from friends . . . over the following few days we let the world know that Roscommon were in the final. Pints were bought for the Dubs . . . we were great ambassadors!'

HAIR-RAISING

For fifty-two years Paddy Joe's barber shop in Roscommon town was the only place where even on the hottest day the hospitality was warmer than the weather. Some of his customers lived isolated existences. His shop was the one place their loneliness took a holiday.

Thirty years ago Paddy Joe gave up cursing for Lent and he has forsaken the practice since. Until he decided to sell it in 2024 his barber shop was the go-to place for GAA fans near and far. The famous walls of fame were populated by wonderful pictures of the great and the good of Roscommon football. The shop was a sanctuary for those who love to talk about football and life in general.

Paddy Joe produced lyrical quotes – notably his tribute to his native county's footballers back in April of 2016 as Roscommon made it to the knock-out stages of the league, with a famous speech about Roscommon playing summer football in Croke Park:

'It's April and the Rossies are in Croke Park. Imagine if it was later in the year, with the ice-cream melting and the tar melting and the cuckoo singing and the Rossies in Croke Park.'

WE NEED TO TALK ABOUT KEVIN

Paddy Joe got up close and personal with an Irish sporting icon.

If begrudgers were to choose a sporting subject for a screenplay they would surely choose Kevin Moran: a success in the academic world and in business and a man who reached the very top of the ladder in not just one but two sports. Moran was the rock on which so many attacks floundered and his courage and commitment earn him a deserved place in any fantasy team of great Gaelic footballers.

Dave Sexton's reign at Manchester United was celebrated in the song 'Onward Sexton Soldiers'. To no United or Dublin player did the metaphor of a soldier apply more appropriately than Kevin Moran. He exploded onto the Irish sporting world like a hurricane with his spectacular displays for the Dublin Gaelic football team.

In 1978 Moran sensationally became a Manchester United player, for a nominal fee, having obtained a degree in business. Initially Dave Sexton deployed him in midfield in United's reserves but when Ron Atkinson arrived on the scene he immediately moved him to centre-half and in October 1981 he made his debut against Wolves. Injuries to Gordon McQueen and Martin Buchan opened the door for Moran to win a place in the heart of United's defence.

Having won an FA Cup medal in 1983, in 1985 Moran became the first player to be sent off in an FA Cup final by Peter Willis for a clumsy, rather than a malicious tackle on Peter Reid. A major controversy developed when Moran's medal was initially withheld.

Inevitably, given Moran's bravery, throwing his head and body where no sane person would go, injuries came his way. The United manager Ron Atkinson once joked that he was going to give him a part-time contract because he never finished a match!

Paddy Joe is a big fan:

'I think back to FA Cup Final day in 1985 when Man Utd beat Everton by a magnificent Norman Whiteside goal and myself and a few friends were seeing history in the making,' he says with characteristic enthusiasm. 'Peter Reid was in possession of the ball as Kevin Moran came in to tackle. It was a red card despite Reid's plea not to send Kevin off. Kevin was the first winning player to be refused a winner's medal when he went up the steps to collect it. That action prompted the late Val McCrann, George Bannon and myself to send Kevin a medal on behalf of the Church Street Traders Association, Roscommon town. Kevin was delighted with our response and forwarded a letter of thanks back to the Church Street traders. When he was next in Ireland he came to meet us and thank us personally. A great gesture from a great man and one of the greats of Gaelic football.'

A CUT ABOVE THE REST

For fifty-two years, Paddy Joe enjoyed interacting with many customers from all walks of life. He is now living in Sligo with his wife Maura. They met in 2013 but the flames of romance are still burning brightly: 'Love is like porridge. It needs to be made anew every day.'

The shop, though, still has a hold over him:

'Every emotion that can be expressed has been done so inside those four walls. It has been a privilege to meet and listen to some of the most wonderful people anyone could meet.

'We had some mighty fun over the years. We've written best man speeches, grooms' speeches, father of the bride speeches! We've helped with eulogies, winning captains' speeches . . . every emotion that could be shared has been shared here. I got educated about world politics and local politics. One man was a walking encyclopaedia on the Middle East, which I was anxious to understand. I learned about cattle prices, sheep prices, what lambs were making. About grants from the EU. I learnt that I needed to listen to the man in the chair, to be present for him. They are two of the greatest things you can give.'

There were tales of the unexpected:

'These two local men, who will have to remain anonymous, arrived into town every Friday. God help them, they were cursed on the double . . . they were fond of money and fond of drink. They'd collect the pension in the post office and then go to the pub where they'd order two glasses (half-pints) of Guinness, one each.

'When the first man got his glass and had it paid for, he looked at the barman and asked if he could have an empty pint glass. When he received the glass he emptied the contents of his half-pint into the pint glass, draining the froth into it. The barman put the emptied half-pint glass into the sink, then asked the customer would he mind explaining. "No problem," said the man. "It's just in case someone comes in and wants to stand me a drink, it'll be a pint I'm having!"'

There was also an occasional disagreement:

'I remember one particularly heated row over politics. All of a sudden the man in the chair hopped up and went out the door! I had to go out into the street after him to retrieve the gown! He'd heard enough from the fella he was arguing with . . . it was pure Civil War politics.'

ALL CREATURES GREAT AND SMALL

His last day included a special haircut for his very first customer, Fuerty native Martin Mulhern, who now lives in Westmeath.

One of the tribe loves Liverpool FC more than Roscommon. I thought about naming and shaming him, but I will Klopp out.

Special mention for local legend Christy Grogan. His conversation is punctuated by talk about the Rossies with occasional diversions into golf. He caught me on the hop when he told me that he always wears two pairs of socks on the fairways. When I asked why he informed me: 'In case I get a hole in one.'

HAIR AND THERE

Paddy Joe could trade quips with the best of them. Witness his musings on becoming a teenager: 'Too old for Santa Claus. Too young for Rockfords (Roscommon's premier nightclub).'

THE LATE LATE

The shop became even more famous in 2023 when Paddy made his *Late Late Show* debut at the launch of the new Championship season. He was there to represent fans. The invitation to join Ryan Tubridy came as quite the shock:

'They called me on the Thursday and I was in the middle of a haircut. I thought it was someone having me on so I hung up the phone! The man called me back straight away and told me he was a researcher with *The Late Late* and gave me his name and told me to Google him. I couldn't believe it.

'I asked them would they let me wear my Rossie jersey and bandana and they said they would. But then we got a message telling us it was a smart dress code . . . so I called them back and thankfully they said I was an exception.'

Asked on live television if he was confident of a Rossie win against Mayo on the following Sunday, Paddy Joe replied: 'I love going to MacHale Park. We were down in 1972, we were down in 1978, we were there in 2010 and we were there in 2019 when the rain was beautiful . . . and what a magnificent occasion it was when we won. You couldn't play bad football in Castlebar, it is one of the best stadia in the country. The Rossies are going there on Sunday . . . nobody gives us a chance . . . Don't tell anyone, but the Rossies are on tour on Sunday.'

After the programme Ryan Turbidy went up to Paddy Joe and told him never to 'lose your beautiful Roscommon accent'. When he turned on his phone as he prepared to drive home he found that he had 627 new messages. The sweetest part of the story, though, was that Roscommon beat Mayo.

Paddy Joe announced his retirement shortly before Roscommon's All-Ireland SFC Group 2 clash with Mayo in 2024. After the match Aidan O'Shea, who he had never met before, was one of the people who approached him to congratulate him on his news.

WORD PERFECT

The shop was a mecca for football chat. Its closing coincided with the death of a noted Roscommon footballer, Adrian O'Sullivan. He was the only player in the county's history to have captained Roscommon to Connacht minor, under-21 and senior football titles in 1965, 1969 and 1972 respectively. Gerry O'Malley once said of him that he was the greatest centre-back that he had seen playing when he retired. Some compliment.

Paddy Joe's barber shop was so sought out, though, because of the host's unique ability to come up with a great turn of phrase. He went viral after the 2017 Connacht final when Roscommon shocked Galway in a downpour in Salthill with his comment: 'We blew them into Galway Bay.'

A STRANGER CALLS

The 2022 All-Ireland final was a shootout between Kerry's David Clifford and Galway's Shane Walsh. A few weeks later Paddy Joe was cutting a regular customer's hair. The man asked him a question: if there was a transfer system in Gaelic football, who would he take for the Roscommon team, Clifford or Walsh. Paddy Joe went for Walsh explaining that while Clifford was lethal close in, Walsh's overall contribution to the team was superior as he would take possession of the ball back in his own goal-line and work the ball up the field to get a score. As he waxed lyrical about the merits of Walsh, a stranger who had been sitting quietly in the corner got up from his seat and walked right up to the barber's chair and was very emotional as he said to his host: 'Thanks so much for the lovely things you have just said about my son.'

It was agreed that Paddy Joe had to meet Shane. When the two met the barber took the star forward by surprise when he asked him who was the cleanest player he ever marked. Walsh picked Lee Keegan because: 'he never "mouthed me" or blackguarded me or struck me off the ball. He just played his own game and always did it very well.'

TWO FUNERALS AND A WEDDING

Stories were a powerful currency in the barber's chair and hoarded for the perfect moment. Like the one about Finbarr the farmer's wife Nancy who nagged him constantly. The only moments of relief came when he was out in the fields. One day Finbarr was ploughing when Nancy came storming out to nag him about his lack of money, bitterness lacing her every word. Suddenly Finbarr's donkey kicked up his back legs and struck her in the head, killing her instantly. At the funeral, the priest noticed that when the women offered their sympathy, Finbarr would nod his head up and down. However, when the men came up and spoke quietly to him, he would shake his head. Afterwards the priest said to Finbarr, 'Why did you nod your head up and down to all the women and shake your head from side to side to all the men?' 'Well,' Finbarr replied, 'the women all said how nice her dress was, so I agreed by nodding my head up and down. All the men, though, asked me: "Is the donkey for sale?"'

Paddy Joe's skill as a barber was matched, if not surpassed, by his people skills with compassion to the forefront. He has a kind of Dostoyevsky-like empathy with the outsider, whoever might pass by unnoticed and unheeded.

WHERE HEROES ARE MADE

One of his last customers was a man in great form because he had just celebrated his fiftieth wedding anniversary. Paddy Joe asked him what was the spark that kept the marriage together. He was shocked when the man burst into tears. After he regained his composure he said: 'Every week I put my money on the table for my wife. My father never gave my mother a penny. The only money of her own was when she sold the turkeys to pay for the Christmas expenses.' With characteristic insight Paddy Joe observed: 'Buried trauma never decomposes.'

He not only listened to people, he watched their hands because of the insights they offer to a person's mind: 'Hands are the feet of the heart.'

He has not only cut hair but his wisdom has changed lives. Once, a man called into the shop on the way from the airport to his mother's funeral. The man was seething with fury towards his sister and resolved 'to have it out with her' as soon as he returned to the family home. Paddy Joe gently suggested that maybe he should hold off on the conversation until after his anger subsided. A week later the man returned to the shop on his way back to the airport. He thanked Paddy Joe for his good advice and explained that he had only spoken properly with his sister after the funeral when he was calmer and they had talked for hours and resolved their differences. He was returning to the airport at peace with himself, his sister and the world.

Some time ago Paddy Joe was surprised when a young woman came in to the shop in a state of extreme distress. She explained that she had broken up with her boyfriend two weeks previously and he had not texted her since but she missed him terribly. Paddy Joe probed and established that her boyfriend had a shy disposition. The barber suggested that she should take the initiative and text him. Six months later she returned

HAIR AND THERE

to the shop to present him with an invitation to her wedding. Paddy Joe shared a waltz with her at the wedding reception.

The barber shop was a haven for football fans but above all it was a place where the owner's mantra came to life: 'Kindness has a long memory.'

Beannachtai na Chàirdì.

The blessings of friends.

11

THE TIES THAT BIND

The Family

Ah! There is nothing like staying at home, for real comfort.
JANE AUSTEN

It is the place where we take our first steps and cry our first tears.

There was a little old lady who was nearly blind, and she had three sons who wanted to prove which one was the best to her. The eldest son bought her a fifteen-room mansion, thinking this would surely be the best that any of them could offer her. The second son bought her a beautiful Rolls Royce with a chauffeur included, thinking this would surely win her approval.

The last son had to do something even better, so he bought her a parrot that he had trained for fifteen years to memorise the entire Bible. You could ask the parrot any verse in the Bible, and he could quote it word for word. What a gift that would be.

Well, the old lady went to her first son and said, 'Son, the house is just gorgeous, but it's really much too big for me. I only live in one room, and it's too large to clean and take care of. I really don't need the house, but thank you anyway.' Then she confronted her second son with, 'Son, the car is beautiful. It has everything you could ever want on it, but I don't drive and really don't like the chauffeur, so please return the car.'

Next, she went to her youngest son and said, 'Son, I just want to thank you for your most thoughtful gift. That chicken was delicious.'

Danielle Caldwell comes from a very different type of family.

In 2022 she won her first All-Star. But more important to her is her bond with her sisters, Anna and Katie. Anna has a translocation of her chromosome 17, which results in her having special needs. She is the beating heart of the family as Danielle acknowledges. Their friendship feels ancient, as though they both have known each other for lifetimes:

'When Anna first got diagnosed, mum had just found out she was pregnant with me. There's only a year and a month between us and growing up, I kind of grew up a bit earlier than other kids. I was defending her, I suppose. I was nearly a big sister to her rather than a little sister.

'I wouldn't change anything for the world, she's absolutely amazing. We're better people in our house because of her. She taught us how to be kind and patient and she makes us better people in general.

'She doesn't take anything for granted and she's so happy. There's not a care in the world on her.'

ENERGY AND VISION

Given their back stories it is no surprise that Danielle and Katie became healthcare professionals. After studying in Manchester as a physiotherapist Danielle returned to work in a nursing home in Knock. Katie trained as an occupational therapist and both sisters assist their parents, Josephine and Daniel, to care for Anna, as Danielle observes:

'Both of us went into healthcare just because we wanted to help people. We've cared for Anna our whole life so it kind of stems from that as well, to work with people. Katie and I are in the rehab section so it's to get a patient and help them in some way to get back to their baseline function, or to discharge them home from hospital. But I do think the reason we're in this kind of line of work is from Anna. We've been caring for her since we were kids. It's a natural role to fall into.

'Anna would never really be left by herself. So, for instance, when our family are out and it is me minding her, Anna would come to training with me. She absolutely loves coming to training and socialising with the girls. The girls are so good to her; they always make her feel so welcome. She is quite dependent on my mum and dad but she does attend a rehab centre from Monday to Thursday in Castlebar, which is a great social outlet for her. She has loads of friends in there. We are really blessed that Anna has full mobility and she can communicate her wants and needs. It is great that she can because I know there are people who aren't fortunate enough to have that.'

ON THE MOVE
Danielle has become such an integral part of the Mayo full-back line that it is difficult to imagine she spent her early years in another county:

'I grew up in Greystones in Wicklow, so the only sports that I played were athletics and field hockey. I had no real concept of Gaelic up there. I don't know was it because of the school I was in but I was just never introduced to it really. It was only athletics and hockey. So when I moved down to Mayo, I tried to find an athletics and field hockey club but I just didn't really enjoy them that much. And of course, I began secondary school so I just thought the best way to make friends and get into the community would be to join a Gaelic team. I joined it and I haven't looked back since.'

The Caldwell family moved to Castlebar and Danielle attended Davitt College, where her teacher would be a formative influence:

'I couldn't praise my PE teacher enough, Ms Flynn. Sinéad created such a nurturing environment for me to excel in. She put me in goals for my first few games but as soon as she saw that I was trying to learn how to solo and hop at training, she threw me into the mix. And she never once gave out to me or benched me if I made a mistake. She was just so nurturing and really helped me develop as a player.'

There would be a domino effect for the family. Daniel Caldwell was introduced to ladies football by his daughter and went on to become the Chairperson of the Higher Education Colleges. Football has brought father and daughter closer together:

'The main thing we bond over is football and it's great. But he's probably the one person that would know what I'm thinking before I even say it. And he knows when I'm lacking confidence, he would know me inside out. He's like my personal therapist, I always say. We are open with each other. If I think he can do something better, I tell him and if I can do something better, he tells me. We have a great bond over football.'

In the GAA context home is often literally home.

It is common to speak of the GAA as a family.

As the Caldwell example illustrates, the GAA is often a family of families.

Of course, families have disagreements from time to time. Think of the Gallagher brothers, Noel and Liam from Oasis, who have strong family ties to Mayo. Noel said: 'I used to like my mother until she gave birth to Liam.'

WHERE HEROES ARE MADE

Music fans went into a frenzy when it was announced that the Gallaghers would perform a major Oasis reunion concert in Croke Park in August 2025. Noel is no stranger to the field after lining out for Manchester club Oisín's in an exhibition match in 1983. A club photograph shows Noel alongside his teammates ahead of the exhibition match with Kilmacud Crokes, alongside another Gallagher brother, Paul.

THREE ANGELS

Another illustration of the centrality of family within the GAA came after the 2024 All-Ireland final. Niall Grimley dedicated Armagh's All-Ireland win to his late brother Patrick, who tragically died in a car accident the previous November. The Orchard County beat Galway to lift the Sam Maguire for the first time since 2002 and for just the second time ever. Grimley shared the success with his brother's children, with father of three Patrick dying shortly after his fortieth birthday. Patrick's wife, Ciera Grimley, also died, a week later following a four-vehicle collision near Markethill, County Armagh. The couple had been returning home from Patrick's fortieth birthday party when the accident happened. Ciara McElvanna, wife of Armagh 2002 All-Ireland winner Kevin McElvanna, was also killed in the same incident.

After the All-Ireland Niall remarked:

'There were three angels looking down on us today. I'll go see my family [to celebrate] because this isn't about the medal or the cup for me. I've been through a lot this past eight and a half months. I lost my brother and there's not a minute goes by where I don't think about him. That was for him and I just wish he was here to see it. He wouldn't believe it. Every night I was turning out to train, I was just doing it for him. I just wanted to put a smile on his children's faces because they deserve it. They're amazing.'

THE TIES THAT BIND

The team stopped at the site of the crash on the way back from Dublin to remember his brother:

'We were coming down the Newry road, there was singing and beers and the craic was ninety,' he said. 'I knew it was approaching, and I was a bit tense, and the next thing I can see the bus slowing down. The bus pulled over and Geezer (Kieran McGeeney, the team's manager) asked myself and a few of us to go out. We took Sam out and we said a wee prayer for Patrick, Ciera and Ciara. Moments like that are moments I'll never forget and that's coming from one man and that's Geezer.'

Following the team's visit to the crash site, an Armagh flag was left at the scene. Later McGeeney said about his Armagh team:

'They were told they couldn't beat teams above them. They beat teams above them.

'They were told they would never get out of the group of death. They topped the group of death.

'They were told they couldn't win tight games. They won tight games.

'Everybody said they wouldn't win the All-Ireland. And they won the All-Ireland.'

NO SHOW LIKE A JOE SHOW

Joe Brolly has never been one to mince his words. He claimed that Mickey Harte was the first manager to apply an offside tactic, even though the rule doesn't exist in Gaelic football.

Armagh's triumph created an almost unique occasion – when the tables were turned on Joe Brolly, who had also been a frequent critic of the Armagh manager Kieran McGeeney. Alongside a photo of him kissing the Sam Maguire Cup, star player Blaine Hughes tweeted: 'What do ya think of that Joe Brolly!!'

WHERE HEROES ARE MADE

Hughes was using the exact same line uttered by Kieran Donaghy – who was part of the Armagh backroom team in 2024 – after winning Sam Maguire with Kerry in 2014.

Donaghy speaks movingly about his own fraught relationship with his late father:

'My dad had some issues with drink and gambling, and he'd a tough enough journey on his own. And then it just got to the point where it was unworkable at the time. But it was a fierce thing, you know, when your parents were broken up, you were nearly cast aside by other people's houses.

'I didn't talk to him for two years before he died. He had a lot of issues but there were good sides to him. I suppose I was around him the most as a youngster. My brother wouldn't have been around too much. I think he might have been a bit bipolar, he used to have fierce highs and fierce lows, and I think the drink might have been a coping mechanism at the time, maybe.

'I felt I always had anger for him for being missing during that part of my life when you need your dad the most, kind of twelve to eighteen age group. It was tough. The funeral was tough. And a few years after it, I was kind of like, there was probably more going on with him. If it was nowadays, I think someone would have grabbed my dad, and said "Listen, you've got three lovely kids, a lovely wife. Grab a hold of yourself," or "Go in and dry out". People just kind of left everybody alone. Everybody kind of minded their own business. There was no one grabbing him and saying, "You're going to mess this up here."'

Joe Brolly had bigger fish to fry than to respond to his 'roasting' in Armagh in 2024. A few weeks later his wife Laurita gave birth to their first child together following an 'emergency' delivery. Joe described the birth of his little girl: 'You sit there with the baby in your arms for three or four hours and it is as close to paradise I think as a human being can get. If you are in the right situation, with the right person.'

Joe Canning was also bound by the bonds of love at the same time. His mother had passed away in January 2022:

'She was sick for a long time. Going back to 2015 when she got breast cancer. She was good then until 2020, and we lost her so it's nice to remember her through Josie (Joe's daughter) so she lives on. Her name is Josie. It's the third generation of the name. My mam was called Josephine, I'm Joe, and we have Josie now.'

12

HOPE AND TEARS

Ellis Island

No one leaves home unless home is the mouth of a shark.
WARSAN SHIRE

The founding of the GAA is part of the story of struggle, the spirit of a nation in chains trying to break free, of wanting something more and finding the courage to run away from the greatest empire the world had ever known.

The Ireland of the 1840s was a vision of hell – the years of a tragedy beyond belief when over a million people on this tiny island died from famine. Nothing prepared people for it. Nothing could prepare anyone for the sight and smell of death on a massive scale – bundles of corpses where once there had been life.

The mid-1840s saw the plagues of Ireland – hunger, disease and government neglect. Each plague compounded the other like a battleground of contending dooms. Fragile lifelines of aid reached only a minority of the population. In the first year there was barely enough potatoes, in the next only a trickle. Then nothing. Potato stalks withered and died. There was nothing for seed. Many people had nothing to live on and nothing to live for.

The death toll was seemingly unending in many districts. Everything had to be rationed. It would have taken too much land to bury the corpses individually so their relatives normally buried them in a mass grave. There were so many people dying it was impossible to make coffins for them all, or even have a coffin for each family. Timber was very scarce. Sometimes villagers decided to build one proper coffin with a sliding bottom. They solemnly put the corpses into the coffin, carried them up to the grave and slid back the bottom of the coffin and the body tumbled into the grave. The coffin was brought back to the village and passed on to the family of the next casualty.

Fear was the only real sign of life as people died slowly in agony. To the embattled, emotionally bankrupt and hopelessly disorganised, the ordinary joys and sorrows were an irrelevance. The chances of survival were slim. For many, death was a welcome escape from pain and heartache. The afterlife was the only dream they could still cherish. For the strong, life was a victory over death. Where possible the corpses were buried under hawthorn trees – because of their alleged special favour in the eyes of God. These trees were long palls in a parched place. They sang a lament to the angel of death. The memories were too sad ever to be healed.

Ireland was a country of extremes, from the beginning to the end. It seemed simultaneously connected to the Garden of Eden in the landlords' palaces and to some foretaste of doomsday destruction where the peasants lived to die. Nowhere were the gardens more luxuriant or a people more miserable. The tragedy was a moral test which those with power failed.

Deep in their psychic memory the famine was still a painful experience for Irish people right through the nineteenth century and beyond. People used the words 'I'm famished' whenever they were cold or hungry. The frequent usage of these words was just one symptom of the lasting effect of the famine. Often Irish people buried their thoughts of the famine deep in their subconscious. The story of the famine years was so horrific they just wanted to erase it from their memory. There was great shame attached to failing to feed one's family. Parents always blamed themselves for their children's deaths. Succeeding generations had inherited their shame. Even in the twentieth century some people in rural Ireland would not travel anywhere without bringing a piece of bread in their pocket because the fear of hunger was so strong.

The term 'Great Famine' is itself a misnomer. It is more accurate to say there was a 'Great Starvation'. Famines are caused by natural disasters. There are not famines when there are large quantities of food in a country. There was plenty of food produced in Ireland during those years. That food was exported while Irish people starved in the country's greatest human tragedy, is an enduring monument to inhumanity, ineffectiveness and indifference.

There were two main options open to these people: emigration if they could afford it or the poorhouse/workhouse. The workhouses had a huge stigma attached to them. Like the infamous coffin ships, where so many Irish emigrants died prematurely, there was so much disease in the workhouse that to sign into the place was often to sign one's death warrant. Generally, the poorhouses postponed death for a short while but no more. In the poorhouses and soup kitchens families were separated from each other. All the men were housed in one section, the women in another. There were separate places for babies, young children, young girls and boys. Once a family went in they might never see each other again. There were strict

HOPE AND TEARS

rules about communication with another section. If one person broke the rules the whole family might be thrown out. Through speaking Irish in the workhouses people could sometimes pass on messages without their masters knowing what was being said. In many ways the poorhouse was worse than jail. At least in jail you could get news from your family. It has often been claimed these places could have been called deathhouses.

THE DEEP BLUE SEA

In many respects people thought they were safer in their own place. There was so much disease in those coffin ships their chances of surviving that long journey in such a weak state were remote. People by and large did not trust the sea. They all heard the stories of the American sailing ship *Stephen Whitney*. On a foggy December night in 1847 the ship sailing on a voyage from America to Bristol, was wrecked off the Irish coast on Bolig Rinn na mBeann on the Western Calf Island. Within days ninety-four bodies were washed up on the beaches. Some people were desperate enough to try anything but the majority preferred to meet their maker on their own land rather than on the other side of the Atlantic Ocean.

Nobody knows how many people went on the coffin ships. The one reliable statistic is about a group who went to Canada where they all died of typhoid fever in a place called Grosse Ile just outside Quebec City. Twelve thousand Irish people were buried in mass graves in Canada. They set out to make their mark in the world but the only mark they made was in a grave – a people with no name. It was their final indignity. They lived to the point of tears.

Historically, in Ireland the shadow of emigration lurked like a vulture hovering over its prey. It was the traditional Irish solution to economic problems. It churned out an assembly line of bodies for the boat to England and America. There were many scenes of families travelling in block to the train station. Everyone wore their Sunday best. The mother was blind with tears. The father's eyes were dry but his heart was breaking. Men did not betray emotion. It would have been seen as a sign of weakness. The young people leaving leaned out of the window choking with sadness as they saw their parents for perhaps the last time. Younger brothers and sisters raced after the train shouting words of parting. Sometimes white handkerchiefs were produced and waved until the train went out of sight. Those handkerchiefs gave a ritual, almost sacramental solemnity, to the goodbyes. Their presence was a symbol of defeat, a damning indictment of an economy unable to provide for its brightest and most talented. Few people have better captured the imprint of emigration on the Irish psyche than Brendan Graham.

MELODY MAKER
Born in Tipperary his songs have sold more than 100 million units. His anthem 'You Raise Me Up' has been recorded in over forty languages by almost one thousand artists and has been performed at official Ground Zero 9/11 commemorations, the Nobel Peace Prize ceremony, the Super Bowl, the White House, the Olympic Games, Queen Elizabeth's visit to Ireland, Pope Francis' visit to the United States and Ireland's 1916 Centenary Concert. He also penned Ireland's last two Eurovision-winning songs – 'Rock 'n' Roll Kids' (1994) by Paul Harrington and Charlie McGettigan and 'The Voice' (1996) by Eimear Quinn.

What is less known about him is that he was once part of the GAA's diaspora. The inaugural meeting of the Gaelic Athletic Association of Western Australia took place on Sunday 2 August 1970, at Perth's Irish Club. Sixty-four men came together to

HOPE AND TEARS

sanction the official formation of the association which was to be affiliated with the GAA in Ireland. Reflecting the close relationship between the Catholic Church and Gaelic sports in Ireland, two priests and two Christian Brothers attended the meeting, including Padraig Kelly who would become the association's inaugural president.

Unlike many people, emigration to America was not a central part of his family story: 'Not really ... one brother ... a musician went there fifty years ago and is still there.' Yet Graham wrote one of the most heartbreaking songs about emigration: 'Isle of Hope, Isle of Tears'. It is based on the story of the first person to enter America through Ellis Island – a young Irish girl named Annie Moore and describes her leaving everything behind and starting over in a new place. It contrasts Ireland – the isle of tears – with the Isle of Manhattan – the isle of hope. I wondered what was the catalyst to the song?

'A visit to Ellis Island on my return from Nashville on my first-ever trip to America. I saw Jeanne Ryhnart's sculpture of Annie arriving in America with her two younger brothers and I wondered what that must have been like for a fifteen-year-old (as the information at the time suggested Annie was). We now know that she was seventeen and born in May so that 1 January was not her birthday as I thought when I wrote the song.'

Does she represent the Irish emigrant story to America in microcosm? 'Absolutely – she is the emblem for all who travelled there in hope and tears.'

How did the title suggest itself? 'I came across something that it was a name by which Ellis Island was known.'

Graham was inspired by a personal visit to Ellis Island: 'I have always felt that so much of our history is abroad ... in Britain, Australia and America, so visiting there was like coming face to face with an unknown part of "my own" history.'

'Hopes and Tears' captures the ambiguity of the emigrant experience. It was important for him to focus on both 'sides' of the story:

'Of course, you get it straight away not everybody reached Manhattan after making the long journey to America. Some were sent home again. So, hope was dashed to be replaced by tears.'

The celebrated songwriter believes that it was important for these emigrants to hold on to their Irish identity in America rather than experiencing their own sense of longing and identity crisis: 'Well, we see this every day ... hear it time and time again – as one American lady said to me: "I'm a hundred per cent Irish". Her accent belied that so I asked her and her answer was: "Both of my grandmothers were Irish". That was a powerful insight into what being "Irish" in America meant.'

Graham believes that the GAA have a role to play for some of the new emigrants hankering for home where the hills are winter green; where the water's clear and the air is cleaner: 'Of course it has. It's a natural bond with the collective of "home", a home away from home and easily slipped-into community that is both supportive and informative ... that gives you "the suss" on the place. I lived in Australia for five years and one of the first things I did was to join the GAA playing community in Perth even though my background was not GAA but rugby and basketball. I was a youth international at the latter.'

Harry Truman told the US Congress in 1952: 'One of the reasons we lead the free world today is that we are a nation of immigrants.' In contrast today Donald Trump is hostile to immigrants especially from Haiti and other 'sh*thole countries'. As a consequence, some Irish people living in the US are avoiding going to GAA matches and Irish dances amid rising fears over being deported under Trump. New York lawyer

Brian O'Dwyer claims he is aware of Irish people being quietly detained and deported.

PAT ON THE BACK

In 2023 the Irish government committed €500,000 for a revamp of New York's GAA stadium. Situated in the Bronx, Gaelic Park has been a home for Gaelic games in New York City since 1926. The funding was made available through the government's Emigrant Support Programme.

Trips to New York to play in club matches has been a regular feature of many a glittering career. A case in point was Pat Spillane:

'On one trip, the team manager brought us to a pub he owned on the Friday night and let us drink for free all night. He hoped this might deter us from going out again the night before the game. From memory, I don't think it worked.

'On another occasion, I was due to play for a junior club side. In the middle of the night, I got a call from Aer Lingus to inform me that my ticket had been cancelled. Apparently, the sponsor of the club's senior side didn't want me playing with the junior team and persuaded the travel agent who had made the booking to cancel it. I still made it to New York. Somebody turned up in Shannon and paid for my flight in cash.

'On another trip, I was due to play alongside a star player who was also travelling from Ireland. However, by the time we had made it through immigration in New York, he had changed sides. I think the Jerry Maguire "show me the money" approach had worked.

'The 1984 New York final between Donegal and Cavan really took the biscuit. Up to thirty high-profile players from Ireland were flown out. How high was the standard? Well, lads who had played in the All-Ireland final a couple of weeks earlier were substitutes. The New York Board was not affiliated with the GAA at the time so normal playing rules didn't apply – at least as far as Donegal was concerned. They brought on ten replacements.

'My happiest memories, and you'll struggle with this, are from the times I lined out with Tyrone and wore their white-and-red jersey. Little did I think that a few years later I would be public enemy number one in the county after my "puke football" comments.'

DEDICATED FOLLOWER OF FASHION

Another former Kerry footballer has special memories of the Big Apple. It was not in the stands of Croke Park or at a local club, but a fashion show that Paul Galvin was struck by cupid's arrow. The RTÉ presenter Louise Duffy hadn't a clue who Paul was as she wasn't interested in football. The smooth-talking Galvin used the chat-up line 'Is your jacket Balmain?' and before Louise knew it, the pair were smitten. Sparks began to fly and they went on a date in Ranelagh. That was in 2011 and three years later Galvin popped the question while the pair were on holiday in New York.

KING HENRY

Henry Shefflin became the undisputed king of hurling. Now in retirement his career can be fully appraised.

Even in his most sublime moments he played with a competitiveness that was as essential to him as breathing. He brought a no-nonsense approach to the game, believing that if something is worth doing, it is worth doing well, with everybody mucking in. He was a stickler for preparing properly. At the height of the Championship season everything else was an intrusion that tended to be pushed to one side as much as was practicable as he immersed himself in what really mattered – hurling.

His performances were central to Kilkenny winning League, Leinster and All-Ireland titles. As early in his career as 2002 he was the unanimous choice as Hurler of the Year. Yet to speak to him is to appreciate that even the greatest and most successful players are still haunted by memories of past disappointments. In 1997 he had tasted defeat in a minor All-Ireland final to Clare:

'A few of us didn't perform that day. I hit a few frees and missed a good few of them. There was a breeze flowing in the second half and I went out to hit a few 65s, right into the Clare crowd. All I could see was these lads waving behind the goal – the Clare hurlers as well as umpires. It was a tough and lonely place. When you're a minor you'll always remember those kind of days, you'll take it to heart. You heap some of the blame on yourself when you're hitting the frees. It was a day I wouldn't like to go back to again.'

He lost his first senior All-Ireland title in 1999, when hot favourites Kilkenny lost to Cork on a miserable day. He is still pained by the memory:

'They came back and to see point after point flowing from Cork was a sickening thing. I know Seánie McGrath got a few points but I can't remember if they were left or right. I just remember it slipping from us. It just went. I remember standing in the rain, listening to the 'Banks of the Lee' roaring out over the microphones. You're there on your own and you have your thoughts. You could have done this, you could have done that. To think you have it and then it's just snatched from you.

'We were kind of in shock. I remember walking out of Croke Park and there were still Kilkenny people around, coming over congratulating us, saying "well done" and all this. It just rubbed it in more. To think you have to go home and face these people the following night. They come out clapping you and you're after losing an All-Ireland. It's gut-wrenching. I took it badly. It upset me a lot.'

Despite his status within the game Henry has not had his head turned by success. He refuses to take the credit for Kilkenny's great performances:

'We never depend on one or two individuals to produce the goods. If I was having an off day the likes of Eddie Brennan produced a big performance. We were very much a team. Brian Cody did not want to see anyone come off the field happy after a defeat. There was no point in saying I played well but the others let me down. We won as a team and we lost as a team. We used defeats to motivate us to achieve even more success.'

Henry is keen to pay tribute to his coach with Kilkenny, Brian Cody:

'It is vital to a team to have a coach who thinks about the game, especially about improving our game but in particular a manager who can read a game and when things are going badly never lose their composure and can turn things around. He gave inspired leadership. His man-management skills were excellent, he instilled belief and got us right physically and mentally for the big days. He also knew how to motivate us. When it comes to motivation it is different strokes for different folks. He knew what buttons to push to motivate us individually and collectively. He always provided us with good feedback. Above all, he was a winner. Winners have critical skills, don't leave winning to chance, leave no stone unturned and make things happen.'

There is more to Henry Shefflin than hurling. He studied at Waterford IT and emerged with an honours degree in Business Studies and Financial Services. As a student at Waterford he lived in a house designed for four, with six others. First to bed got the bed.

HOPE AND TEARS

In 2000 he won his first senior All-Ireland against Offaly. The next year, though, Shefflin was to experience the bitter taste of defeat again when Kilkenny were sensationally beaten by Galway in the All-Ireland semi-final:

'After winning the All-Ireland in 2000 there was great hype about us. We thought we were great lads and a small bit of that seeped through to our hurling. We probably didn't think we'd have to put in the hard work and we definitely didn't put in the hard work. Training was very poor and you could feel in training that it wasn't going well.

'It was a turning point for some of us, that we had to cop on. It was a wake-up call. I didn't hurl well all year. I think I was a small bit gone away from the game concentrating on maybe other things, certainly not focused on the game and the things you have to do. And doing the simple things instead of doing the great things.

'Against Galway we were horsed out of it, simple as that. We weren't hungry enough. We weren't able for the physical battle. Hopefully it was a turning point for myself. I went looking for protection that day. I went on to the referee and the umpire and the linesman. You don't do that. Hurling is a man's game. Rather than look for protection you have to drive out and try to win the next ball and horse on.'

9/11

Later that summer Henry and two friends went to New York. Shefflin played a match on the Sunday. Two days later the twin towers of the World Trade Centre were attacked:

'I don't know how many blocks we were from it but it was a crazy feeling. Unbelievable. Unbelievable. We didn't know what hit us. Three Irish lads over in the fastest city in the world. We didn't even have any experience of going to New York. We ended up staying for about a week. Couldn't get out of there. We walked down Times Square and we were looking at the big screen. It was only that night when we sat down and watched telly the same as everyone else did for days.

'We rang home and our parents were there. "Are ye all right, are ye all right?"

'"Ah, we're grand."'

13

FACE THE MUSIC

Cúil Aodha

If the game of hurling was an old dog, the GAA would be telling us that good old hurling was being taken to live on a lovely farm in the country, while texting the local vet about having hurling put to sleep because hurling has become a bit too whiny.

DÓNAL ÓG CUSACK

This is primarily a place of love, not loss.

His name is carved on the collective consciousness of the nation.

Seán Ó Riada died in 1971 at the young age of forty. A weak liver curtailed his life cruelly. His funeral was televised and public sympathy was that of the loss of a great chieftain. His legacy to Irish music and culture is immense and remains vibrant.

John Reidy was born in Cork City in 1931. His formative years were spent between Cork and Limerick; he was the son of a Garda from Clare while his mother was from the West Muskerry Gaeltacht. He began his studies in University College

Cork on a scholarship in 1948, reading Classics and Irish, before moving to the music department. He graduated as a Bachelor of Music from UCC in 1951. He was already assistant director of music in RTÉ when he graduated and moved to Dublin, but the work's administrative nature frustrated him. His initial motivation was a hunger for success in classical music.

Leaving behind the marginal classical music scene in Ireland, as well as his wife and first-born child, Ó Riada attempted a music career in Europe in 1955. He moved to Italy and France where he adopted a more bohemian lifestyle and composed several avant-garde compositions for orchestra called Nomos. Just as he was on the verge of becoming Ireland's first avant-garde composer, he decided to return to Ireland, gradually rejecting modern 'Classical' music, as he began to devote his time to the study of all things Irish. Although he was inspired by Paris and gave some recitals and broadcasts of his work there his wife fetched him home and he settled back with his family in Dublin. He said to her: 'I'd rather be breaking stones in Ireland than be the richest man living in Europe.'

THE PRODIGAL SON
At about this time he changed his name from John Reidy to Seán Ó Riada.

He took over as the musical director in the famed Abbey Theatre in 1957 where he remained until 1962. In 1950s Ireland traditional music was often held in low regard by some elements of Irish society. Ó Riada's first attempt to combine Irish song with the classical tradition was in 1959, he composed the score for the documentaries *Mise Éire* and *Saoirse?* in 1960 and, most famously, the score for the film version of *The Playboy of the Western World* in 1963. This last piece made him a household name in Ireland.

FACE THE MUSIC

He also composed *Mná na hÉireann* ('The Women of Ireland') which confirmed the musical eloquence of his writing. In this period, he sought to create a sort of Irish flavoured classical music, i.e. Irish folk tunes arranged for orchestra, as Vaughan Williams had done in England and other nationalist composers had done in Europe towards the end of the previous century. He studied and collected old Irish music and produced a series for RTÉ called *Our Musical Heritage*. Ó Riada was the founder of the modern school (the authentic ancient style of playing) Irish folk music.

We all need a supporting cast. The beautiful St Colman's Cathedral in Cobh is 'held up' by several pretty houses known locally as 'the deck of cards'. Between 1961 and 1969 Ó Riada was leader of a 'Celtic chamber orchestra' called *Ceoltóirí Chualann*. It included Ó Riada, Martin Fay (fiddle), Paddy Moloney (pipes) Seán Keane (fiddle) Michael Tubridy (flute) Seán Ó Sé (singer) and Seán Potts (whistle).

Although they played in concert halls dressed in black suits with white shirts and black bow ties, they played traditional songs and tunes which were arranged in a more interesting way than was usual in Irish music until then. Ó Riada sat in the middle at the front playing bodhrán, an instrument that had almost died out, being played only by small boys in street parades. He also wanted to use the wire-strung harp for authenticity, but as these were as yet unavailable, he played the harpsichord instead. Arrangements of tunes like Brian Boru's March and much of the music of the seventeenth century harper O'Carolan went on to inspire the formation of The Chieftains.

Ó Riada also had an impact on popular culture through the song 'An Poc ar Buile'. He was one of a trio with composer Dónall Ó Mulláin and tenor Seán Ó Sé, responsible for what has come to be regarded as the first pop record 'hit' in the Irish language. The tape of 'An Poc ar Buile' was made just for the fun of it by the three men who took turns singing the verses and joined together for the rousing '*ailliliú, puilliliú*' chorus.

The song became an overnight success. Seán Ó Sé has explained the background to its recording:

'One evening Seán Ó Riada and myself went up to (Ó Mulláin's) house in Screathan and on an old reel-to-reel tape recorder we recorded it, each of us taking verses, the three of us singing every third verse and we did the chorus together, just for the fun of it.

'Straight away he (Ó Riada) liked the voice and he decided there and then that we would go into a small studio at the corner of Stephen's Green, up on the fifth floor – it was called Peter Hunt's Studio – and we recorded a voice and piano version of 'An Poc ar Buile'. The minute it came out it became a hit. There was no official top ten on any of the radio stations but it was certainly the first hit in the Irish language.'

The lyrics, detailing the exploits of a puck goat, were written by Ó Mulláin in the 1940s, rejuvenating an older song relating to a man or 'buck' and called 'An Boc ar Buile'. This concerned an incident involving a local landlord's attempt to exercise the 'right' of 'droit du seigneur', which allowed feudal lords to have sexual relations with tenants' brides on their wedding night.

'An Poc ar Buile', along with three further tracks by Ó Sé and Ceoltóirí Cualann – 'Tórramh an Bhairille', 'An Spealadóir', and 'Amhráinín Síodraimín' – became Gael Linn's second extended play (EP) record.

In 1964 Ó Riada moved to Cúil Aodha in West Cork, an Irish speaking area where he established Cór Chúil Aodha, a male voice choir. In his later years Ó Riada composed Irish church music, including 'Aifreann 2', to be sung by un-trained voices in his choir. He died at the young age of forty in 1971, but his enormous influence on others was only beginning.

In 2008 a statue of him was unveiled at a ceremony opposite St Gobnait's Church in Cúil Aodha. One of the organisers of the event, Eoin Ó Súilleabháin, said locals were pleased to finally be able to honour one of Irish music's biggest ever influences.

YOU DON'T KNOW JACK

One of the most memorable evenings of my life came when a mutual friend arranged for me to meet Jack Lynch some years after he had retired from the political stage. My heart was beating like a bodhran. Outside through the glass window a silvered swirl of stars settled in. He seemed possessed of a kind of wisdom, an ancientness.

I sat in silence and stillness and, like the soloist in an orchestra moving towards the centre of the podium, he took control. There is no easy way to describe the next few hours other than to say 'something happened'. The experience felt like a sacred time when the perpetual restlessness of the human heart was stilled and transformed in the face of this heartfelt, rhythmic, and charismatic character. Time shimmered and paused, slowing its relentless pace as I sat enthralled. He shared the story of his great Cork team with me at a leisurely pace.

While I was intrigued by his sporting career I had to ask him about his involvement in one of the most controversial events in Irish history: the Arms Trial. It is indicative of his sensitivities around the topic that he said he would only speak about it on the condition that I would only publish the piece 'long after' he died. He was standing on the edge of the past that was terrifying as he recalled with a studied eloquence:

'The North was to be my major preoccupation as taoiseach. Very shortly after I took office in 1966, I travelled to Stormont to see the Northern Premier, Captain Terence O'Neill – this was the time when my car was snowballed, by a handful of Ian Paisley's supporters.

'There can be no unity through force or coercion – the unity we seek can come only through agreement and the IRA was making that unity, immeasurably more difficult.

'This is quite apart from the revulsion which we all feel towards their repeated acts of barbarity. The catalogue of such barbarism is long but one incident sticks out in my mind. This was the bombing of the Abercorn restaurant in Belfast (on Saturday, 4 March, 1972). No warning of the bomb was given and two young women died and 130 people were injured, many losing limbs and otherwise being maimed for life. One young woman lost both her legs and an arm and many others suffered similar injury.

'I was absolutely appalled to realise that on this island, an organisation, claiming to act in the name of the Irish people, should perpetrate such an atrocity. What is the point of a united Ireland if this is the price to be paid for achieving it?'

Things would escalate for Lynch with the Arms Crisis:

'There was a time during that period, when it was widely believed we would be decimated at the polls whenever an election took place. This was, of course, due largely to the dismissal of ministers on 6 May 1970 and the resignation of another minister. Naturally this was a very trying period for me personally. Although I was not close socially to any of the people involved, I had grown up in politics with them and a bond of camaraderie had grown up between us. To have had to dismiss them from office was a very painful thing to do, as was the subsequent recrimination.

'History will adjudicate on the rights and wrongs of that period, but I felt I had no option but to act as I did, given the information placed at my disposal by the security forces. There have been suggestions that I orchestrated the prosecutions throughout the affair, but again the fact of the matter is that I had no involvement whatsoever in anything to do with the prosecution, or with the conduct of the case, once I handed the papers over to the Attorney General.

'Almost overnight in May of 1970, we lost four senior members of the Government – Charlie Haughey, Neil Blaney, Kevin Boland and Michael Moran. These were difficult ministers to replace, especially given the fact that a taoiseach really has only a one in two choice, from which to make government appointments. In the circumstances, I don't think we did badly, in spite of continued, opportunistic harassment by the opposition. The growth rate for those years in the early seventies was very high. We dealt competently with the security situation, and we began to make substantial progress with the British on a solution to the Northern Ireland problem.

'One of the difficulties I experienced in dealing with British prime ministers or ministers on the North, is that they often were not very well acquainted with the issue and didn't rate it high in their order of priorities. This is understandable, given the relative importance of the Northern Ireland issue in the context of the overall British political situation, but it did mean that the Northern problem was allowed to drag on, sometimes unnecessarily.'

We also had a great chat about Eddie Keher who he had a huge admiration for. Nonetheless he would have been thrilled that in March 2025 Cork ace Patrick Horgan moved past the Kilkenny legend as the top scorer in league history. He passed Keher's 72-524 (740) – to move on to 26-673 (751).

A TWIST IN THE TALE

It turned out that our conversation was Jack's last interview. At the end the conversation took an unexpected turn. He told me that the soul of Ireland was to be found in hurling and in the music of Seán Ó Riada and that one of his regrets was not in seeing that while Ó Riada was alive. If he had he would as taoiseach have commissioned Ó Riada to write an epic musical work inspired by hurling on the lines of the musical epic tribute to the *Brendan Voyage* with the ability to stir the blood like Ó Riada's own score for *Mise Éire*. His eyebrows moved upwards, and something flashed in his eyes.

I am including Cúil Aodha in this collection as a small apology on the part of Jack Lynch for failing to harness the genius of Ó Riada to celebrate our national game.

EDGE OF GLORY
Kerry's Paul Geaney launches the Allianz League against the stunning backdrop of the Cliffs of Moher.
© INPHO/DAN SHERIDAN

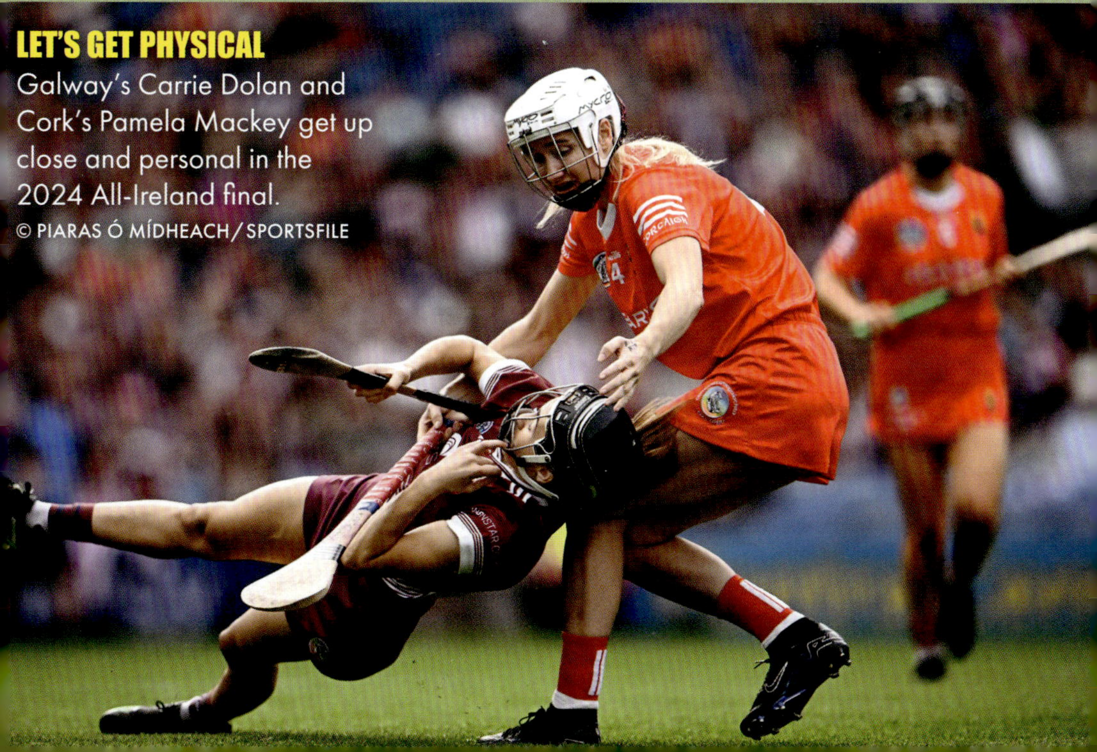

LET'S GET PHYSICAL
Galway's Carrie Dolan and Cork's Pamela Mackey get up close and personal in the 2024 All-Ireland final.
© PIARAS Ó MÍDHEACH/SPORTSFILE

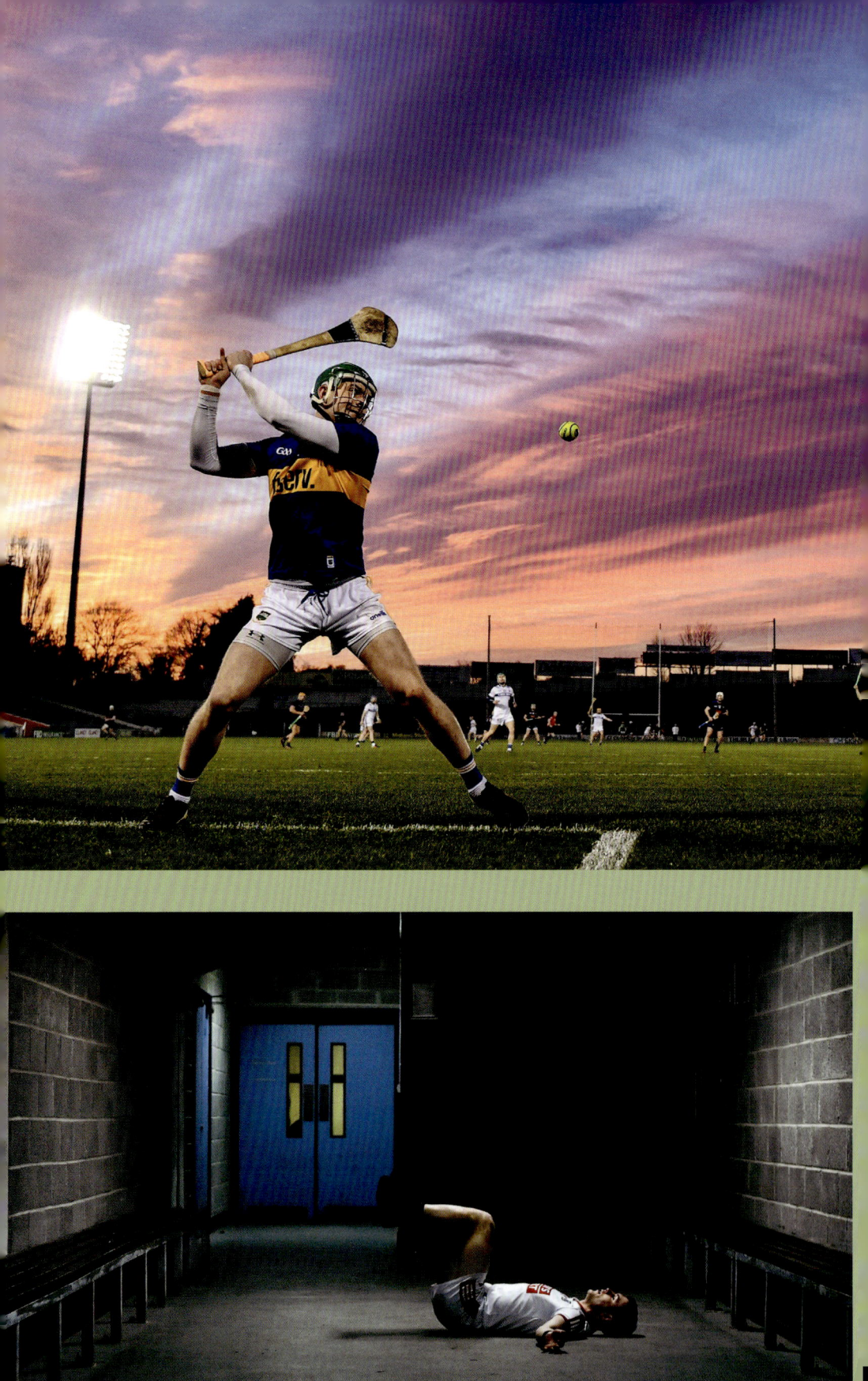

JEEPERS KEEPERS
TOP LEFT Tipperary goalie Barry Hogan launches an attack in Semple Stadium.
© SAM BARNES / SPORTSFILE

WE'RE WALKING IN THE AIR
TOP RIGHT Dublin's Brian Fenton celebrates after dispatching Kerry in the 2023 All-Ireland final.
© BRENDAN MORAN / SPORTSFILE

FALL BACK
BOTTOM LEFT Cork's Seán O'Leary Hayes gets in the zone before facing Galway in Pearse Stadium.
© SEB DALY / SPORTSFILE

THE BLUE JERSEY BOYS
Carter Sludds, age six, and cousin Leo, age seven, cheer on the Oylegate-Glenbrien team as they run on the pitch before the Wexford County final.
© PIARAS Ó MÍDHEACH/SPORTSFI

DADDY'S GIRL
Ben Conneely celebrates Offaly's Joe McDonagh Cup triumph with his daughter Rua.
© PIARAS Ó MÍDHEACH/SPORTSFI

ROAR OF APPROVAL
Former Kilkenny manager Brian Cody lends his vocal support to the Cats in the 2023 Leinster final.
© PIARAS Ó MÍDHEACH/SPORTSFILE

KEEP YOUR EYE ON THE BALL
Umpire David Coady watches on alongside Mayo goalkeeper Rory Byrne as Roscommon attack in Hyde Park.
© PIARAS Ó MÍDHEACH/SPORTSFILE

GIANT ON MY SHOULDER
TOP LEFT Armagh's Aaron McKay climbs over Roscommon's Conor Cox in Croke Park.
© INPHO/RYAN BYRNE

PUBLIC DISPLAY OF AFFECTION
TOP RIGHT Nicky Kennedy hugs Ballygunner captain Stephen O'Keeffe after they won the Waterford County final.
© DAVID FITZGERALD/SPORTSFILE

OUT OF FOCUS
BOTTOM RIGHT Monaghan's Niall Garland is goalbound when a hurl is thrown at him.
© HARRY MURPHY/SPORTSFILE

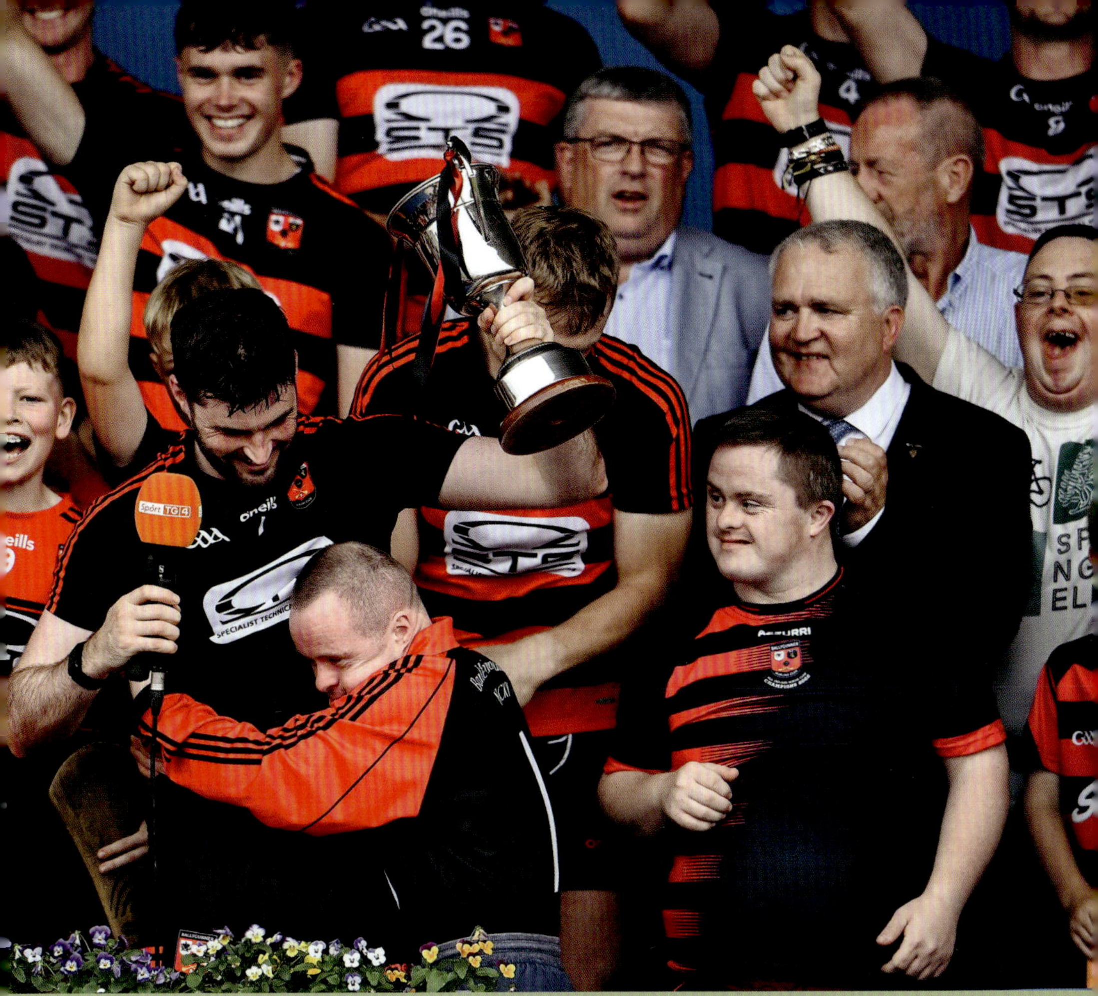
26
Spórt TG4
SPECIALIST TECHNICAL

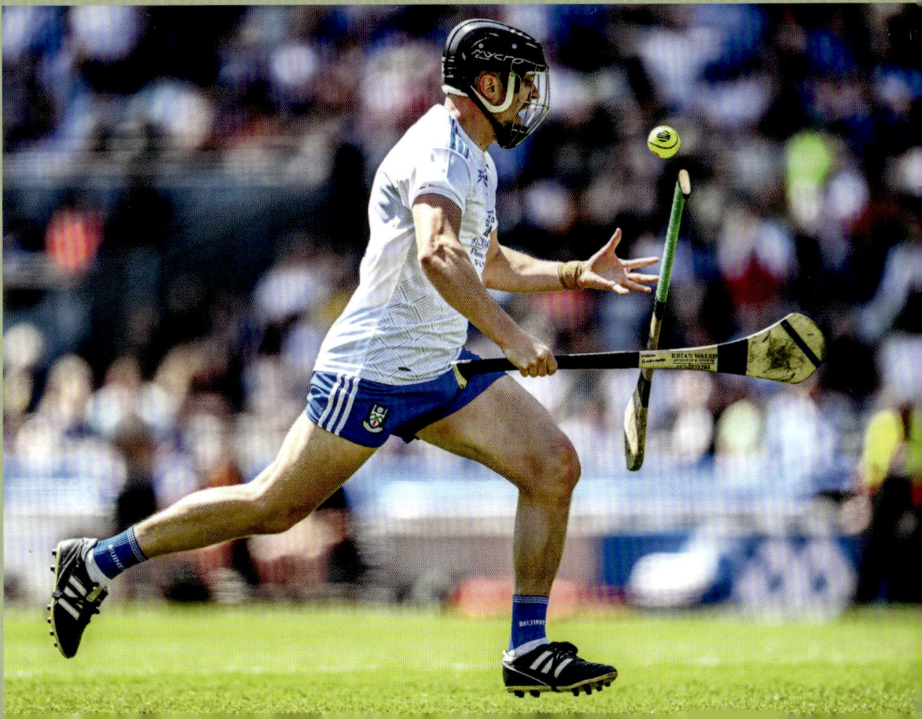
BRIAN WALSH

TAKE IT ON THE CHIN
Annaghdown's Jemma Burke collides with Aoibhín Webb of Bennekerry/Tinryland in the Ladies Club Intermediate Final.
© INPHO/LEAH SCHOLES

CHIN UP
Wexford ace Lee Chin evades the Clare defence in Semple Stadium.
© INPHO/RYAN BYRNE

14

WHO FEARS TO SPEAK OF 98?

Wexford

I love me county.

JOHN MULLANE

Roly Meates was an Irish rugby coach in the 1970s. At the time the coach was not part of the selection committee. Given the political nature of the selection process then, he found that if he was keen on a particular player the best way to ensure that he was selected was to publicly lobby for his rival for the jersey.

Liam Griffin cultivated a different approach to selection. He is a man with a very strong sense of Wexford's place in Irish history. He grew up in the 1950s when the names of the Rackards (Bobby, Billy and Nicky), Art Foley, Nick O'Donnell, Ned Wheeler, Jim English, Tim Flood and many more were assuming legendary status not alone in Wexford but all over the country. In earlier years the Wexford footballers had contested six All-Ireland finals in a row from 1913 to 1918 winning the last four, the first ever four-in-a-row for any county. In 1968 Griffin watched Wexford reach the Holy Grail again. They played Kilkenny, the reigning All-Ireland champions, and after an epic struggle came out on top by the minimum margin of one point.

As Galway played in the Munster championship at that time and Antrim did not have a senior team, the win over Kilkenny saw them through to the All-Ireland final against Munster champions Tipperary, the fourth time in the 1960s for the teams to clash for the Liam MacCarthy Cup. The score stood at 2-1 in Tipperary's favour and the Purple and Gold were determined to level things up.

Tipperary completely dominated the first thirty minutes – the duration of games at that time was sixty minutes. Although Jack Berry scored a Wexford goal shortly before the interval, Tipp led at half-time by eight points. With two goals from Tony Doran and Jack Berry notching up his second goal, Wexford went eight ahead – a turnaround of sixteen points with time running out. Tipperary did hit back with two late goals but the Yellowbellies won by 5-8 to 3-12.

THE HEATHER BLAZING

Wexford have a tradition of heroic defence. Cromwell, after the sacking of Drogheda, set his eye on Wexford. He sent a company under Lt. Gen Jones to attack it from the Rosslare side. Captain Sinnott and his comrades put up a fearless defence until, outgunned and outnumbered, they were forced to surrender. After the destruction of the Fort, the Puritans, as Cromwell's troops were called locally, marched the survivors and any inhabitants they could capture to the large valley in the sand dunes opposite Lambert's Corner, known as 'the Murder Hole' and executed them.

Liam Griffin believes that Wexford people carry the DNA of the 1798 Rising in their genes because it was their 'rebel hands' that 'set the heather blazing'. It was they alone who followed the call to 'Arm, arm'. They were martyrs to the cause, 'For Ireland's freedom we fight or die'. It was then that 'Father Murphy from County Wexford' swept 'oer the land like a mighty wave'.

Amidst the hotbed of political intrigue and the reams of revolutionary rhetoric that rampaged the nation it was Wexford people, and Wexford people alone, who put their pikes where their mouths were 'o'er the bright May meadows of Shelmalier'.

In his classic poem 'Requiem for the Croppies' Seamus Heaney describes Vinegar Hill as 'the final conclave'. He captures the inequality of the battle and the heroism and bravery of Wexford people in battling superior forces as they were 'shaking scythes at cannon'. Faced with this uneven battle 'The hillside blushed'.

The famous ballad 'The Wind that Shakes the Barley', first published in 1861, tells the story of an Irish rebel from County Wexford who leaves his lover behind to help fight against British colonial rule.

Liam Griffin argues: 'We were the only ones who stood up when Ireland needed someone to take on the Empire.'

In this perspective, winning the All-Ireland in 1996 was much more than winning a match; it was another instalment in the county's unique tradition of defiance, determination and dignity. It is indicative of the place of the hurley in Wexford life that camogie ace Ursula Jacob was chosen as Wexford Woman of the Year in March 2025.

NO SMALL WONDER
Without wonder the people perish. Wonder is a lovely quality that enables us to see into the freshness of things, to be able to look with a new eye on every day that dawns, on every sun that sets. Wonder it is that sends a thrill through our being when spring sends the sap through the trees and makes the heart leap

up when it spots a rainbow in the sky. In the summer of 1996 Liam Griffin's band of merry men created a purple and gold wonderland in Wexford. He did get inspiration from an unlikely source. RTÉ sent cameras down to Offaly before the Leinster final to capture the mood of the county and former taoiseach Brian Cowen was prominent on the news when he was filmed singing the 'Offaly Rover' in a local pub. Liam Griffin was sitting at home in front of his television and saw Cowen singing 'A rover I have been and a rover I will stay':

'They were singing the "Offaly Rover" and I suddenly thought to myself, "The Boys of Wexford" and "Kelly the Boy from Killane". That was me, to use a sports psychology term, finding an anchor. I decided that this was where we needed to make a stand. So I got up at five o'clock in the morning and I walked the beach in St Helen's up and down. I was saying to myself, "This is much more than a hurling match."

'This was way bigger than any game. I began to think, "We're actually fighting for a way of life here. This hurling is on the way out in this county. We haven't won an All-Ireland Final since 1968. We're nobodies now. We're hurling for the actual saving of this game here." And then I thought of my own dad. All the matches that my father brought me as a kid.

'So, I wrote a speech, and the speech was all about who we were and where we came from. I spoke to Niamh Fitzpatrick (their psychologist) about what I was going to do and I said, "Am I going to drive them mental?"

'She said, "No, I think it's brilliant." I said, "I want them to come back into Wexford with that Cup. So I'm going to stop the bus." Then she said, "Walk them out of Wexford then again. And let them walk back in again with it."'

He didn't tell anyone else about his plan, so when he asked the Wexford team bus driver to stop just before the Wexford–

Wicklow border on the way to the Leinster Final and then ordered everyone off, there were puzzled looks all around:

'We were going to walk out of Wexford and we were going to walk back and we were going to do whatever it took to bring that Cup back. That's what we were focused on from the minute we began walking. And if that meant bringing death itself, then we were going to put our bodies on the line. We did everything we were supposed to do and everybody knew what they were supposed to do. Tackle, hook, block, discipline. They're the things that you've got to do. And if you do that, then we'd a great chance of bringing back that Cup. And if we resolved to do it, then nothing was going to stop us. We were ready. And were going to walk out of Wexford.

'I remember Niamh saying to me, "You make them deep-breathe when they're walking up that road." So I said to them, "Breathe long and hard, we're walking out of Wexford. And when we put our feet outside this county, you remember that when we put them back in here we'll be carrying that Leinster Cup."

'I got back into the bus and I sat down beside Rory Kinsella. There was silence for a minute, and he said to me, "Where the f**k did that come from?! You know now that if we lose this match you'll be the laughing stock of County Wexford."'

Wexford beat Offaly by 2-23 to 2-15 and went on to beat Limerick in the All-Ireland final.

WEXFORD ROYALTY

Today the most glittering star in the county's hurling firmament is Lee Chin. Wexford is part of his DNA:

'Growing up in Wexford, I was involved in football, hurling and soccer from an early age. I always played outfield in football and soccer but in hurling I had a short stint in goal at Faythe

WHERE HEROES ARE MADE

Harriers. I only lasted a game there at my age level but I sometimes played in goal if I was playing an age level or two up. We played a county final and I was in goal for it, but conceded about six goals. That sporting career didn't have any longevity! I made some early strides outfield in hurling but my first chance to play at Croke Park came as somewhat of a surprise. It was a Thursday when I got a phone call asking would I go to play for Wexford under-14s. That call was from Joe Kearns, who was part of the Wexford panel when they won the All-Ireland Final in 1996. I told him that I might need to get hold of my mam to ask could I take the day off school. He said, "I don't think she'd have a problem with that!" Sure enough, he was right.

'I remember they had a bus arranged and off we set. Mam and my grandmother followed up in the car. This was a place that I had only ever dreamed of playing in. The dressing room, walking out from the tunnel – it is all so clear, even to this day. I scored a point at the Davin Stand end that afternoon. If you asked me now, I could still point out the exact spot that I scored it from. That game impacted me so much. It made me feel I was chasing the right thing.'

15

THE TORTURE CHAMBER

The Sand Dunes at Bettystown

Success is no accident. It is hard work, perseverance, learning, studying, sacrifice and most of all, love of what you are doing or learning to do.

PELÉ

He knows that the key to a full life was taking it. He understands that it is not about having less fear, but more courage.

He believes that the main thing is to ensure that the main thing remains the main thing.

Star forward Bernard Flynn believes one location was pivotal to Seán Boylan's success as Meath manager that would bring four All-Irelands to the Royal County. Flynn would discover in a brutal way that there were severe consequences if you broke the code that drove the squad with the fervour of medieval monks:

'The training in Bettystown was savage. I hated the running sessions. I would always be at the back while fellas like Joe Cassells, Terry Ferguson and Gerry McEntee would be up at the front. Even when I was vomiting down my top I kept going because you dare not stop.

'The biggest single lesson I got about Boylan's psyche came one night when he brought us over the sand dunes in Bettystown early in my career. It was minus four or five degrees and we were made to go into the water because he loved the healing and therapeutic powers of water and the whole spirituality of that. But we were worried about getting hypothermia. Seán was way ahead of his times because he had a back-up team with him from early on. One of his first nights in Bettystown he had his crew and they had jeeps with their lights on and they were providing the light in the sand dunes.

'It got so bad I was scared I was dying. I actually felt death was coming over me. I had never felt so bad before or since. I was at the back and I fell down and I got sick and I hid in the bush where it was pitch dark. When the lads came running around again I jumped into the middle and I thought I had got away with it. Seán had been watching me, though, and he saw what I was at and he stopped everybody. He knew I was a young lad and needed a bit of a reality check of what was expected and demanded of me. I was still wiping away the vomit from my top but he gave me such a lecture and a lesson that I never stopped again in my entire life.

'The lads were looking me in the eyes and some were shaking their heads and I knew they thought less of me because of that incident. It took me a lot of hard work to rebuild some of their trust after that. I felt I had let myself down and I had let them down but the one thing I learned was that you never give up. It wasn't a case of Seán putting his arm around my shoulder. He devoured me and tore strips off me and had me nearly crying. I got no sympathy from anybody else and that was the kind of thing that was needed. He has the image of being a lovely man but underneath he is a silent assassin in a way!'

You don't win four All-Irelands just by being nice.

THE TORTURE CHAMBER

THE SCHOOL OF HARD KNOCKS

In case Flynn was to forget that lesson there was another painful reminder of the etiquette that was required in the Meath camp, which put a premium on a widely shared sense of purpose and values:

'At one stage the All-Stars were going to play in the Skydome in Toronto. Robbie O'Malley, myself and a few players from other counties were asked to go over in advance to promote the games and generate the maximum level of interest. We ran it by Seán Boylan and somehow he said yes because we were going to be playing Dublin in the quarter-final of the National League, which was big for us at the time. When we arrived in Toronto we were met by a limousine and we were on the equivalent of *The Late, Late Show* in Canada. There were three live television shows and three or four of the top radio shows. We were treated like royalty and we had never known anything like this. We got a few bob for it at a time when we had nothing.

'We had a great break and we were asked to extend the trip for an extra two days for more promotion. We managed to get the word back to Seán. We came back on a wet night and the quarter-final was the following Sunday and we went straight to training.

'As soon as we walked into the dressing room the hatred we felt from the rest of the players because we had overstepped the mark in their eyes, or they were just plain jealous they didn't get to go and do something that was unacceptable for Meath players to do, was unreal. I have no doubt but if it was Liam Harnan or Mick Lyons who had been asked to go to Toronto they would have said: "Go f**k off and get somebody else."

'We didn't think there was anything wrong in what we had done. What was done to me that night in training meant I physically couldn't walk at the end and stumbled into a car to get me home. I got thumped and belted all over the field that night. It was not the first time I got thumped but what was different that night was that nobody said anything to me. We were ignored because we had missed one training session and that was sacrosanct.'

A MISUNDERSTOOD MAN

Part of the problem for Flynn was that his colleagues made assumptions about him that did not reflect him in the best possible light:

'I was often underestimated within the Meath squad for my dedication. When I was going out with my wife nearly all of her dates were spent just kicking the ball back to me. I knew there were many attributes of the game I didn't have but the one thing I could do was kick equally well with both feet which was not exactly commonplace at the time. I only got this skill with savage practice. There were some Meath players, though, who thought I liked to enjoy myself a bit more than the others because these guys were so serious and sure of themselves. Maybe I just was different to the dressing room.

'I dressed a little differently. The boys never knew what gel was or creams were till I came into the dressing room. I was a little different. They saw colours on me that they had never seen. They thought I was something from outer space. It was much later till I realised this and I wondered back then why they were kicking the sh*t out of me at times.'

On one occasion Flynn added fuel to that fire in Seán Boylan's eyes. Yet, like all great leaders, Boylan had the capacity for the counter-intuitive response and could understand the voice of resistance. He could change the rules of the game when he felt it was needed and find new possibilities and stay calm and engaged when there was a threat to his authority. Flynn also experienced this side of his manager at first hand:

THE TORTURE CHAMBER

'I know there was always a culture within the Dublin squad, for example, of going for a few drinks on the Monday night after a big match. I got into my head that one Monday night I would go out for a few drinks. Back then Bad Bobs was the place to go and I thought as I was away from Meath nobody would know. I had a great night and made it into work the next morning on time as I always did.

'That evening I went to training having literally no sleep the night before and having had what might be nicely termed as "a rough night". It was one of the few times when I simply couldn't run and a bit like that night in Bettystown I was really scared that I was going to die because my head was spinning. Seán was running us up and down the hills and he could see the way I was struggling badly. Normally he would pull up a fella in front of the whole squad but he knew I was a younger guy and there was a danger that he might push me over the edge.

'Although I had the height of respect for him, I was fiery and I would take him on on the odd time and that was well known within the squad. He probably felt that if he started eating the face off me that night there could be a reaction and who knew where it would end? There was a bit of a rebel in me and some of the lads would say more than a bit.

'It was only afterwards that I realised how brilliantly Seán handled the situation that night. He pulled me up and he said to the lads: "Bernard is not feeling well. I chatted with him beforehand and I'm pulling him out." I knew that was not the case and I didn't know what was going on. He got me into a corner on my own and never discussed the incident with any other players. I know because I asked several of them about it subsequently. He said: "If you f**king ever do again what you did since Sunday evening you're finished." He then proceeded to go through all my movements from Monday evening to

Tuesday morning: every pub and club I had been to and what time I came and left. He then said: "You are getting one chance, now go home and rest."

'His psychology was brilliant. He weighed me up and felt that this was the best way to handle me because there could have been a major row and there were a few of them. I respected him and had a little fear of him and there was no way I was going to try anything like that again. I didn't think he would be able to track my movements but he was letting me know he was.

'That was his genius. He knew the right card to play in nearly every situation.'

16

WHAT IT SAYS IN THE PAPERS

The Kildare Nationalist

Success is not final; failure is not fatal: It is the courage to continue that counts.

WINSTON CHURCHILL

Quem deus vult perdere, dementat prius (The person whom God wants to destroy, he first makes mad).

In Ger Loughnane's latter years as Clare manager he would frequently be mad because of journalists. Clare felt they had been unfairly treated by the media in 1998. On an RTÉ programme Loughnane had been pilloried – ran through and placed on a spit to burn. Legal eagles called him afterwards to tell him he could not lose the case if he sued the national broadcaster, but he declined to do so. However, when he was annoyed there were safer jobs than being a GAA journalist. Lion-taming for example. At the time he attracted trouble like pollen attracts bees.

1999 would be a year for some retribution as he recalled for me looking over an endless canopy of trees – a scene of almost unimaginable beauty. The scene was enchanting, bewitching and with a soft babble of a stream in the distance:

WHERE HEROES ARE MADE

'I admired the writing of a lot of journalists. To take one example I appreciated the writing of Vincent Hogan, even though he gave Clare a hard time now and again. He thought he was right and fair enough. I respect that. He is a quality writer and has great insights into the game. I've always enjoyed reading his stuff and he's one of the first guys I would read before or after a game.

'I wrote to him once after he wrote a book about Nicky English to tell him how much I enjoyed it. I do think, like many others, he went way over the top on the Colin Lynch controversy in 1998. He was part of the clique.

'He asked if he could come down to interview me in 1999. I agreed and told him to come down to training one particular night and that I would meet him in Cusack Park, knowing that we weren't training there. When he arrived he was told we were training in Crusheen. When he got there he discovered we were actually training in Flannan's. When he got to Flannan's I stopped the training exercise we were doing and told Mike Mac to take over. Every time I saw a journalist attending one of our training sessions I handed over to Mike because I wanted to reinforce the view that all the Clare team did in training was run around the field. The more they believed that the better I liked it. Hogan began talking to someone on the sideline so that I went over and told Mike Mac to take the players away, away over to the far end so that he would see as little as possible.

'The rest of the training session went on for about an hour on a wet, miserable evening. As we finished he asked where he could talk to me. I told him to meet me in the Sherwood because all the players would be going in afterwards. When he heard this Tony Considine asked me privately, "Are you going to talk to him after what he wrote about Clare?" I replied, "No danger. I won't be in the Sherwood." I went straight home and he was hanging around all night in the Sherwood. No one he asked had a clue where I was. He drove back to Dublin without getting his interview.

'You could say it was very petty on my part. I just wanted to give him something of what he gave us. I can't remember who said: "If you don't read the newspaper, you're uninformed. If you read the newspaper, you're misinformed." It is not correct but sometimes it is the case.'

Ná bris do loirgín ar stól nach bhfuil i do shlí.

This translates literally as don't break your shin on a stool that's not in your way but essentially means don't go out of your way to get in trouble. As Clare manager this was not Loughnane's way.

Retirement has done nothing to diminish Loughnane's capacity to surprise and the old bloody-mindedness surfaces occasionally. Asked if he had any regrets about the way he played the media as Clare manager, a look of granite hardness appears and his answer is typically forthright:

'Yes. My slight regret is that I didn't really go to town on them and that I ever let them into the dressing room.'

LOCAL NEWS

Newspapers have always played a huge part of Irish life – none more so than in Cork. Towards the end of the nineteenth century there was intense competition in Cork between the rival papers.

The *Skibbereen Eagle* sought to carve out a distinctive identity for itself by focusing on international affairs. Famously it took a stance against what it saw as Russian oppression. It boldly stated that it: 'will still keep its eye on the Emperor of Russia and all such despotic enemies – whether at home or abroad – of human progression and man's natural rights which undoubtedly include a nation's right to self-government. "Truth",

"Liberty", "Justice" and the "Land for the People" are the solid foundations on which the *Eagle*'s policy is based.' The comments were picked up all over the world as an example of resistance to tyranny.

In marked contrast *The Kerryman* newspaper was playing a significant part in the fabric of life in the county but without concerning itself with global politics by positioning itself as a paper of Kerry, for Kerry by Kerry.

Every Saturday one girl received two copies of it in her posh boarding school in Cork. One was ostentatiously decorated with the message 'Love from Mummy' but was actually from her boyfriend and hidden inside were pages and pages of his letters filled with his angst-ridden declarations of undying love. The other paper was actually from her mother. The letters had the desired effect because within a few years the happy couple were married and they both lived happily ever after in the Kingdom.

KILDARE KIN

For their part sportswriters are often dismissed as fans with typewriters. The implication is that such an idea is a damning indictment. But is that necessarily the case? Consider the case of the award-winning Kildare sportswriter Brendan Coffey who has an insider's perspective of the role of the local media as a former sports editor of the *Kildare Nationalist*. He had the good fortune to grow up at a time when Kildare were flourishing under Mick O'Dwyer – when after winning Leinster in 1998, Kildare captain Glenn Ryan referred to him as a 'God':

'Like most of my childhood friends, I was mad about sport. Our games followed the seasons: soccer in winter, GAA in spring, and all sorts during the summer, including July's two-week spell of tennis. I watched the darts at Christmas and the Dublin Horse Show in August. April was a magical month: it began with The Masters and kept us enthralled for another two weeks during the World Snooker Championships.

'Both of my parents had grown up on a small farm in the West and migrated east after school, like so many of their peers. They were reared in conservative Catholic homes but they wore those labels lightly and moved easily in the burgeoning suburban world around Dublin. We lived in a three-bed semi-detached and our neighbourhood was full of similar families. There were enough young dads around the estate to form a competitive soccer team. I remember travelling to matches and playing ball on the sideline with other kids. More vivid are the trips home, which usually involved a stop at some pub. Apparently I swiped the cue ball off a pool table one time but my crime was not detected until we were home. I think I am on safe ground pleading innocence still: I could only have been five or six at the time. The snooker bug had probably hit by then. Within a couple of years, I had my own small table, courtesy of Santa.

'If soccer was the first game I encountered, Gaelic games were not far behind. Unusually, Dad fared best as a hurler despite his roots in a player wasteland. Aged thirty-seven, he won a Junior championship with his adopted club, a big thing at the time. Maynooth was predominant in football, naturally, for a club in North Kildare. At that time, they were struggling in both codes. 1994 was the beginning of a revival and a Junior football championship followed the year after.

'1999 brought remarkable success. Maynooth completed a double, winning the Intermediate grade in hurling and football. The millennium dawned with a senior club in the town. Those heady days sealed my love of GAA.

'The urge to write about sport came from my father. He had taken on the role of PRO in the club and spent his evenings compiling match reports for the local papers. I took this approach to be standard. Later experiences taught me that he was unusually dedicated to the role.

'Then the notion dawned: "Why not try this lark for myself?" So, pen in hand, I watched a Connacht championship match between All-Ireland champions Galway and my father's native Sligo. My report can still be found in a press at home.

'"Yeats casts a cold eye as Galway snatch a late draw with Sligo" reads my bold headline. My handwriting – neat and cursive – is far better than the report but, as the first line indicates, I was nothing if not ambitious. The report runs to five foolscap pages and signs off on an even note: "Analysts will say Galway have the ball in their court but on the face of it, it was a poor game which nearly ended with a fairytale story."

'The piece, recently re-read, was not as bad as I feared. A lot to work on, certainly, but some potential too. At that stage, I was fourteen and terribly green. I was like a young footballer who might get better if he stuck at it. Or I could have lost interest and drifted away.

'For whatever reason, I decided to write a letter to Liam Horan of the *Irish Independent*, then the paper's Gaelic Games correspondent. I sent a copy of my match report as well, hoping for a few pointers presumably. Time has shown me how incredibly lucky I was to seek out Liam's guidance. Someone else might have put that letter aside and never looked at it again. I know how easy it is to forget about such things. I can still remember my excitement when his return letter came through the post. Even the paper it was written on had a sense of prestige: cream colour, subtle weighting, elegant insignia.

'His letter is dated "6/7/99". In it, he writes: "Dear Brendan, Many thanks for your letter. The report is excellent. Well done. You are going about things in the right way – get plenty of stuff published while you're young."

WHAT IT SAYS IN THE PAPERS

'The generosity of his encouragement is remarkable, even now. And he went further: "If you like, ring me and I'll go through your report with you. And you can tag along with me to a match in Croke Park some Sunday to see how it operates, and to meet a few of the journalists. I'd be delighted to give you a hand."

'His sincerity still shines through. I would love to think that I could be that kind to some youngster starting out. Liam could have responded in any number of ways (or not at all) and none would surpass his actual response.

'He left his contact number at the bottom and added a postscript: "Excuse my terrible handwriting!" At least I had the edge on him in one respect.

'I dialled the number, not realising it would take me through to the sports desk. Liam was out of the office. I left my details and, good as his letter, he got in touch. We discussed my match report on the Galway Sligo game and then he asked if I fancied coming into the office for an afternoon. If I had known things would turn out this way, I might not have written to him in the first place. Suddenly I was preparing to visit the man at work. What would I say? What would I do?

'The journey into Dublin was no big deal: hop on the 66 in Maynooth and it would take you all the way in, to Middle Abbey Street. Before the Luas came along and reorientated the bus routes, I only knew that side of the city. Strictly speaking, we were neither northsiders nor southsiders, not that those terms meant much at that stage. But there was a sense, even then, of being more at home on the northside. The Savoy, Arnotts, Eason's on O'Connell Street: they seemed like our kind of scene.

'Independent House loomed close to the bus stop on Middle Abbey. In I went, a mixture of nerves and quiet pride. Liam came down to the lobby and we headed for lunch. The venue was new to me but I realise now it must have been the Peacock

WHERE HEROES ARE MADE

Theatre Cafe. Not a bad start for a schoolboy. Apart from his obvious interpersonal skills, Liam possessed a salesman's instinct. Not surprisingly, he subsequently moved into the business world – I remember being so disappointed when he left the *Indo* in 2000 – with much success.

'For the duration of lunch, I felt like a fish caught in headlights. The place was packed and my anxiety, with no table free, peaked as I stepped away from the counter first. Liam spotted two seats available at a table for four. I had neither the gumption nor the tact to think of that option.

'Once we began to chat, I began to relax. Yet, for some reason, I found my sandwich almost impossible to manage. Each time I tried to take a bite, the whole slice of ham emerged from between the bread. My abiding memory remains that impenetrable piece of bacon. Perhaps it was an aid to conversation. The more I spoke, the less time spent contemplating my food.

'Afterwards, we went to the office. Liam introduced the other journalists on the desk and got me to update his statistical records for that year's hurling and football championships. While I poured through match reports, he seemed to juggle numerous jobs: emails, meetings, phone calls. He was coming off a good week, too, having landed a couple of scoops.

'I learned a lot that day, more than I was entitled to learn from someone who had no obligation to me, a random teenager. I will always be grateful for his decency. Liam taught me much about journalism but the most valuable lessons did not dawn immediately. Respect, integrity, patience: these qualities Liam embodied. He was light-hearted and good-natured, the kind of company you want to keep.

'I cannot say I travelled home that day convinced about my future as a sports journalist. Yet the virtues Liam displayed would stand to any person in any walk of life.

WHAT IT SAYS IN THE PAPERS

'For Bruce Springsteen, the glorious days revolved around high school baseball. Under-16 football was about as big as it got for me. We reached a Division 1 League final and I had nailed down the full-back position. We were going places. I had even got a few match reports published in our local paper, the *Liffey Champion*.

'We won most games in that league campaign and I enjoyed writing about them. The hard part was trying to remember how the game had unfolded. Our coach kept tabs on the scorers and I pieced it together with a few teammates after the game. We would play around with headlines down the back of the bus.

'Maynooth leave Celbridge feeling blue' was an obvious choice when we picked up the win against the Hazelhatch crowd, who played in the melancholy colour.

'I enjoyed my football that season but probably knew I was near the limit of my potential. Most departments, I was middling and not driven enough to push myself beyond those levels. Physically, I viewed the pain barrier as the point at which to stop. I would never win a fight to the death.

'We played indoor soccer after school on Fridays. The week of our league final, disaster struck. I went to shoot but another foot beat me to the ball. The first wave of pain came pulsing through my big toe. Even the thought of it now makes me wince. While my foot throbbed, I hopped off the pitch and cursed my luck. What a stupid way to get hurt. If I had injured myself during a match or a training session, it would have been easier to take.

'After the worst of the physical pain subsided, a new anguish took hold. The thought of missing the final hurt more than the injury. Maybe I could have hobbled through it but not in the full-back line.

'The game turned out a cracker. We played Na Fianna, who were top dogs at underage level around that time. They were an amalgamation from Mid Kildare. Allenwood, who reached the county final that year, were the only senior club. The rest – Ballyteague, Milltown, Robertstown – played Junior or Intermediate. Together, they covered a vast area stretching from the edge of the Curragh over the Hill of Allen and on as far as Coill Dubh (home to their hurling club, who were then the county's leading force). Any trip along those routes is a journey through GAA heartlands. Maynooth, for all its modern industry and transport links to the city, was unfashionable by comparison. The club had only emerged from the Junior ranks a few years before. There were senior championships on the club's roll of honour but they belonged to bygone eras: 1896, 1913 (football); 1937, 1939 (hurling).

'I remember the game being an end-to-end contest, a rollercoaster of emotion. Every time we scored, they seemed to get one back straight away. Numerous times I felt we had it; just as often I thought we were gone. Our star player was Pierre Ennis, who had the physique of a man. Even at that stage, he was being talked about beyond Kildare. His skills as a soccer player had attracted interest from Premier League sides in England. I think we already knew he would be heading to Aston Villa during the summer. So this game would be his last. Selfishly, I wanted him to stay. Not just for our team and our club. In my mind, he was destined to do great things for Kildare. Even at Primary level, everybody knew him by his first name. We would arrive at a school in Leixlip and someone from the other team would be straight over: "Is Pierre playing?" We could have the game won before it began, depending on the answer.

'Every time Pierre got on the ball that day against Na Fianna, time slowed. He would either score or set up a score. His performance was remarkable, the sort of display you only get to see from a preternaturally gifted young player. Maybe a truth hit me: playing football would never compare to the thrill of watching someone like him soloing up the field.

'The final went down to the wire, everybody on tenterhooks. I think we went ahead and then they got a goal. Whatever way those final minutes panned out, I know they hit us with a sucker punch. Suddenly time ran out. Pierre could not slow the seconds any more; he had none left. We were crushed. But I also felt the result was unjust: no way should Pierre have finished on the losing side.

'There was a low hum in the dressing room when we got back inside. Some lads were quietly crying, others flung their boots on the concrete floor in frustration. The room had a hollow atmosphere: everyone there but mentally elsewhere. Then the club chairman landed in, making an impassioned speech about the pride he felt in our performance. He captured the mood but his words could not take from the feeling of loss. Only teenage dreams can be so thoroughly shattered.

'Maynooth had a reputation for being a poor championship outfit. I have since realised that the GAA is full of such clichés. I had heard similar things said about Kildare: not tough enough, folding when the pressure comes on. Amazing how labels can stick with teams. Before I had a chance to form my own mind, older voices were putting these fixed ideas in my head.

'As we prepared for the under-16 Championship that summer, I heard the opposite being said about Carbury. Supposedly they were a great championship club. No doubt we were being fed this narrative to keep us on our toes but I just found it created confusion. We rarely had trouble with Carbury in the past. Why should we be so apprehensive now?

'Maybe the primacy of championship was not as strong in a place like Maynooth. Every game counted the same in my head. A lot of us played soccer as well, where the league was the most important competition. The distinction between league and championship took some time to hit home. I got the feeling that the players, in a club like Carbury, had it drilled into them from a young age.

'We were drawn away. Down to the lion's den we travelled, confident of a win. Carbury were no great shakes in the league and no amount of talk about tradition could convince me they would trouble us now.

'From the throw in, the pace was frenetic. They did everything faster than us. The penny had finally dropped but it was too late. We were chasing shadows all night. The sinking feeling never left me during the game. I lost my rag with an umpire midway through the second half. He was a Carbury man, a hard chaw who spent most of the game barracking our goalkeeper. The two of them were at it, to be fair, but an adult should have had more sense. Eventually I had a pop.

'"I'd say you were a great player in your day, ya fat f**ker."

'He went quiet for a while, which I took as a mini victory, but the game was gone from us. If our heads were right, we would not have wasted so much energy arguing with an official. The final whistle came as a relief. Just like that, the year was over. What a change from the league final.

'We scattered for the summer. Pierre began life as an apprentice cross channel. He was named under-16 International Player of the Year at the FAI Awards in 2001. We heard that he was breaking into the Villa reserves. His path to the top seemed clear.

'I picked up some summer work with the local papers, writing reports on club games. But it was all about the Lilies in those years. I had really caught the bug by 2000. I felt detached in 1998 because I spent the month of June in the Gaeltacht and my mother's Galway connection left me divided. My uncle had taken me to the Connacht Final, a miserable day in Tuam.

While Niall Finnegan's late free salvaged a draw for Galway, Roscommon should have won. Would Kildare have claimed Sam Maguire if Finnegan missed? Sporting history hinges on such moments.

'Play sport seriously and it will eventually bring you face to face with your own mortality. Injuries, losses, rows: painful reminders of human frailty. Success undoubtedly keeps underage teams together because the players get a taste for something that is so hard to resist. Defeat dulls the senses. The real test of desire comes in adversity. No wonder most young fellas drift away from sport as they reach eighteen. How badly do you want to play football when a world of alternatives is on offer?

'My playing interest, in time-honoured fashion, diminished. Sports writing gradually took its place.

'I got a kick from seeing my byline in print. On Wednesday evenings, I checked the local shop to see if the paper had come in early. There is a buzz in being published. And it never leaves you.'

The GAA owes a huge debt to RTÉ because of its role in bringing Gaelic games into people's homes. But all across the country the local papers have played a huge role in spreading the GAA gospel. They cover the big games and the ones that the national media have no interest in. Like the GAA itself they are of the community, for the community and by the community.

VIDEO DIDN'T KILL THE RADIO STAR

In 1989 Ireland experienced something of a broadcasting revolution station, in the shape of local radio and TV3. Then Sky arrived in 1992.

Local radio has also been a huge boost for the GAA and created a new class of local star. A case in point is Shannonside Radio's legendary commentator Willie Hegarty. So many of his games are remembered more for his commentaries than the matches themselves and each one becomes nothing less than an epic.

In November 2024, Roscommon's Padraig Pearses shocked Corofin in the Connacht club championship. The final nail in the coffin came when Jack Nevin scored into an empty net because the Corofin goalkeeper had joined his team's attack. Willie compared it to a householder leaving all the doors and windows open. Then he compared it to sheep wandering into a neighbour's field.

17

THE POET FOR ALL SEASONS

Inniskeen

The only certainty is that nothing is certain.
                                    PLINY THE ELDER

Monaghan have made a major contribution to GAA lore and legend. Their most famous poet Patrick Kavanagh was, like Pope John Paul II, a goalkeeper. Patrick was a proud Inniskeen Rover (their original name until it changed to Inniskeen Grattans), having played in goals and also acted as club secretary for a while. He also wrote a great piece evoking a match called *Gut Yer Man*.

He explains that 'the team we were playing were a disgusting class of a team, who used every form of psychological warfare. For instance, when one of them was knocked down he rolled on the ground and bawled like a bull a-gelding.

'The man responsible for my deposition (as captain) was a huge fellow, a blacksmith, a sort of Hindenburg, whose word carried weight. He was a great master of the cliché, but sometimes he broke into originality, as the time we were going for the county final and he wouldn't let us touch a ball for a week previous as he wanted us to be "ball hungry".

'Then there was the time I pulled the ball over the goal-line and a most useless non-playing member of the opposing team kicked it back into play. We argued and there was a normal row.'

He was in goals for Inniskeen Rovers against Latton in Carrickmacross in the 1931 Monaghan County final, when the pitch was invaded by fans. In the time it took them to clear off, Kavanagh ditched his post for an ice cream and, by the time he returned, Latton had scored a goal.

As club treasurer he used to keep the club money in an attaché case under his bed and admitted that occasionally he 'visited the attaché case for the price of a packet of cigarettes but nothing serious'. This disclosure led former Leitrim county footballer Colin O'Regan to observe that Kavanagh was the first exponent of 'pay for play'.

Kavanagh recalled his time as his club's captain, secretary, and treasurer:

'Ball hungry as we may have been, we lost the match, and I was blamed, for I was "in the sticks" and let the ball roll through my legs. The crowd roared in anguish. "Go home and put an apron on you". And various other unfriendly remarks were made such as "Me oul' mother would make a better goalie."'

Kavanagh also wrote a poem entitled 'Camogie Match'. It includes the memorable line: 'A shout from the sideline: Mark your man, Kathleen Cody.'

Kavanagh summed up the GAA: 'No man can adequately describe Irish life who ignores the Gaelic Athletic Association, which is true in a way, for football runs women a hard race as a topic of conversation.'

CONVERSATION WITH CON

I had a great chat about Kavanagh with Con Houlihan one fine Thursday evening in July. In his heart Con was a poet:

'Vincent Van Gogh said that you could see poetry in a furrow. Patrick Kavanagh spoke about the undying difference in a corner of a field.

'Kavanagh was the best company ever born for the first three drinks and then he would just turn. He could be very nasty then. Once I wrote about him in glowing terms in *The Irish Press* morning paper. He came up to me on the street and said "you were just f**king patronising me". He knew I was genuine but that was Kavanagh, just the way he was. But his influence on me was enormous. He made you see your own fields, your own little rivers and cows, as important. T.S. Eliot said in a moment of enlightenment – and he hadn't many of those – that art was about taking the here and the now and making it rich and strange. Kavanagh practised that. He didn't preach it.

'Flann O'Brien, I admired his work enormously, but he was no company. And it wasn't drink, he was as bad sober. Kavanagh used to call me the biggest pygmy in Ireland. That gang when together would compete to see who could be the cleverest. It was holding court.'

18

DUNNES' DEAL

Dunnes' Car Park Castlebar

Mistakes are the portals of discovery.

JAMES JOYCE

Dunnes Stores has a special place in GAA folklore. More precisely its car park in Castlebar has a unique notoriety in the association. On a damp Saturday morning I visited there in the company of Mayo's All-Star midfielder T.J. Kilgallon. He explained the context to me:

'When I broke into the Mayo team first in 1980 we had no real management but in 1982 Liam O'Neill took charge of us and brought us up to the mark. Roscommon had given us many a hiding so in 1985 we were determined we would "dog into them" and match them physically. We beat them convincingly.

'Although we lost in a replay to Dublin in the All-Ireland semi-final it was a real learning experience and a first for a lot of the players. One of the things I remember is one of our selectors Billy Fitzpatrick who was forty-one coming on and scoring a point. Despite his age he had only played ten or twelve games for Mayo.'

DUNNES' DEAL

The following year Mayo fans and players had great expectations for the Connacht Championship after the apparent breakthrough in 1985:

'Ten days before we faced Roscommon we played Cavan in a challenge and we were brilliant. However, before the Roscomon game Dermot Flanagan got shingles and we ended up playing the game without five key players because of injuries. We were missing the spine of our team and were flat on the day and the Rossies beat us. I was talking to Martin Carney about this recently and we agreed that if there had been a backdoor that year we would have done really, really well because we had been flying before the Roscommon game. If we got our injured players back we would have mounted a strong challenge for Sam.

'That's probably the big regret of my career. In 1986 and 1987 a lot of us were at our peak but on neither occasion did we deliver on our potential. We were a very skilful team and in our prime, more so than when we got to the final in 1989, and I see those two years as the time we really missed the boat. Emigration was a problem. We lost some good players like Eugene Griffin and an outstanding player in Ger Geraghty. Both our managers back in those years, Liam O'Neill and John O'Mahony, tried to get him back and it nearly happened a few times but he never made it.'

Things did improve in 1988:

'When John O'Mahony came in to manage us he was a confident man who believed in his own ability. He brought new ways and new ideas. Meath beat us in the All-Ireland semi-final but we ran them close and that gave us hope that better things were coming.'

1989 would see Kilgallon in an unfamiliar role:

'The year started badly for me. I severed my medial ligament and there was a possibility that I would never play again. Our physio, Martin Carney's wife, did a great job with me but when

I got back to fitness Willie Joe Padden and Seán Maher were going very well at midfield. In my life I only ever played three games at centre half-back but they were a Connacht final replay, an All-Ireland semi-final and an All-Ireland final. The first time was against Roscommon and I went back to my spot to pick up Eamon McManus Jnr. He turned and said to me: "I think you're in the wrong place." I had a bit of a laugh with him about it. It wasn't that he was playing mind games or anything.'

So who did play mind games?

'Meath. Gerry McEntee would always stand nearer the opposing free-taker than he was supposed to and would try and put the kicker off by saying something like: "You're going to miss." He would tell you that you would put it to the right or the left but never over the bar. Colm O'Rourke was not shy on the field. He would always be passing a smart comment to you. Some of the lads thought he was trying to get you irked enough to punch him so that you would be sent off. He was certainly trying to distract you and put you off your game. I think Ryan McMenamin became probably the main exponent of that "art".'

SO NEAR YET SO FAR

T.J. Kilgallon believes the 1989 All-Ireland is yet another case of what might have been for Mayo:

'After Anthony Finnerty got the goal we were in the driving seat because having lost the previous two years they were starting to doubt themselves, but in the last ten minutes we went into disarray and let them off the hook. They finished strongly and got the final three points.

'There were 10,000 people waiting for us when we flew back to Knock. It was awfully moving. There was a real party atmosphere and we went on the beer for three or four days to kill the pain. There was none of the backstabbing you normally have after a defeat.

DUNNES' DEAL

It was almost a mini-celebreation and Mayo people were proud of us for getting there and playing well. There was a feeling that we needed to do a tour of the county as a political move as much as anything else. I went back to work on the Wednesday, though, because for me it was over and done with – but not achieved.'

Mayo's next attempt at redemption would come in the All-Ireland semi-final in 1992:

'There was kind of a bad vibe all year and even though we won the Connacht final there was a sense in the camp that things were not going well. Probably the most memorable incident that happened in that game was that Enon Gavin broke the crossbar in Castlebar and the match had to be delayed. The management had brought back Padraig Brogan earlier that year – I'm not saying it was a popular move with the players. When we played Donegal in the All-Ireland semi-final it was probably the worst game ever seen in Croke Park. Padraig had played for Donegal the previous year and when the Donegal lads saw him warming up, you could see that it gave them new energy.

'Things got ugly after that. It was more personal than it should have been. It was probably an early example of player power. We said that if there wasn't a change of management a lot of us would walk away. I was asked recently if we really did spend a training session pushing cars. We did! It was here in the Dunnes Stores car park in Castlebar and the cars were really big. There was not a great humour in the camp and the manager had to walk the plank. John O'Mahony had stepped down in 1991 because he was not allowed to choose his own selectors and maybe that's when we should have acted.'

BLOOD AND BANDAGES

Some players have their careers defined in moments. Willie Joe Padden is such a player. In the All-Ireland semi-final in 1989 against Tyrone he was forced to the sideline with a dangerous cut to his head. In one of the most iconic images in the history of the GAA he later returned to the fray, covered in blood, his head wrapped in a bandage, his shirt splattered in blood:

'Everybody had written us off before the match. I got an injury. I'm not too sure which Tyrone player it was. He was going for a ball and he hit his knee off my head and I got a few stiches in it. You don't mind getting a few things like that as long as you win the game. It was our first experience of getting to a final after all our endeavours from the previous years. From our point of view and from a spectator's point of view, it was a great period because we were basking in the build-up to the final, especially being in our first All-Ireland for so long.

'1989 was one of the more open All-Irelands. Unfortunately, Jimmy Burke, our full-forward, got injured and he had to go off. That really took the wind out of our sails because he was in there as a target-man and did that job very well. We were forced to rejig the team. Having said that, when we took the lead in the second half we looked as if we were in the driving seat but we got another injury and had to rejig the team again. I think it was that cost us the game rather than a lack of concentration. We were just as well prepared as Cork so it certainly wasn't a lack of fitness. We didn't press home our initiative so we didn't get the extra couple of points up to have the cushion there for the end of the game. Cork rallied and pipped us in the end.'

The promise of reaching the All-Ireland final in 1989 was not built on by Mayo and their All-Star defender Dermot Flanagan looks back on the experience as a lost opportunity:

'The winter of 1989 saw a form of euphoria because we had reached a final after such a long time and had played well which really took away from our focus. What should have happened is that we should have cleared off for a week and realised we had lost. People thought we were on the crest of winning an All-Ireland which created a lot of distractions and left us vulnerable in 1990.'

To this day Flanagan finds it difficult to assess the way events unfolded after Mayo's defeat in the Connacht final replay to Roscommon in 1991:

'John O'Mahony departed in controversial circumstances. John never spoke in public about all the details and I suppose we should let him bring them to heaven with him. It is probably fair to say that part of the reason was that he was not allowed to choose his own selectors. Looking back, the circumstances of Mayo football were not right then.

'Brian McDonald came in as his replacement and a year later would find himself in a huge controversy. Were there any winners? Everybody was a loser to a greater or lesser extent. Brian had been a selector with Liam O'Neill in 1985. To be fair to Brian he had a lot of good ideas about the game but whether he was the man to get the best out of players was another question. The first thing he asked me when he took over as manager was if I was committed to Mayo football. I was totally committed. I was the first guy to do stretching before training and after training. Long before it was fashionable I was doing acupuncture, watching my diet, reading sports injury books and doing power weightlifting – anything that would give me an edge or improve me as a player, so it came as a shock to be asked that.

'The issue that got into the media was about the players pushing cars as part of a training session. That was not the underlying problem. You needed to have a very strong skin to be able to handle Brian's comments in a training session. That was okay for the senior players but repeated exposure to this for the younger players could have undermined their confidence. We had a lot of younger players in the squad at the time.

'Again, in fairness to Brian, we did win a Connacht final in 1992 and could have beaten Donegal in the All-Ireland semi-final. We were not in the right frame of mind for an All-Ireland semi-final. There were a lot of problems with organisation. I was a man marker and I was on Tony Boyle for a short time in the game and did well on him, but I wasn't left on him and he played havoc with us.

'Afterwards the controversy broke in the media. The team was going nowhere. There were no winners in that situation. The tumultuous saga reflected very badly on the whole scene in Mayo. The county board had been deaf to any complaints. John O'Mahony had left under a cloud. These situations don't come from nowhere. A lot of mistakes were made.'

The sins of the father were revisited on Flanagan:

'My dad wouldn't have been hugely popular with the county board in his playing days. One day he turned around and asked the County Chairman if he wouldn't mind leaving the dressing room. For that reason some people believed that I was the most likely instigator of the "revolt" against Brian, but I had nothing to do with it. I never had to push cars because I was training in Dublin and was too busy in my legal career to be "masterminding a coup".'

MAGIC HANDS

In more recent years Castlebar is probably best known as the power base of former taoiseach Enda Kenny. The first Connacht team to win an All-Ireland was Galway in 1934. Two years later, Mayo won their first All-Ireland. The star of the Mayo team was Henry Kenny, father of Enda:

'A mythology developed in the county about the 1936 team, not least because they went fifty-three games without defeat. People thought they could jump over telegraph poles.

DUNNES' DEAL

'My father went to teacher training college in De La Salle, Waterford. Times were very tough and the food was so scarce there that my father said you needed to have the plates nailed to the tables! After he qualified, he went to teach in Connemara and cycled sixteen miles to train for the club team and sixty miles to Castlebar to play for Mayo. One of his teammates was Paddy Moclair, who was the first bank official to play county football, and he cycled from Clare. I've seen telegrams from the time from the Mayo County Board and they were told: "Train yourself – you've been selected to play."

'My father was particularly famous for his fielding of the ball. He grew up on the same street with Patsy Flannelly, another of the stars of the 1936 team. They had no football as kids so they went to the butcher's shop and got pigs' bladders from him to use instead of footballs. Dad always said: "If you could catch those, you could catch anything."

'The other thing he was noted for was his ability after he caught the ball in the air to turn before his feet touched the ground. When my brothers and I started playing, his advice to us was always: "Be moving before the ball comes." He found a big change in the way the game was played, especially when they started wearing lighter boots like the soccer players. When he saw a pair of them, he said: "These boots are like slippers." He didn't have much time for the solo runs and that's why he called it "the tippy toe". He said he would "beat the solo runner with his cap".

'Dad had great admiration for athletes. That's probably why the player he admired most was Kildare's Larry Stanley, who of course holds a unique distinction of winning All-Irelands with Kildare (1919) and Dublin (1923) and of representing Ireland in the Olympics (in the high jump at the 1924 games in Paris).

'In 1936, Séamus O'Malley captained the Mayo team to the All-Ireland. He travelled to Dublin by train the evening before the match. On the day of the match, he announced that he could not stay for the celebrations and got a lift back to Mayo after the match. The Sam Maguire Cup was put in the boot of the car. He had to go to his work as a teacher the next morning, so he left for work by bicycle with the Sam Maguire Cup strapped on his back! The times have changed!'

Tom McNicholas was the last survivor of the 1936 Mayo team. At ninety-five years of age, he was still driving his car, and his former career as a teacher was evident in the clarity of his directions to his home. He retained vivid memories of that team and was best equipped to give me an objective assessment of Henry Kenny.

'There wasn't the same cult of personality back then, but there was no question that the star of our team was Henry. He was wonderful at catching balls in the air. He had great duels with the mighty Kerry midfielder Paddy Kennedy and was probably one of the very few players, if not the only footballer, who could hold his own with Kennedy. This was particularly the case in the All-Ireland semi-final in Roscommon when we beat Kerry 1-5 to 0-6 in 1936, when Kennedy was the new star in the game.

'Henry was known as "the man with the magic hands". He had big hands and he could hold the ball in one hand. Now our game has become more like basketball, there is so much hand passing. Back then, though, it was a game of catch and kick, and nobody did it better than Henry. I don't think any of our team would believe the way the game has changed, especially the emphasis on stopping teams from playing and above all the number of times people pass the ball backwards. We believed in positive football and playing your own game rather than the opposition's.'

19

THE HOME OF HURLING

Hayes Hotel

Success is neither magical nor mysterious. Success is the natural consequence of consistently applying basic fundamentals.

E. JAMES ROHN

A meeting here had the same effect as opening a window into a darkened room. It is where the story of the GAA begins.

For considerable time Michael Cusack had been perturbed about the decline of native Irish games in the face of growing competition from British sports, like the garrison game soccer and also rugby. Initially Cusack sought to wrestle control over field games and athletics also to introduce a more egalitarian dimension to Irish sport:

'No movement having for its object the social and political advancement of a nation from the tyranny of imported and enforced customs and manners, can be regarded as perfect, if it has not made adequate provision for the preservation and cultivation of the national pastimes of the people. Voluntary neglect of such times is a sure sign of National decay and of approaching dissolution . . .

WHERE HEROES ARE MADE

'A so-called revival of athletics was inaugurated in Ireland. The new movement did not originate with those who have ever had any sympathy with Ireland or the Irish people. Accordingly, labourers, tradesmen, artisans, and even policemen and soldiers were excluded from the few competitions which constituted the lame and halting programme of the promoters . . .

'We tell the Irish people to take the management of their games into their own hands, to encourage and promote in every way, every form of athletics that is peculiarly Irish and to remove with one sweep everything that is foreign and iniquitous in the present system. The vast majority of the best athletes in Ireland are Nationalists. These gentlemen should take the matter in hand at once, and draft laws for the guidance of promoters of meetings in Ireland next year . . .

'It is only by such an arrangement that pure Irish athletics will be revived, and that the incomparable strength and physique of our race will be preserved.'

In the billiards room of Hayes Hotel in Thurles on 1 November 1884 were schoolteacher Michael Cusack, athlete Maurice Davin (a world record holder in the hammer), stonemason John K. Bracken, District Inspector Thomas St George McCarthy, journalists John McKay and John Wyse Power and solicitor P.J. O'Ryan. Two days later *The Cork Examiner* reported:

'A meeting of athletes and friends of athletics was held on Saturday at three o'clock in Miss Hayes's Commercial Hotel Thurles for the purpose of forming an association for the preservation and cultivation of our national pastimes.

'Mr Michael Cusack of Dublin and Mr Maurice Davin of Carrick-on-Suir had the meeting convened by the following circular: "You are earnestly requested to attend a meeting, which will be held in the on 1st of November, to take steps for the formation of a Gaelic Association for the preservation and cultivation of our national pastimes, and for providing rational amusements for the Irish people during their leisure hours."

'Mr Davin was called to the chair and Mr Cusack read the circular convening the meeting ... Mr Cusack then proposed that Mr Maurice Davin – an athlete who had distinguished himself much both in Ireland and in England – should be the president of the association.'

The two most important political figures of nationalist Ireland, the leader of the Irish Party, Charles Stewart Parnell, and the founder of Land League, Michael Davitt, were quickly persuaded to act as patrons and crucially so too was the Archbishop of Cashel Thomas William Croke, to give an ecclesiastical imprimatur to the fledging body – beginning the patronage of the Archbishop of Cashel at national level which continues to this day.

The Thurles location was no accident. Cusack had written to Maurice Davin on 26 August 1884, that 'The business must be worked from Munster. Suppose we held a meeting of delegates in some central place in Tipperary on the 1st of Nov. next. Don't bother your head about Dublin. The place couldn't be worse than it is. We'll have to look to the provinces for men.'

Since then, the acclaim for the event has gone to Cusack and Davin. Political agendas may have played a part here with an attempt to accentuate the Nationalist significance. In 1899, Cusack wrote in *The United Irishman*, about a conversation with the Fenian P. W. Nally in Phoenix Park two decades previously, which he claimed inspired the idea of the GAA. However, as we head to the 150th anniversary it is likely that the role of the other founding members will achieve more recognition.

WHERE HEROES ARE MADE

THE HURLING IMMORTAL

Since that first meeting in Hayes Hotel, Tipperary has rejoiced in the name of the 'home of hurling'. Semple Stadium remains the cathedral of hurling.

Down through the ages Tipperary has gifted the GAA with some of the giants of the ash such as Nicky English, Eoin Kelly, Michael 'Babs' Keating, Tommy Doyle and Lar Corbett. Apart from his skill on the field of play Lar will be remembered for explaining to Prince Philip during the visit of Queen Elizabeth II to Croke Park that a player must learn to play the game from a very young age.

Tipperary hurling is not without its humour. John Doyle enjoyed the story of the former hurler who is in an accident and is rushed into hospital. Two men are in the ward with him. One dies almost immediately. Then the second. The player in panic screams when the consultant appears: 'Doctor, doctor. Get me out of here quick and stick me in the backs. Things aren't going well in the forwards.' Another example was the headline in the *Tipperary Star*: 'Death of hurling immortal.'

THE DOYEN

There continues to be a swathe of the Tipperary population who believe that football is a game for hurlers with bad eyesight. When talking about the great Tipperary hurlers it is not a case of who to put on the list but who to leave out. One example serves to illustrate the richness of the county's tradition. In the Tipperary colours he was as eager as a lamb in springtime.

In the closets of Jimmy Doyle's mind as a boy all his dreams were consumed by thoughts of playing in an All-Ireland final. Like so many of his generation he was converted to Gaelic games by the GAA's answer to St Paul, Micheál O'Hehir. The famous RTÉ commentator's conversions did not take place on

THE HOME OF HURLING

the Road to Damascus but from the 'magic box' on kitchen tables throughout the country. Doyle grew up in an era when Micheál O'Hehir was at the height of his extraordinary career, in the days of wet batteries and communal radios. For hundreds of thousands of Irish people he was the only mediator. A phenomenon never to be emulated, he alone had the power to bring Gaelic games to the people. And he did. It was he who made Doyle aware for the first time of the unlimited potential that Gaelic games have for excitement, drama, tension, spectacle, elation and heartbreak, all packaged together in the ebb and flow of the enthralling broadcasts of the man with the golden voice. As one of the greatest forwards in the history of hurling, Doyle would weave his own magic into the lush tapestry of the GAA.

This was a golden era for hurling because there were great teams like Cork, Tipperary, and Wexford. Not only that but these teams had five or six great players competing for each position. In an era of outstanding defenders like John Lyons and Willie John Daly of Cork, Diamond Hayden of Kilkenny and Billy Rackard and Nick O'Donnell of Wexford it was going to take a formidable talent to shine but Jimmy Doyle lit up the hurling pitch like a Christmas tree. He could get scores from left or right. However, it comes as a shock that such a classy forward should start and finish his career as a goalkeeper. His Tipperary career was bookended by appearances as goalkeeper on the losing All-Ireland minor final to Dublin in 1954, when he was just fourteen and a stand-in appearance in goals against Waterford in 1973.

Even when early childhood memories are fading, almost every child can recall their first football or hurling match. They can remember the score, who got a great goal, who had a bad miss. But mostly they remember their parents. And that is the magic of the GAA. Hurling was part of Jimmy Doyle's family tree. His father Gerry was sub goalie when Tipperary won

WHERE HEROES ARE MADE

All-Irelands in 1937 and 1945 and his uncle Tommy was one of the legends of Tipperary hurling, winning five All-Irelands. As a result, Jimmy grew up almost from the cradle hearing stories about the Tipperary teams that featured some of the greatest characters in the game like Mick 'The Rattler' Byrne who was a small man but, pound for pound, he was the toughest man you could ever meet. He would mark guys from Wexford three or four stone heavier than him but he would never be beaten. He was a great corner-back for Tipp but also a wonderful story-teller. He did not have much time for all the talk players have today about their injuries, especially about their 'hamstrings'. He always said that the only time in his playing days he heard anybody talking about hamstrings was when they were hanging outside a butcher's shop.

Having won three minor All-Ireland medals Jimmy Doyle won six senior All-Ireland medals in 1958, 1961, '62, '64, '65 and 1971, captaining the teams in 1962 and 1965. He also won six National League medals and seven Railway Cups. The ultimate accolade came for the Thurles Sarsfields man when he was chosen on both the GAA official Team of the Century and the Team of the Millennium.

Of course, it helped that his Tipperary team were a well-oiled machine with outstanding players like Babs Keating, Donie Nealon and of course Tony Wall who was one of the great centre-backs of all time. For Babs Keating, Jimmy Doyle was a great role model:

'Long before players were handed out gear for free we were very conscious of the importance of equipment. Jimmy Doyle was one of the best hurlers I ever saw. He would always arrive in the dressing room with five spare hurleys. I learned from him the importance of proper preparation.'

20

JUST A LAD OF EIGHTEEN SUMMERS

The City of Brotherly Love

Some are bound to die young. By dying young a person stays young in people's memory. If he burns brightly before he dies, his brightness shines for all time.

ALEKSANDR SOLZHENITSYN

The streets of Philadelphia are immortalised in Bruce Springsteen's Academy Award winning song of the same name. They are also home to a GAA club.

A striking photograph shows the fifteen-year-old Kevin Barry playing rugby at Lansdowne Road in 1917. It shows the teenager about to score a try for his school, Belvedere College, and help defeat Blackrock College in the Leinster Schools Rugby Junior Cup final. Three years later he lay in his coffin, hanged at Mountjoy Gaol for his role in a fatal ambush of British soldiers in central Dublin during the War of Independence.

He was born in Dublin in 1902. His family had a farm in Co Carlow and a dairy in Fleet Street, Dublin. He attended primary school in Rathvilly, Co Carlow and then moved to St Mary's

College in Rathmines before switching to Belvedere College. At the age of fifteen he joined the IRA.

He was convicted by court martial of killing Private Marshall Whitehead, a nineteen-year-old soldier from Halifax in Yorkshire, in an IRA attack on a military lorry outside Monks Bakery on Church Street in Dublin on 20 September 1920. Two other soldiers were killed, one aged twenty and one fifteen (although the British army believed he was nineteen). The soldiers were collecting supplies from a bakery for delivery to Collinstown Aerodrome. They were the first military fatalities attributed to the IRA in Dublin in 1920.

After Barry's conviction, his destiny hung in the balance. Tensions in Ireland were already simmering close to boiling point, especially after the lengthy hunger strike in Brixton prison of Terence MacSwiney, the Lord Mayor of Cork. Pleas for mercy for Barry came from unexpected quarters. The Unionist Sir James Campbell, Lord Chancellor of Ireland, who had lost a son in the war, claimed that the student's 'extreme' youth was crucial and argued that he had clearly been naively manipulated by older immoral men. One significant cause of the cross-party support was the iconography of pictures of the youth in his distinctive black and white hooped Belvedere College rugby jersey. The pictures were of a player, like so many British public schoolboys and university students lost during the Great War. His 'vocation' as a 'medical student', 'Student der Medizen', and 'estudiante de medicina', made headlines across the globe. His execution, by hangman John Ellis on 1 November 1920, enflamed the court of Irish public opinion and was a key event in Ireland's struggle for independence.

Sport in Ireland takes place in a wider political context. During the War of Independence, Barry's execution had a profound effect on the national psyche. His club Old Belvedere, in an act of sheer defiance, re-appointed Michael O'Brien as captain for a second season – even though he was interned at the time.

IN MEMORY
In 2023 Kevin Barry GFC in Philadelphia celebrated its fiftieth anniversary and is named after the icon of Irish history. The club earned praise from the wider community in Philadelphia during the pandemic for its community reach, when members made food deliveries to emergency rooms and other places in need. On the pitch the club has also made its mark winning a North American championship in 2007, and a Philadelphia championship in 2011.

THE STREETS OF LONDON
The Irish have had a great sway in other cities for a long time. Irish immigrants flocked to London after the 1845 Famine that decimated our people. The Irish were the dominant immigrant community for many decades in London. The links between Ireland and London are found all over the city. An example is the stunning stained-glass window of Saint Brigid, complete with detailed use of Irish and Celtic lettering which was installed in 1952 to honour our Irish emigrants, labourers and their families, who have lived and worked in London since the nineteenth century. The window is in Saint Etheldreda's Church, Ely Place. It is the oldest Catholic church in London, founded in 1260.

Another significant glass window image is of young Saint Patrick (without a beard) in St Patrick's Church, Soho. It was built by poor Irish immigrants in 1790. It is the first Catholic church that was allowed to be built in London after the Reformation. It is a reminder of Saint Patrick's gift to us: No Sham – just a solid Rock of Trust.

WHERE HEROES ARE MADE

Liverpool (often said to be Ireland's thirty-third county because of the number of its inhabitants with Irish ancestry), Manchester, Birmingham, Northampton, Nottingham, Glasgow, Edinburgh, Aberdeen, Cardiff, Swansea and Wrexham have vibrant Irish communities.

Irish people like Terry Wogan and Eamonn Andrews became household names in the UK. This continues today with other Irish people like Graham Norton, Orla Guerin, Dermot O'Leary, Craig Doyle and Caitriona Perry. Liam Brady, Dave O'Leary and Frank Stapleton joined Arsenal Football Club in the 1970s and many think of all the Irish jockeys and horse trainers that have won horse racing in Cheltenham and still continue to do so in flamboyant style. Where the Irish have gone they brought Gaelic games with them. Nobody has documented the Irish emigrant experience better than Shane MacGowan where the love of home endures and is encapsulated in a devotion to 'an old hurley ball'.

After the 2024 All-Ireland hurling final Jarlath Burns captured the importance of the diaspora: 'For those people, who are our diaspora, who left this country because of war and famine, and for your ancestors, we are thinking of you today as you watch us. You are in Croke Park today, if not in body, then in spirit and we thank the countries who took you in and gave you jobs and allowed you to make a new name for yourselves with our native games.'

21

EVERY DAY IS LIKE SUNDAY

Croke Park

Don't judge each day by the harvest you reap
But by the seed you sow.

ROBERT LOUIS STEVENSON

It is the holy of holies.

But it has known tragedy.

Who wants the facts to get in the way of a good story?

One of the most powerful scenes in the film *Michael Collins* was when an armoured British tank opened fire on a crowd at a Gaelic football match in Croke Park in 1920. One of the effects of the film, though, was to cement Croke Park in the popular mind with the events of Bloody Sunday and as a central theatre not just of sport but Irish history.

Within a few hours Ireland seemed to be on the edge of sliding into chaos.

It remains the darkest day in the rich history of the GAA.

It colours all the pages of memory. History is not just the study of the past but an explanation of the present.

It should have been a battle of skill.

It became a battle with bullets.

Thirteen people were shot dead by the Black and Tans in Croke Park during a football match between Tipperary and Dublin on 21 November 1920.

DIFFERENT TIMES

If you praise the sunshine in some parts of Ireland, you'll be told 'it'll never last'. Yet there is ample reason for optimism about the ongoing health of the GAA. As Chief Executive of the Irish Sports Council John Treacy, who famously won the silver medal in the marathon at the 1984 Olympics, is ideally equipped to offer a dispassionate appraisal of the role of the GAA in Irish life:

'I think there's a danger that we take them for granted. A number of years ago we hosted a gathering for all the top sports officials in the EU. We showed them a hurling match and they were watching it with their mouths open. They couldn't believe that amateur players could produce a game of such skill and speed. All through the day they kept asking about it.

'For an amateur organisation it is a staggering achievement to have created an incredible stadium like Croke Park especially in the middle of Dublin. They have shown incredible leadership. The GAA has adapted to the changing times. They are keenly aware of the need to bring modern marketing methods into Gaelic games. I think a critical step came in the 1990s with the decision to introduce live coverage of a large number of games on the TV. Young people get their heroes from television. If you go down to Kilkenny you will see almost every young boy with a hurley because they want to be like their heroes. In recent times you can see some young lads and girls with hurleys walking on the streets of Dublin. You would hardly ever see that thirty years ago. That has not happened by accident and shows the forward-thinking approach the GAA has taken.

'They have shown great creativity in the way they have managed to defy the tide and ensure that they continue to get so many people to volunteer. The Economic and Social Research Institute produced a report on the social capital aspect of sport and it is basically ninety pages of a glowing tribute to the GAA and the way they have harnessed the voluntary capacity. Instead of saying to people as in the past give us all your time – they now say give us two evenings and a Saturday morning to train a juvenile team or whatever. We can't put a price on the kind of social value the organisation brings.

'However, their finest hour for me was when they revoked Rule 42 and opened up Croke Park to Ireland's soccer and rugby games while the old Lansdowne Road stadium was being demolished and the Aviva was being built. Nobody will ever forget the extraordinarily unique atmosphere that day Ireland played England in that never to be forgotten rugby match in 2007. The emotion that day was unreal as evident in the sight of big John Hayes bawling his eyes out while the anthems were being played. You could hear a pin drop when they played God save the Queen. The respect was phenomenal. It was a day when everybody was so proud to be Irish. A special day in the history of a very special sporting body and one I take my hat off to.'

A PILGRIM'S PROGRESS

Father Colm McGlynn is one of the many Dublin fans who regularly make the pilgrimage to Croke Park:

'The magic of the Dubs began to happen in our generation with the emergence of Heffo's Army on that famous All-Ireland day in 1974 when we beat the great Galway team of Liam Sammon and to finally win the Sam Maguire Cup after long years of footballing famine. I guess the game that I remember most is the 1975 hammering by the emerging young Kerry side of probably the greatest GAA manager of all time, Mick O'Dwyer, Then probably the most exciting game I'd seen to that point of my life – Dublin beating Kerry in a magnificent 1977 All-Ireland semi-final when Anton O'Toole, the Synge Street stallion, ran riot and years of epic rivalry and the great friendships made between both those teams. The names flood back: Paddy Cullen who was famously outfoxed by Mikey Sheehy's goal in the 1978 final, Seán Doherty, Brian Mullins, Jimmy Keaveney, Tony Hanahoe, Bobby Doyle, Gay O'Driscoll, Kevin Moran and Kerry's Ogie Moran and Páidí "Mucker" Ó Sé a target for the Hill with their chant "all coppers are b**tards".

'Fortunately the Dubs rose again with other great memories like on a wild wet 1983 day when only twelve Dublin players were left on the pitch beating Galway that day thanks to Brian Mullins' midfield efforts and a boxing match of legendary fame at the half-time tunnel dressing room walk. Heffo's Army's brought so much joy and a lot of heartache too but I look back with immense appreciation of such fantastic memories to savour.'

It is the personal history that moulds Fr Colm's appreciation of Croke Park:

'The last memory of a visit to Croker with the man who introduced me to Hill 16, my father James Victor McGlynn. I'm holding the stub of the ticket. It reads *Saturday 11th August 2007 section 711 row w seat 30 senior football quarter finals, after Nicky Rackard Cup final and ESB minor quarter final*. Earlier we had taken a 14 bus from Rathmines thinking it would stop on O'Connell Street but instead it ended up at Merchants Quay. Very soon Dad got tired walking and for the first time ever I had to flag a taxi to get us to Summerhill.

'We then made our way through the gauntlet of matchday sounds: "Get your team's colours ... official programmes ... programmes of the game ... apples pears or chocolate, four cents each the bananas" and a whole lot more, finally arriving into our seats high up into the newly built Cusack Stand, in which my father, a plasterer by trade, was enthralled by its engineering work. Dublin comfortably beat Derry that day to reach the semi-final and Dad and I were very happy with another victory for the boys in blue. Then suddenly from a place deep within, walking out the gates of Croke Park, I began to cry tears that flowed, doing my best to hide them from Dad. It was the dawning realisation that this would be my last visit with Dad to this Dublin theatre of sporting dreams of heroism, skill, enjoyment, fun and song as well as darker, sadder memories of thrilling games ending in defeats that Dad had initiated me into since my teenage years. I just knew in my bones it was his final goodbye and sure enough three months later, on Remembrance Sunday, 7 November 2007, he died and went to his maker whom he loved so much. 'Molly Malone' was sung as we lowered him down into his Bohernabreena cemetery grave after the religious formal prayers.

'That day we said goodbye to the da who had regaled us with the stories of the heroes of Dublin teams of his generation in both football and hurling: Lar and Des Foley, John Timmons and the great Kevin Heffernan, all who got battered by the county teams the length and breadth of the country.'

More than any other venue, Croke Park is living proof of Mícheál Ó Muircheartaigh's assertion of a place in which reside: 'The dead who shall live forever and the living who shall never die.'

22

CAVAN'S FAIRYTALE IN NEW YORK

The Polo Grounds

Good becomes better by playing against better, but better doesn't become the best by playing against good.

AMIT KALANTRI

Cavan's famous victory over Kerry in the 1947 All-Ireland final is perhaps the most iconic moment in the history of the GAA. To borrow from a native New Yorker, Paul Simon, the nation turned its lonely eyes to New York for 'the Polo Grounds Final'.

As the leading academic Damien Kiberd has noted, many of those republicans who lost the Civil War could not bear to live on in a land which was a sore disappointment to their dreams. A number went to a real republic, the United States, where they made fortunes in business – and bootlegging. Even today if you walk the streets of New York, you see vans plying up and down with names like 'P.J. Brennan, Est 1926' inscribed on their doors. The republican idea has always been linked to entrepreneurship: after all, the French revolutionaries of 1789 were the first politically organised businessmen of the modern

CAVAN'S FAIRYTALE IN NEW YORK

world, keen to replace a parasitic upper-class with a society of 'careers open to talents'.

The loss of such flair to Ireland in the mid-1920s was something which the fragile young state could ill afford. It became a mantra among commentators that the Irish were successful in the US in ways they never could be at home. One reason for this was that Irish-Americans continued to believe in their own culture, long after their 'sophisticated' stay-at-home cousins seemed to have given it up.

Shortly after she was elected president of Ireland in 1990 Mary Robinson coined the phrase 'the Irish diaspora' to describe the intrinsic link between Irish emigrants abroad and 'their native sod'. From the outset Gaelic games have been one of the most formidable imaginative batteries which allow Irish exiles in the four corners of the earth to feel they continue to belong to 'home'.

The 1947 All-Ireland final was held in New York as a gesture by the GAA of goodwill to the Irish people in America. Once it was announced it aroused great interest in every county. To get there was a great prize in itself. The teams left Cobh together for a six-day trip on the *SS Mauritania* to New York, after getting their vaccinations against smallpox, which were compulsory at the time. The fact that it was the first final played abroad gave it a much more exotic quality so it really grabbed the public imagination.

But what kind of machinations were going on behind the scenes in New York to make this event possible on the ground? A breathtaking series of hair-raising machinations behind closed doors involving moral blackmail, bribery of a kind, intimidation and blatant lie-telling allowed this event to happen. Arranging for the 1947 All-Ireland final to be played in the Big Apple was one of the great achievements of Canon Michael Hamilton's active career. Initially almost everyone seemed implacably opposed to the project.

Machiavelli himself would have admired the 'promptings' behind the scenes that finally persuaded a controversial Central Council meeting at Barry's Hotel that it was worth carrying through. Folklore abounds of how Miltown Malby's Bob Fitzpatrick's passionate speech to congress, complemented by the prop of a tear-stained handkerchief, swung the vote as he read from a bogus 'emigrant's letter'.

For Cavan the trip to New York was particularly welcome because in previous years they had experienced many bitter disappointments as one of their biggest stars from that era, Mick Higgins, who later trained Longford to their only Leinster title, explained:

'Initially most of our team would taste the bitter pill of defeat in three All-Ireland finals before getting his hands on the ultimate prize. We lost to Kerry in 1937, Roscommon in 1943 (after a replay) and Cork in 1945. It was a unique occasion in the history of the GAA. Lots of teams have won All-Irelands but only one has won one in New York. We took great pride in that. We knew we had made history and that we would never be forgotten as a result. To this day Cavan people are proud of us because of our achievements.'

THE GALLANT JOHN JOE

The Polo Grounds final made legends of the Cavan players – none more so than their centre half-back John Joe O'Reilly. In 2022 he was immortalised with the unveiling of a life-size statue in the market square in Cavan town. Tears fell from the eyes of older fans; they tried to wipe them quickly away. There was darkness at the sides of their vision, drawing in. Is maith an scáthán súil charad: A friend's eye is a good mirror.

Joe Brolly was spoken about with words that I would need to go to Confession for if I repeated them here – because of the time he called Cavan football 'the Black Death'.

A special occasion was made unforgettable by a speech from an icon of the game, Mick O'Connell:

'My first game in Croke Park was in 1957 against Cavan in a National League semi-final. Many names have been forgotten since as time passes by, but I know for Cavan that day, Jim McDonnell and the Gallagher brothers were playing. Among the Cavan players were a couple of colleagues of John Joe's: Phil "the Gunner" Brady and Victor Sherlock. So that was a link in my playing days to John Joe.

'The following year, I played in an Ulster verses Munster game here in Breffni Park. I was staying in the Farnham Hotel here and that morning, I met Micheál O'Hehir. I have great memories of my connection with Cavan from a way, way back and for that reason, I'm delighted to be here today.

'It's very nostalgic for me. The name O'Reilly is very close to me. My wife Rosaleen was a native of Poles and she was an O'Reilly as well, so the name is very, very close to me. Walking through the town and its outskirts, it brings home to me that it's a very special place and it will always be in my mind.'

23

SING A SONG FOR IRELAND

Frognoch

Our main business is not to see what lies dimly at a distance but to do what lies clearly at hand.

THOMAS CARLYLE

The phone rang loudly as he was in mid-sentence in our interview.

He looked at it with disdain but eventually he answered.

It was one of his former ministerial colleagues who was asking for a small favour. He made him work for it but eventually he graciously agreed to the request.

As he put down the phone he asked me what I thought of that formerly prominent politician. I was about to give a diplomatic answer but when he stared at me with such intensity through his steely eyes I knew I was being tested. So I gave a frank, and unflattering, appraisal. He favoured me with a broad smile in response before quoting Gandhi: 'If there is an idiot in power, it is because those who elected him are well represented.'

Charles J. Haughey would have been 100 on 16 September 2025.

Meeting him was a journey into a different world, like a slumbering country village replaced by the noise and fury of a capital city. His eyes spoke without the necessity of words or gesture, some intuitive seismic register caught the slightest tremor of variance from the norm.

Although best known for his involvement in racing, the former taoiseach played Gaelic football and hurling at club level with some distinction. Born in Donnycarney he was educated by the Christian Brothers in Fairview, a noted GAA nursery. He won a county medal with Parnells in 1945 – a noteworthy year for him because he also achieved notoriety then for allegedly burning the Union Jack outside Trinity College. He smiled enigmatically when I asked him about this incident but would neither confirm nor deny it.

On the pitch he was known for his fiery temperament. He was suspended for a year for striking a linesman. His brother Jock won an All-Ireland medal in 1958 when Dublin beat Derry, the county of birth to both his parents. Charlie regularly engaged in what Donald Trump calls 'plausible hyperbole'. He was fond of talking up his interest in the GAA.

He recognised the potential of major GAA personalities to win elections as Mick O'Dwyer told me with a mischievous grin:

'I often marked Charlie's brother Pádraig, or Jock as he was known, and that's how I got to know the Haugheys. In 1982 Charlie sent two ministers down to Coláiste Íosagáin in Ballyvourney where my sons were at school. They put huge pressure on me. I got as far as the door of the Convention Centre in Killarney. But when I had a look at what was ahead of me, I decided: "This is not for me." I turned around and walked away.'

THE LAMESTREAM MEDIA

In 1998 I interviewed CJH for a book I was writing at the time. The interview took place at 9 a.m. on a Saturday morning in his stately home in Kinsealy. When I was shown in he greeted me stiffly with a hesitant handshake and a smile so tight it would take a crowbar to prize it open. He was clearly weighing me up. Throughout the encounter he was clearly suspicious especially after I produced a recording machine.

Stories of his lavish hospitality were legendary so after he showed me in to his study and said 'we will have refreshments' I was intrigued to see what magnificent hospitality awaited me. How was I literally going to taste the high life for the first time? Would it be croissants specially flown in from Paris that morning or would it be smoked salmon sent from Kinsale? He made a call on the telephone at his desk. Shortly afterwards a 'maid' entered with extraordinary deference – to him – not as much to me!

She had a beautiful tray with a stunning silver teapot and cutlery and China to match. At the risk of sounding ungracious I was a little disappointed to see that in this sea of splendour the refreshments amounted to ... a plate with four Digestive biscuits.

As we ate and drank I expressed great surprise that he had a copy of a biography of Mary Robinson on his desk. The end of his time as taoiseach had coincided with her time as president of Ireland and relations between them could be described politely as 'tetchy'.

She had been an outspoken campaigner on issues including decriminalisation of homosexuality, contraception and divorce legislation, and changing the law so women could sit on juries. At one point in her presidency she enjoyed a ninety-three per cent approval rating among the electorate, making her Ireland's most popular president ever.

She was the first president not to be elected with the support of Fianna Fáil. In 1991, Charles Haughey prevented her from leaving the country to deliver the famous BBC Dimbleby Lecture in London, which had been delivered the year before by

German chancellor Helmut Schmidt whose lecture was titled 'Europe in the Nineties'. Robinson was scheduled to speak on the position of women and the family in Ireland. Fearful of the negative publicity, Haughey refused to allow her to travel.

He was surprisingly sparing of her in his comments. However, he absolutely lacerated her adviser Bride Rosney.

When I talked, he looked out the window and did not seem to be paying attention but then out of the blue he would make the most incisive comment. I was in no doubt that whatever else he might have been this was a man of a formidable intellect, one who got one hundred per cent in his Leaving Certificate Latin exam.

At the end of the conversation, when I prepared to leave, Charlie said, 'And of course you will let me see the piece before publication.' It was said in a way that was a command not a request by a man not used to having his authority questioned. Despite my misgivings I duly sent him what I had written. Shortly afterwards I received a letter back from him inviting me to Kinsealy a second time to discuss some minor amendments he wished me to make. Another Saturday morning I duly made my way there again for 9 a.m. I arrived to meet a different man. All his suspicion had melted away and he was full of the charm that I had seen often during some of his television appearances. When I apologised for bringing an umbrella on what had turned into a sunny day he replied: 'Better have and not need, than need and not have.'

He spoke about the late Irish rugby coach Mick Doyle who had invited him to launch his autobiography. He had asked Doyler if it was only about rugby. Doyler replied, 'It's twenty per cent rugby and eighty per cent sex.' CHJ said in response, 'You got the balance just right.' We parted after a few more Digestive biscuits.

WHERE HEROES ARE MADE

I thought that would be the end of my dealings with him. Not so. The following Friday evening I received a phone call. The conversation was short and sweet. 'This is Mr Haughey. Could you come out to see me tomorrow morning at nine?' His tone indicated that he clearly did not expect me to decline his invitation, but he gave me no clue as to why he wanted to see me.

The next morning I had the same anxious feeling in my stomach as I journeyed out to his home that I had the morning of my Leaving Cert Irish exam. In our original interview he had spoken to me about when his horse Flashing Steel won the Irish Grand National in 1995 and that the trophy had been presented to him by the former taoiseach John Bruton. He had made a complimentary comment about his political adversary. However, that week a series of revelations had appeared in the media about 'irregularities' in his finances. John Bruton was publicly very critical about CJH. Charlie 'instructed' me to take out the kind comments about Bruton.

IN CORRESPONDENCE

He also had a surprise for me. In our previous conversation I had pressed him if his much-spoken-of interest in the Kerry team of the 1980s was genuine or a political ploy to court publicity. When he replied no, he gathered by my expression that I was not fully convinced. To my amazement he showed me a copy of a letter he wrote to Mick O'Dwyer after Offaly deprived them of the five-in-a-row in 1982. The letter stated:

> Dear Mick, You very very nearly did it!
> It was by pure chance in the end that you should have lost.
> But you and all your team can be well satisfied that in the best traditions of all Kerry teams you were as magnificent in defeat as you have been glorious in so many victories.

> *You may have lost the Sam Maguire Cup this year but you left Croke Park having won the honour and respect of all.*
> *With every good wish for the future,*
> *Yours sincerely, Charles Haughey.*

RISE AND FOLLOW CHARLIE

As I left, Charlie inquired if I would like a photo of him to use in the book. When I said yes, he invited me back for my fourth visit to Kinsealy.

This was different. Charlie was tied up on the phone so it was his late wife Maureen who greeted me. She showed me into a room which was clearly where the coats were hung up and the sheer size of it gave me an understanding just how big the parties hosted in that house must be. Some time later Haughey arrived and gave me a tour of the bottom floor of the house. What struck me was the sheer volume of photos of him with leading figures on the world stage like President Mitterand and Bob Hawke. Then, as the tour was complete, he brought me back to the cloakroom to collect my coat. I got a revealing insight into what he thought of his cabinets. All his photos with them were hanging there at the very back – where virtually nobody would ever see his ministers. In fact, the photos of his horses were much more prominent than his cabinets.

He was a keen horseman, though he did have a few famous falls in his career. He was once alleged to have said that he chose black and blue as his colours because he was black and blue so often following riding mishaps. He laughed when I quizzed him about the veracity of that remark: 'I think you'd have to take that as apocryphal!'

I asked him what advice he had for me to live a happy life. He answered immediately, 'Life is too short to be drinking bad wine!'

GO TO HELL

I wondered if he was religious. His answer was oblique. He told me the story of the lawyer who went to Heaven. He arrived at the Pearly Gates and Saint Peter said, 'I have some good news and some bad news. The good news is that you get into Heaven. The bad news is that the part of Heaven designated for lawyers is full.'

'No problem. Take me to them and I will sort out that for you.'

Saint Peter guides him to the lawyer section and he summons all seven of them together.

The new lawyer says: 'Have you heard? They've doubled lawyers' fees in hell . . .'

Before he can finish the sentence all seven lawyers race to the elevator and descend to hell.

Saint Peter says: 'That was incredible! Well now you can make your home here.'

'Don't be silly. I'm going straight to hell.'

'But why?'

'Have you not heard? The rumour is that they have doubled lawyers' fees in hell.'

Haughey also advised me to sleep on big decisions: 'The morning is wiser than the evening.' As for paying attention to critics, his riposte was: 'Don't let the seagull run the picnic.'

POETIC PROMPT

The day before our last meeting Charlie had received a letter from a friend. It included a poem which was written in 1923 by Brian O'Higgins, a republican prisoner in an internment camp known as Tintown in the Civil War, which had just been discovered in an old photograph album. He felt it particularly pertinent given the prevailing tide of media comment about him at the time:

SING A SONG FOR IRELAND

The world will strip your failings
And hide the good you do
And with its sharpest thorns
The ways you walk bestrew:
You'll toil for men and they'll curse you:
'Twas thus, and thus 'tis yet.
And thus 'twill be forever.
But God does not forget.

It was then that Charlie introduced me to a place I had never heard of before that point: Frongoch.

THE WEE COUNTY

In the world of Gaelic games Louth has an honourable pedigree, being at the forefront of the Gaelic Athletic Association since its formation in 1884. In May 1885, a branch of the association was set up in the county following Michael Cusack's visit to Drogheda. Shortly after, clubs sprung up the length and breadth of the county. Louth were represented by Young Irelands from Dundalk in the first football All-Ireland final held at the Benburbs club grounds, Donnybrook on 29 April 1888. In the early 1900s Louth qualified for three All-Ireland football finals, losing the 1909 final to Kerry but victorious in 1910 and 1912, wins gained at the expense of Kerry (in a walkover) and Antrim respectively.

This was a turbulent and complex period in Irish history. While many Irish sportsmen fought and died on the Western Front and at Gallipoli, some chose the path of radical nationalism. Seán Etchingham of the Wexford GAA was such a man, and he proposed in November 1914 that the GAA establish rifle clubs so that members could defend Ireland. A speaker at the meeting expressed concern that the weather might not

WHERE HEROES ARE MADE

be suitable for rifle training. Etchingham was infuriated and responded: 'Do you want special weather for war? This opportunity – the like of which you have not had for a century – may pass; an opportunity that may not occur again.'

Sarah explains how her grandfather was caught up in the political turmoil:

'In 1916 he answered the "call to arms" and was interned in Frongoch Prison (North Wales) where he met Michael Collins. Following the 1916 Rising, 1,800 Irish rebels were arrested and interned at that Prisoner of War camp. In the aftermath of the Insurrection, 3,000 Irish rebels were arrested in all, and were marched to Dublin Port to board boats destined for internment camps in Britain. Over the next six months the internees including leading lights of the struggle for independence like Michael Collins, Richard Mulcahy, Terence MacSwiney and Sam Maguire, formed deep bonds of friendship while sharing their knowledge and skills. The lessons of the Rising had been learned and republican networks were strengthened within Frongoch's North and South camps, located at a former Welsh whisky distillery.'

The testimony of one of those men arrested, Johnny Flynn, exists today:

'We were lined up at Richmond barracks, marched down along the quays, and along the North Wall. There were two rows of soldiers either side of us, with a lorry behind us with a machine gun mounted upon it.

'We certainly weren't very popular as we were marched down to the boat. But for the soldiers either side of us, we might have fared very badly with the women of Dublin. Many of them were shouting "shoot the bastards".

'The rebels were brought to Britain on cattle ships, many of them thrown into pens alongside the cattle. Of the 3,000 aboard,

1,800 were interned at Frongoch in Wales: an old, disused distillery which had been used as a Prisoner of War camp for German soldiers during the First World War. Living conditions were atrocious, with many of the German prisoners at the camp dying of TB.

'In spite of the poor conditions, the proximity of so many Irishmen with similar republican ideals led to a community atmosphere among Michael Collins and the other detainees, and the prison became known as Ollscoil Na Réabhlóide or the University of Revolution.'

One of the detainees, Joseph Lawless, recalled the atmosphere in his Bureau of Military History testimony:

'Frongoch has since then been aptly termed the University of the Irish Revolution, and so indeed it was. No more certain way of perpetuating the ideals of the executed leaders and ensuring another and bigger effort to throw off the yoke of foreign domination could have been imagined or desired by them.

'The police in Ireland had done their work well in selecting throughout the country the most likely disaffected persons, most of whom were Volunteers, but not all of them. These, lodged together in a camp with the leaven of those who had had their blood baptism on the streets of Dublin and elsewhere, were bound to be touched by the longing to emulate the heroic deeds of those who fought; and there were those amongst us whose intellects grasped the possibilities of this situation, and strove – to make the best use of the opportunity so unexpectedly provided by the enemy.

'One of the aspects key in fostering this collective identity was Gaelic football,' Sarah continues. 'A number of those interned were Gaelic footballers of considerable repute along with my grandfather. Gaelic football matches were frequently organised between inmates to both keep fit and display their national character. As the prison would not allow the detainees to have hurleys, they were forced to play Gaelic football with a soccer ball. The prisoners renamed the field at the camp – a pitch surrounded by barbed wire – as Croke Park.

'At the time, the Wolfe Tone tournament was the secondary competition in the GAA. Louth – captained by my grandfather – and Kerry had qualified for the final, which was postponed owing to the Rising. Such was the volume of players from both teams interned at Frongoch, it was decided that the Wolfe Tone final would be played on the barbed wire-enclosed field the inmates had deemed as Croke Park. It has become known as the "All Ireland Behind Barbed Wire".

'Attendance at the game was made compulsory, so a crowd of about 1,800 watched a game that has been described as extremely tough and competitive. Perhaps apocryphally, one British officer was recorded as having said: "If that's what they are like at play, they must be bloody awful in a fight!"

'The game was recorded by prisoner Joe Stanley, who was a Louth-based publisher of republican literature. His report of the game itself is sadly rather vague. All that is known is the game lasted forty minutes (comprising two twenty-minute halves) and that Kerry won the game by a point.'

The Proclamation was read out by piper Cormac Bowell during the interval. After the game each player placed a piece of grass from 'Croke Park' into the box with their medals as a tribute to the men interned there in 1916.

There was an unusual marketing strategy for the game. Posters advertising the Wolfe Tone tournament final match in Frongoch between old rivals Kerry and Louth informed fans that 'admission was 5 shillings and wives and sweethearts should be left at home'!

TIME TO SAY GOODBYE

On a day so cold the frost bit the snow, Sarah explained how the saga ended:

'The last Irishman in Frongoch on 23 December 1916 was Dublin priest Fr Laurence Joseph Stafford. The Dublin Diocesan Archives include one letter dated 23 December, which was written to Archbishop William Walsh of Dublin. In it Fr Stafford writes: "Five months ago when they were releasing the men interned here in hundreds, I said I should be the last Irishman left in Frongoch; and today I am."

'Outlining to the archbishop how he lobbied the British authorities for the prisoners' release he had argued "that Christmas was Christmas".

'"Today the gates of the compound are thrown open and tonight there will not be a single Irishman (save myself) left in Frongoch."'

According to Noelle Dowling, archivist at the Dublin Diocesan Archives, when World War I broke out in August 1914, Fr Stafford asked to become a military chaplain and the following March he signed up.

This proved a difficulty when he was appointed to Frongoch because he wore the military chaplain's uniform. The men looked at him as being a sort of 'Khaki chaplain'. Even though he knew some of them, they did not take to him initially. But through his good work and his perseverance they finally did accept him.

Another letter written by Fr Stafford from Frongoch is dated 19 July 1916, shortly after he arrived in the camp. He relates how he celebrated Mass for the men in both camps in Frongoch, as well as Confession and the Rosary: 'I need hardly say, the men appreciate the presence of a priest among them and I am up shortly after five every morning to begin my work.'

WHERE HEROES ARE MADE

POSTSCRIPT

Sarah is proud that her grandfather made a significant contribution to the GAA:

'In 1920 at the behest of Michael Collins he was nominated and elected Secretary of the County Board, a position he held until 1925. He later served four years as County Board Chairman from 1928–31. He refereed the 1928 All-Ireland Final and Tailteann Games and Railway Cup Finals as well as countless Louth Finals. With Drogheda Stars he won two Louth Junior and two Louth Senior medals, before helping to form Wolfe Tones in 1923. He won a third Louth Senior medal with them in 1925. He declined the invitation to represent Leinster in the 1924 Tailteann Games because of his political views. In 1928 he refereed the All-Ireland final, the first occasion Sam Maguire was presented to the winning team – Bill "Squires" Gannon lifting the trophy for Kildare.'

So what became of the camp?

'Today, the barbed wire has been removed from the field, and now it is grazed by sheep. Locals in the Welsh village still refer to the field as "Croke Park". There is a small monument to the memory of the game and the men involved, which was erected by a Liverpool branch of the Gaelic League.'

24

WHEN DAVID BEAT GOLIATH

Mullinalaghta

Let others lead small lives, but not you. Let others argue over small things, but not you. Let others cry over small hurts, but not you. Let others leave their future in someone else's hands, but not you.

JIM ROHN

Sometimes people surprise you. Like when I joined the Botox Support Group. Nobody raised an eyebrow.

A Longford club surprised me.

It was one of those moments that can derange the emotional life – the fulfilment of an ancient dream.

People felt it before they saw it – like eager first-time parents, waiting for their child's first words.

There was a presence in the air, like a shuddering, or a tense moment in a film.

Close your eyes and the years roll back. Great hurling and football matches refuse to be undramatic. If the form-book suggests predictability, there is almost always a subplot to send the blood pressure into orbit.

WHERE HEROES ARE MADE

People who witness miracles, even minor ones of the sporting variety, are wont to carry around forever afterwards a potent cocktail of reminiscence, and any Gaelic football fan who wants to avoid a long monologue on the 2018 Leinster club final better steer miles clear of Longford.

Gaelic games are the ultimate virtual reality because they can take you anywhere you want to go. Contrary to real life sport offers us a state of being that is so rewarding one does it for no other reason than to be a part of it. Such feelings are among the most intense, most memorable experiences one can get in this life. There are moments that stand out from the mundanity of every day as shining beacons.

STATE OF SHOCK

A great charm of the games is that they provide a platform for David to take on and sometimes slay Goliath. In February 2019 the Carlow hurlers shocked Galway by drawing with them in the league. Galway had won the All-Ireland less than eighteen months earlier.

Likewise, joy abounds when counties return to centre stage. A case in point in 2025 came when Meath beat Dublin that same season, ending the Dubs' run of fourteen consecutive Leinster titles. Joe Brolly captured the sense of joy: 'The Dublin wall has fallen. At the final whistle in the Leinster semi-final, people wept. They ran onto the field to grab a blade of grass or a handful of clay.'

Louth qualified for all three Leinster football finals in the same year for the first time. Then on an historic day for Louth football, they became kings of Leinster for the first time since 1957. The icing on the cake was that sixty-eight years of hurt came to an end by beating Meath.

WHEN DAVID BEAT GOLIATH

Louth were a point in front of their closest neighbours and rivals, Meath, in the 2010 Leinster final. Then in the seventy-fourth minute Meath's Graham Reilly launched the ball into the square. It fell to Seamus Kenny who aimed for goal. Paddy Keenan who had been stupendous throughout for 'the Wee County' (and who won a richly deserved All-Star at midfield later that year) threw his body in front of the shot and blocked the ball. Neither Dessie Finnegan nor Andy McDonnell could hold the rebound and it was grabbed by Joe Sheridan. He stumbled, fell and was almost prostrate on the goal-line before throwing the ball in the net.

A number of Louth players then surrounded the referee, Martin Sludden, who appeared to have noted the score in his book, even though the umpires' flags stayed down. Aaron Hoey urged Sludden to speak to the umpires and the Tyrone man went towards one of them. The television replays showed the umpire cupping his ear, Sludden saying something and the umpire raising his flag.

After the ensuing kick-out, the referee blew the whistle to finish the game. Sludden remained on the pitch, and in the eyes of Louth fans added to the injustice by booking a number of Louth players, including Aaron Hoey. The anger came from them like the rustle of leaves in a forest.

Then some angry Louth fans confronted Sludden. The Louth manager Peter Fitzpatrick (who would subsequently become a T.D.) and some Louth players stood around the referee to protect him as he was approached by other fans. A Garda started to escort him off the pitch. Two years later two Louth fans were convicted and each fined €1,000 for attacking Sludden. After the game Peter Fitzpatrick claimed Sludden was: 'Dick Turpin without a mask. It was pure daylight robbery'.

An Lú abú.

WHERE HEROES ARE MADE

SEASON'S GREETINGS

Christmas came early for GAA romantics in December 2018 when Mullinalaghta St Columba's team completed one of the most remarkable stories in the history of Gaelic football by winning the Leinster Football Championship title and beating the famed Kilmacud Crokes in a perfectly constructed rollercoaster. They are the first ever Longford team to win the Leinster title.

Mullinalaghta's name, *Mullach na Leachta* means 'Hill of the Standing Stones' and is derived from a hill which was the original site of the local church that dates back to 1839. There are just 447 people living in this half-parish in County Longford and the other part of the parish is Gowna, which is in County Cavan.

The Mullinalaghta GAA membership is just 155, in contrast to Kilmacud's 4,800 members. This win was an incredible tale on many levels, not least the fact that Mullinalaghta were not even rated as a team to ever win a Leinster title. They did the unthinkable, that nobody believed they could do – except themselves and their self-belief. To dream the impossible dream and make it a reality is what Mullinalaghta have taught us all.

Some sporting moments transcend the realm of sport itself and assume a significance in terms of the human spirit that no mere sporting victory ever could. This match was one of them.

Mighty Mullinalaghta we salute you.

25

SEASONS OF SUNDAYS

RTÉ

I find television very educating. Every time somebody turns on the set, I go into the other room and read a book.

GROUCHO MARX

Gaelic games have been at the heart of broadcasting in Ireland from its earliest days. On New Year's Day 1926, '2RN', Ireland's national radio station began its transmission. On 29 August that year a Gaelic game was transmitted live for the first time. The All-Ireland hurling semi-final between Kilkenny and Galway was the first radio commentary outside America of a field game. When RTÉ television came on air in 1961–2 the GAA initially adopted a cautious approach, restricting this coverage annually to the two All-Ireland finals, the two football semi-finals and the Railway Cup finals on St Patrick's Day. Over the years, the GAA has spotted that television is not a threat but a useful ally in attracting people to our national games.

In this respect the old enemy – soccer – showed the way.

WHERE HEROES ARE MADE

WIRED FOR SOUND

Despite all the incredible advances in technology, television is not everything. Most people, given the chance, prefer to 'be there'. From its earliest days, sport was a great spectator attraction. The great Roman architects laid out their stadia not just for the Russell Crowes and Charlton Hestons of their time, as gladiators and chariot-racers to showcase their talents, but to create 'atmosphere'. Sport is so popular now that only a tiny fraction who would like to get the opportunity to attend All-Ireland finals or rugby internationals can get tickets. Hence the importance of television because it is now the medium through which the vast majority of people have access to their favourite sports. Indeed, some sports like snooker owe their popularity almost entirely to television exposure. New satellite technology brings even more opportunities.

George Bernard Shaw once said: 'Men trifle with their business and their politics but never trifle with their games. It brings truth home to them.' From the earliest times there were people who reported on sporting events. Greek and Roman writers recorded many sporting events. In the *Iliad*, Homer recorded in considerable detail the games organised at the funeral of Patroclus. The attraction of sport is that it provides drama, tension, excitement, winners and losers, pain, laughter and sometimes even tragedy. It is uncertain, often to the very finish (remember the 1982 All-Ireland?) and it is intensely human. It makes headlines, it provides a good read, it makes great pictures.

Television creates heroes and anti-heroes! Muhammad Ali was the first true world star of the TV age. Paul Gascoigne's fame soared after the 1990 World Cup not because of his skills but because he struck an emotional chord in the massive worldwide TV audience for shedding tears on the pitch when it looked as if a yellow card from the referee might rule him out of the World Cup final. Within months he was endorsing a wide range of products, many outside football – board games, deodorants, jewellery, calendars, school lunch boxes, to name just a handful. He also had a hit record even though he has a dreadful voice. Mind you, that's not a unique achievement!

Even losers can find temporary fame and sometimes fortune through the universal appeal of sport, as the disastrous British ski jumper Eddie 'the Eagle' Edwards has shown in recent times. Sports stars have been used to endorse products since 1947 when the English cricketer Denis Compton, a kind of James Bond figure, became the face of Brylcreem. His face and slicked-down hair became one of the best-known pictures in Britain, used in magazines and on billboards all over the country.

Every rose has its thorns. Television has created its own problems for sport. Back in 1983 Sir Denis Follows, Chairman of the British Olympic Association, observed: 'We have now reached a stage where sport at top level has become almost completely show business with everything that one associates with showbiz; the cult of the individual, high salaries, the desire to present a game as a spectacle – with more money, less sportsmanship, more emphasis on winning. All this has come through television.' The following year Jack Nicklaus observed: 'Television controls the game of golf. It's a matter of the tail wagging the dog.'

Sport is vicarious living. It is tense, immediate, glamorous. Television generally, although Gaelic games is something of an exception, pays large sums of money to bring the drama and entertainment of the major sports events into our homes. Sport is so popular with television companies because they are acutely aware that nothing stops the world in its tracks more effectively. In relative terms, compared with many other forms of entertainment, such as film, it is cheap. The bustling cities of

Ireland were a ghost town when the boys in green were playing in the World Cup finals. Scarcely a bus moved on the streets. Sport is so important to television companies because it generates a large viewing audience. As such it is a powerful weapon in the ratings war. An example serves to illustrate.

It was not until 1964 that the BBC initiated what was to become the hallmark of British soccer coverage for an entire generation – recorded highlights on *Match of the Day*. ITV was quick to respond and initiated *The Big Match* on Sunday afternoons, featuring recorded highlights of one of the previous day's top games. For the first time, British viewers were given the benefit of expert analysis to complement the action. The BBC had the advantage of having no commercial breaks. To give them an advantage over the Beeb, ITV invested £60,000 in a slow-motion machine, which was a massive sum in the 1960s.

By the World Cup of 1970, when national interest was high and England's chances of retaining the trophy supposedly even higher, ITV boldly announced it had discovered 'the formula'. A panel of provocative experts would enliven half-times and post-match discussions through a combination of informed comment, passionate debate and full-scale abuse. Malcolm Allison, Bob McNab, Pat Crerand and Derek Dougan, 'the two goodies and the two baddies', sought to establish ITV's credentials as a legitimate alternative to the BBC in bringing soccer to the television audience. The science, using the term loosely, of football punditry was born. Neither Pat Spillane nor Joe Brolly realised at the time but a new career had been created for them!

THE SUNDAY GAME
On New Year's Eve 1961, Éamon de Valera stared into a camera to launch a new television service: 'Now it is you the people who will ultimately determine what the programmes in Teilifís

Éireann are to be. If you insist on having presented to you the good and the true and the beautiful, you will get these.'

He urged viewers to demand 'sturdiness and vigour and confidence' from the new station rather than 'decadence and disillusion'. I wonder what he would have made of *Normal People*.

Initially watching television was the preserve of the elite because there were only 30,000 television sets in existence when RTÉ went on air, mostly in well-to-do homes along the east coast. Newsreaders like Maurice O'Doherty and Charles Mitchel became household names, while continuity announcers Thelma Mansfield and Kathleen Watkins became leaders in the fashion stakes. Gay Byrne created the most discussed show on the station. It became a national obsession as he brought Ireland kicking and screaming into more modern sensibilities.

Seán Óg Ó Ceallacháin was the first presenter of *The Sunday Game* in 1979, a rare programme then devoted exclusively to Gaelic games. Seán Óg's contribution to Gaelic games was multilayered. He lined out in both hurling and Gaelic football with the Eoghan Ruadh club and represented Dublin in the 1940s and 1950s. He scored a goal in Dublin's defeat to Waterford in the 1948 All-Ireland hurling final and was also a referee of note and took charge of the 1952 All-Ireland minor hurling final. After helping his father for some years with the programme, in 1953 he commenced his Sunday night slot *Gaelic Sports Results* with RTÉ. Starting with the words 'Go mBeannaí Dia Díobh Go Léir', Seán's programme ran for all of fifty-eight years, until his retirement in 2011. Such endurance placed *Gaelic Sports Results* amongst *The Guinness Book of Records*. It was hugely popular with Irish people the world over.

In fact, so associated was he in the popular mind with Gaelic games that people had great difficulty thinking that he had an interest in any other sports. This was memorably demonstrated

WHERE HEROES ARE MADE

when a caller to RTÉ Radio Sport rang to ask about Manchester United. The conversation went as follows:

'Is this Seán Óg?'

'It is indeed.'

'Seán Óg Ó Ceallacháin?'

'The one and the same?'

'Off the radio?'

'That's me!'

'Sure, what the f**k would you know about soccer?'

A FAN

David Hickey still recalls Seán Óg with great affection:

'One of my earliest memories of football was listening to him on the radio late on Sunday night when for ten to fifteen minutes he would read the football and hurling results from around the country. Van Morrison's song "In the Days Before Rock and Roll" captures those days before TV became commonplace. "I am down on my knees at the wireless knobs . . . Telefunken, Hilversum, Helvetia, Athlone."

'I remember it exactly as Van describes it, the crackling as you went over the "Red Band" to get your station, which for Van was Luxemburg, but for me was Athlone at least on Sunday night for Seán Óg. As Van sang "Fats did not come in without those wireless knobs" and neither did Seán Óg. I can still hear his lovely voice, "Longford Junior Championship: Longford Slashers 1-10, Clonguish 2-3. Dublin Senior Championship: St Vincents 1-23, Na Fianna 1-10 and on and on till we got all the results we were interested in. They were all jumbled so you had to listen to the whole show to get the games you were particularly interested in.

'His voice still reverberates in the windmill of my mind as does a story about him. Before one of the All-Ireland finals in the 1970s Seán got stopped speeding. The cop said he would "throw the book" at him, but if he could get him two tickets for Sunday it would go away.

'Seán went and asked the GAA secretary general for the two tickets. They were good friends so he said to Seán: "I have two tickets that I keep for this type of situation". The tickets were at the junction of the Hogan and Nally stands with a stanchion between them. From one seat you could only see from the fourteen yard to the Hill, the other you could kinda see all the pitch except from the fourteen yard line to the Hill. I can still see the "boy in blue" and his friend's faces, when they shuffled into these "two fingers" seats. What a brilliant use of useless tickets! Absolutely brilliant.'

THE FINGER OF BLAME

Seán Óg had a good team behind him in RTÉ with Maurice Reidy as the editor and John D. O'Brien as director. They made the brave decision to have Liz Howard as one of their main analysts. Liz was an All-Ireland camogie player brought up in a hurling household; her father was the great Limerick All-Ireland star Garrett Howard. For years she was PRO for the Tipperary County Board.

In 1979 Liz hit the headlines following her comments about the Leinster football final on *The Sunday Game*. Legendary Dublin full-forward Jimmy Keaveney was sent off for an elbow offence on Offaly defender Ollie Minnock. Liz was in no doubt that the sending off was very harsh. The next day *The Irish Press* carried the headline 'TV personality supports Jimmy Keaveney' over a front-page story. Keaveney was asked to attend a meeting of the Leinster Council Disciplinary Committee, to explain his actions. The Dublin County Board invited Liz to attend the meeting and give evidence in support of Jimmy. She did and so did Ollie

WHERE HEROES ARE MADE

Minnock, who pleaded for leniency on Keaveney's behalf. Their pleas for mercy fell on deaf ears and Keaveney was suspended for a month, ruling him out of the All-Ireland semi-final against Roscommon. On the day of the match Liz was going into Croke Park when she was accosted by a big Dublin fan who shouted at the top of his voice: 'Look at her. She's the wan who shafted Jimmy Keaveney.' It shows the hazards of being an analyst!

You just can't win.

26

ISLAND IN THE SUN

Fiji

Champions aren't made in gyms. Champions are made from something they have deep inside them – a desire, a dream, a vision. They have to have the skill, and the will. But the will must be stronger than the skill.

MUHAMMAD ALI

Is dóchas an dochtúir do gach anó (Hope is the physician of every misery).

This proverb is a celebration of the undefeated spirit – like his.

The most famous quote in the hurling vernacular is Mícheál Ó Muircheartaigh's observation: 'A mighty poc from the hurl of Seán Óg Ó hAilpín. Seán Óg Ó hAilpín . . . his father was from Fermanagh, his mother from Fiji, neither a hurling stronghold.'

Ó Muircheartaigh also had a great quote about the Cork legend's famous brother: 'Setanta Ó hAilpín . . . the original Setanta from the old Gaelic stories was ten feet tall, had ten fingers on each hand and ten toes on each foot but even he couldn't be playing better hurling than his namesake here today.'

On the pitch he looked as one carved of granite. Off the pitch one of Seán Óg Ó hAilpín's most enduring legacies is to place Fiji on the hurling map.

THE DUAL STAR

Seán Óg Ó hAilpín was one of the last great dual stars, playing at left half-back when winning an All-Ireland hurling medal with Cork in the one-point victory over Kilkenny in 1999, and playing in the full-back line for the footballers when they lost by three points to Meath a few weeks later in the All-Ireland football final.

In 2003 in the Munster Championship, after getting over the grievances with the county board and with a new management team, Cork were all out to prove that they were right to strike and the only way to do that was to win something. They won the Munster title. In 2003, in the course of Cork's triumphant march to the All-Ireland final, a new sporting icon was launched on Leeside. Seán Óg's younger brother Setanta thrilled the Cork public in a way Jimmy Barry-Murphy inspired Cork to All-Ireland final glory at nineteen years of age in 1973. Cork fans were bitterly disappointed losing the final to Kilkenny. Their sense of misery was compounded when they heard that Setanta had gone down under to carve out a new career for himself as an Aussie Rules player. Yet the following year Cork were able to reverse the previous year's form when they beat Kilkenny by 0-17 to 0-9 to win another All-Ireland.

ON A CLARE DAY

The hand of fate is especially fickle when it comes to sport. Accordingly, after a single victory or defeat the hurlers on the ditch can change their colours faster than Manchester United. For all the benefits of leading a confident and unchanged side,

ISLAND IN THE SUN

Cork really struggled in the 2005 All-Ireland semi-final against Clare. With the minutes slipping away it seemed that Cork were on their way out of the championship. Resignation was actually what the Cork fans in the stands had in common, even if none of them had a language which could express it.

Ní bhíonn an rath, ach mar a mbíonn an smacht: To fully excel at something regardless of what it may be, you must be fully committed to it.

The Cork team were.

It was a real test on and off the field, Seán Óg recalled:

'Even the Cork fans felt sorry for Clare. They were arguably the better team, they just didn't take their chances. With twenty minutes to go, we were six points behind and hadn't raised a single flag in the second half. Clare had scored points and were rampant.'

Brian Lohan, memorably described by Mícheál Ó Muircheartaigh as the man 'with the strength of two horses' was giving one of his greatest ever displays at full-back and was 'cleaning' the great Brian Corcoran:

'Clare's Tony Carmody was on fire and causing us untold damage in the centre-half-forward position. Something had to be done. John Allen courageously took off Corcoran and Ronan Curran, two All-Stars the previous year, and sent on Wayne Sherlock and Neil Ronan. Wayne went to wing-back and John Gardiner moved to the centre. Neither Carmody nor Lohan exercised the same dominance again. Neil scored a crucial point.

'John Allen rightly said afterwards, "We had to make the call. We would have been lacerated if we didn't. We were five points down and the game was slipping from us. We have twenty-nine people on our panel. I mean, it was a case of what do we do here? Do we throw in the towel or do we try and stem the tide?"'

WHERE HEROES ARE MADE

Cork scored seven of the game's closing nine points to sneak a one-point win and then won the All-Ireland against Galway with more comfort by 1-21 to 1-16. To add to the occasion for Seán Óg, he captained the team, in the process giving one of the great acceptance speeches in the Irish language.

It was a beautiful fable of the 'new Ireland' as it is meant to be. The GAA's work and volunteering ethos form the beating hearts of many communities not just all over the island of Ireland, but increasingly further afield, as Gaelic games are now played on every continent.

It is home to all – irrespective of whether from Fiji, Fermanagh or Fermoy.

A PARABLE

My favourite story of the year offers a lovely parable – regardless of its veracity. One sunny afternoon, Big Shaq, known for his towering presence and fame as a basketball legend, decided to visit his usual corner store. Despite his celebrity status and impressive physique – standing over two meters tall – he enjoyed the simple pleasure of grocery shopping. It was his way of unwinding after long, demanding days.

Casually dressed in a grey T-shirt, jeans, and a shiny watch, Shaq strolled into the bustling store with his usual friendly demeanour. The staff, familiar with his visits, greeted him warmly, and he returned their smiles as he picked up a basket and began walking through the aisles.

Stopping at the cereal section, Shaq browsed the shelves with focused attention, carefully reading labels to find something nutritious. He was so absorbed in his task that he didn't notice an elderly woman, Mrs Margaret, approaching behind him. She was a petite lady with snow-white hair, leaning on a cane and pushing a squeaky cart.

ISLAND IN THE SUN

'Excuse me, young man!' her voice rang out sharply. 'How am I supposed to get my cereal when you're standing in the way?'

Startled, Shaq turned around to face her. Seeing her stern expression, he quickly stepped aside with a polite smile. 'Sorry about that, ma'am,' he said warmly.

But Mrs Margaret wasn't finished. Glancing up at him with a disapproving look, she muttered, 'They'll let anyone in here these days. No standards any more.'

Her words carried a tone of prejudice that Shaq couldn't ignore. Though her remark stung, he chose to remain calm, a principle he'd held onto throughout his life. With a deep breath, he resumed browsing, determined not to let her words ruin his day.

As Shaq moved to leave the aisle, Mrs Margaret suddenly shouted, her voice loud and accusatory, 'Security! Someone get security here now!'

The store fell silent as customers turned to see what was happening. A young security guard hurried over, looking bewildered. Mrs Margaret pointed at Shaq with a trembling finger.

'Get him out of here! People like him don't belong here. Send him back to Africa!'

Time seemed to stand still. Shaq stood motionless, processing the hateful words. Though his expression remained composed, the hurt was evident in his eyes. He had faced prejudice before, but the blatant venom in her words was a painful reminder of the challenges he still endured.

The security guard hesitated, glancing between Mrs Margaret and Shaq. 'Ma'am,' he said carefully, 'he hasn't done anything wrong. He's just shopping.'

Mrs Margaret's face flushed with anger. 'Are you refusing to listen to me?' she demanded, banging her cane on the floor. 'Get the manager!'

Moments later, the store manager arrived, looking serious. Mrs Margaret wasted no time, pointing again at Shaq. 'I want him out of this store. Now!'

Before the manager could respond, Shaq stepped forward. His deep, steady voice filled the aisle. 'Ma'am,' he began, his tone calm but firm, 'I understand that you may not be used to seeing someone like me here. But I'm just here to shop, like you and everyone else. I'm a son, a friend, a hardworking man, and a citizen of this community. My skin colour doesn't change that.'

The store remained silent as Shaq continued, his words powerful yet full of grace. 'I've faced comments like yours before. They're hurtful, but I choose not to respond with anger. Instead, I feel sad – sad that someone who has lived as long as you have could hold onto such outdated views.'

Mrs Margaret faltered, her eyes dropping to the floor. Shaq's voice softened. 'I have a grandmother about your age. She taught me to respect my elders because they've seen and experienced things I never will. But if she were here and heard the words you said to me, I think she'd feel disappointed.'

The room was heavy with emotion. A few shoppers wiped their eyes, moved by Shaq's composure and sincerity.

'You've seen the world change,' Shaq said gently. 'If your grandchildren heard what happened here today, would they be proud? Is this the legacy you want to leave behind?'

Mrs Margaret's hands trembled as tears welled in her eyes. Her voice quivered as she finally spoke.

'I . . . I didn't think of it that way. You're right. I'm sorry.'

Shaq gave her a kind smile. 'It's okay, ma'am. We all make mistakes. What's important is learning from them.'

The aisle erupted in applause. Mrs Margaret reached out, placing a hand on Shaq's arm. Her voice was now soft and genuine. 'Thank you for teaching me this,' she said.

ISLAND IN THE SUN

Shaq nodded. 'We can all learn from one another. That's how we grow.'

The tension in the store dissolved. The manager thanked Shaq for his grace, and customers approached to express their admiration. Even Mrs Margaret, now visibly humbled, left with a warm smile.

As Shaq exited the store that evening, the golden sunset bathed the street in a peaceful glow. He felt a sense of fulfilment, knowing he had transformed a moment of hostility into one of understanding and humanity.

The story spread through the community, becoming a powerful reminder of compassion and forgiveness. Mrs Margaret, once known for her biases, began greeting everyone with kindness, while Shaq continued to inspire others with his big heart and unshakable belief in the power of kindness.

Back in the real world, increasingly GAA stars are getting immersed in efforts to build bridges.

Like Jason Sherlock, Lee Chin has experienced the less welcoming side of the GAA in the form of racist comments. In April 2025, after the Leinster Championship victory over Antrim, the Wexford ace approached Gerard Walsh to give his condolences after the death of his sister Fionnuala. The gesture was revealed by Antrim performance coach Neil McManus after the match: 'Gerard very sadly buried his sister last week. Gerard played really well for Antrim yesterday in the middle of the park. And as soon as the game was over, you see Lee Chin making a beeline to share his condolences with him. A class act on-and-off the pitch.'

27

THE LYNCH MOB

Bray

There are heroes and then there are legends; heroes get remembered but legends never die.

BONEY KAPOOR

He was proud of his identity.

He enjoyed people who had a similar pride – like George Foreman who was married five times, had five sons and called each of them George.

He was tickled by the story that in 1994, Hulk Hogan's agent left a voicemail saying, 'I've got a grill and I've got a blender, which one do you want to pick?' Hogan couldn't answer the phone because he was picking up his kids from school so his agent offered the grill endorsement to another client, George Foreman. The legendary boxer went on to pocket $550 million from that missed call.

One of my favourite places to visit was Bray because it was home to Brendan Lynch, one of four Roscommon players to be selected on the Connacht team of the millennium. On my final visit to his house, night had fallen early but the shroud of snow reflected a light that gave eerie life to hedges and houses, and by a celestial miracle night was transformed into day. Only the purring car engine shattered the spell of silence. When I arrived I plodded up the pathway, through the thickening snowstorm, leaving big, deep footprints in the fresh snow. The trees seemed to be standing and shivering together, hugging bare limbs and grumbling about the cold.

I never knew where a conversation with Brendan would take me. He once told me he had a particular reverence for Benediction. He loved the choir's singing, the air warm and heavy with incense and bodies and the tinkling of a bell. There always seemed to be a chorus of shrouded coughing coming from the pews from nervous parishioners, answering awkwardly to the priest's promptings. In silence and solemnity the man of the cloth climbed towards the tabernacle. The monstrance glittered like a metallic sun as he moved it in the shape of a cross before a mass of adoring eyes. He marvelled as the altar boys were in scarlet and white as they left the altar in twos in front of the priest bearing the empty monstrance, the light from the candles dancing daringly on the gold of his cloak.

There were few greater pleasures than sharing a slice of apple tart listening to Brendan recalling his memories of his glory days with Roscommon. He had the most wonderful laugh in Bray. His laugh could be heard miles away. When he laughed his entire body shook and his tummy went up and down like a yo-yo. His laugh made me laugh, and when I laughed that made him laugh again, only louder and longer. Tears of joy rolled down his face.

GENESIS

It was Jimmy Murray who catapulted Brendan Lynch into national prominence:

'I was playing a senior club match for Oran in 1941 and this man approached me and asked me if I was a minor. I thought he was asking me if I worked as a miner because in my innocence at the time I didn't know what minor meant as a football term. I told him I wasn't but that I was in the reserves. He was a bit frustrated by my response but explained that Roscommon were playing Mayo in the Connacht minor final and if they won I could be playing in the All-Ireland semi-final a week later in Tralee. At the time, travelling to Tralee was as unimaginable to me as travelling to the Antarctic today. I asked him who he was and he told me he was Jimmy Murray from Knockcroghery. That night I listened to the news on the battery set radio which was the only programme we were allowed to listen to because of the Emergency but I kept it on to hear Seán Ó Ceallacháin reading the sports news. I heard that Roscommon had won. The problem was I didn't know then if I would play or not. I went back to the Curragh and when I heard nothing by Friday lunchtime I was despondent. Then later that afternoon I was on duty when I was relieved at my post and told I had to get the train home to Roscommon and join up with the team. The problem was that I had very little time to get to the station. The hackney car wasn't there so I started to run the few miles to the station. With ten minutes left I stopped running because I knew I couldn't make it. Then I saw a private coming on his bicycle in the opposite direction. I was a corporal so I had one stripe and he had none so I told him to give me the bike and I left it at the station for him.

'We sneaked a draw in Austin Stack Park and beat them easily in a replay. Then we beat Louth in the final. I had played three matches and won an All-Ireland medal.'

CORR VALUES

A human history book, Lynch's mind was as sharp as an executioner's axe. Over sixty years on he was amused by the amateur nature of Roscommon football which saw him left on the subs' bench in favour of an established player with a big name in the county, Purty Kelly, who was over the hill for the 1942 Connacht Championship. In 1943, though, Lynch had established the right half-back position as his own and would announce his arrival on the national stage in bold print in the All-Ireland semi-final against Louth:

'I was marking Peter Corr who had been the player of the year that stage. He had scored thirteen points in the Leinster final. I decided it was his career or mine. I handled him roughly and kept him scoreless. Peter, who was related to the singers the Corrs, went on to play for Everton.

'My lasting memory from the game was when the County Secretary John Joe Fahy came running up to me at the end of the game and said: "Ye'll beat them in the second half if you play like that." I turned to him and said: "We have already." He looked shocked and said: "God, did I miss it?" He was so embroiled in the whole game and the tension it created he had lost all track of time.

'I remember seeing Tom Shevlin playing when I was a boy. He was Roscommon's greatest player in the 1920s. I met him as I came out of Croke Park. He said to me: "Ye were lucky." I said: "We won." He laughed and replied: "That's the end of the argument."

'We beat Cavan in the All-Ireland final after a replay. I marked Mick Higgins who was very quiet and a very clean and good footballer. What I remember most was the mayhem at the end. First Cavan's Joe Stafford was sent off after having a go at Owensie Hoare. We got a point but Barney Cully didn't agree and put the umpire into the net with a box. Big Tom O'Reilly, the captain of Cavan, came in to remonstrate and T.P. O'Reilly threw the referee in the air.'

It was not the medal that mattered to Lynch:

'The euphoria of winning was incredible. I felt like jumping out of my skin. I was on top of the world. I was twenty years of age and the world seemed my oyster.'

SLIGO SETBACK

Roscommon had a slice of luck before claiming a second title in 1944:

'Sligo drew with us in the first round of the Connacht Championship in Boyle. They should have beaten us. We were lucky to survive. There were only 2,000 people in attendance when we played Mayo in the Connacht final because of the transport problems during the war. We were worried by Cavan at half-time in the All-Ireland semi-final but they collapsed completely in the second half and we had an easy win. The belief then was that you hadn't really won an All-Ireland until you beat Kerry in a final so we were all keen to do that. I was marking the famous Paddy Bawn Brosnan. He was a fisherman and fond of the women, fond of the porter and fond of the rough and tumble!

'I made the most impact on their great midfielder, Paddy Kennedy, when I had a head collision with him and he had to be stretchered off. He asked me: "Jaysus, what did you do to me?"'

Roscommon were not to recapture the same winning feeling again:

'We were unlucky with illness. Phelim Murray got TB and spent twelve months in a sanatorium. I would consider Phelim to be Roscommon's best-ever footballer. The nearest to him I have seen since was Dermot Earley who was close to perfect. TB also finished Liam Gilmartin's career. We also lost John Joe Nerney so we were never the same force again.

THE LYNCH MOB

'Mayo beat us in the first round of the Championship in 1945. We were suffering from burn-out and they were hungry. It was a relief in a way because you had the chance to take holidays. I met Jimmy Murray that summer and he asked me how I was finding the summer without football. When I said I thought it was great he told me he felt the same.'

Roscommon were to come within a whisker of taking another All-Ireland in 1946:

'It was a Mickey Mouse ruling in the GAA that cost us the title. We played Mayo in the Connacht final in Ballinasloe. They had a goal disallowed and then we got a goal that was going to be disallowed. Jimmy Murray grabbed the green flag and waved it, and we were awarded the goal. After the game, Mayo lodged an objection. What should have happened was that the referee should have produced his report saying Roscommon won the match and that would have been that. Instead, we had to go into a replay and on top of the heavy collective training we were doing we didn't need another match. We lost Frank Kinlough with a leaky valve in his heart and Doc Callaghan our full-back was injured. By the time we faced Kerry in the All-Ireland final replay they were getting stronger and we were getting weaker. I was never as happy as when the final whistle sounded in that game because the whole year had been absolutely exhausting with the two replays and all the collective training. To quote Shakespeare:

If all the year were playing holidays
To sport would be as tedious as to work.

'It finished us a team. We lost to Cavan in the All-Ireland semi-final in 1947 which meant they went on to play in the Polo Grounds instead of us. I didn't begrudge them. It was only right that players like John Joe O'Reilly finally won an All-Ireland.'

HARSH LESSONS

As Roscommon's fortunes faded, Lynch found himself, in a fit of desperation by the selectors, playing at full-forward. From his point of view the initial experiment worked disastrously well as he scored two goals and was kept in the purgatory of the full-forward position for longer than he wished:

'I found out that full-backs are really kicking jennets. A full-forward needs to be an animal. Our great midfielder Eamon Boland might have survived up there. I always thought he had four elbows and four joints.'

Injury meant that Lynch's career ended prematurely after another Connacht title victory in 1952. His work as a garda superintendent continued to bring him into contact with some famous GAA figures.

'When I moved to Tralee I got to know Dan Spring, father of Dick and an All-Ireland winning captain in 1940 himself, very well. He would contact me before court day to let me know he "had an interest" in a particular case. Once the verdict was in he would be back to me and generally the penalty was light, like a small fine, so he just wanted to be the first to tell the family the good news.'

Le grá i gcónaí.

28

THE MASTER STORYTELLER

John B's Pub

Being a Kerry man, in my opinion, is the greatest gift that God can bestow on any man. When you belong to Kerry you know you have a head start on the other fellow. In belonging to Kerry you belong to the elements, to the spheres spinning in the heavens. You belong to history and language and romance and ancient song. It's almost unbearable being a Kerry man and it's an awesome responsibility.

JOHN B. KEANE

Late one Saturday night I was walking home from a concert in Dublin. It was only two weeks before Christmas so taxis were as scarce as hen's teeth. As I got to the suburbs I saw a man I recognised, having watched him being interviewed on television a few weeks earlier, walking towards me. To my surprise as I walked past him he swung a punch at me for reasons that eluded me. Happily for me he was too drunk and too slow to do any real damage. Knowing that a rational discussion was not a possibility in the circumstances I walked away to a chorus of slurred obscenities.

WHERE HEROES ARE MADE

Since then he has become an elected politician of some acclaim. Now I see him interviewed on TV pontificating on whatever issue has got his levels of moral indignation soaring to new heights. In those moments I say a silent prayer of thanks that he is not in one of the government parties so hopefully he will never get into a position of serious power. People like him are not a great advertisement for heavy drinking.

As a non-drinker I have only darkened the door of a handful of pubs. Yet I have to acknowledge the central place of pubs in the GAA. In my limited experience one stood out for me. It was home to a million great nights. So good were they that many are not remembered by the participants.

In our fast-changing world one of the few constants of my experience of Christmas has always been the festive tales of John B. Keane. Through the intercession of our mutual friend Brendan Kennelly I met the great man himself in his pub in Listowel. He informed me that 'the writer's greatest asset is his indignation'. I told him that as a young boy I had read his stories religiously every Christmas in newspapers and magazines as well as listened to his frequent radio broadcasts over the season of goodwill. Like *The Late Late Toy Show* John B's new seasonal story was a staple of the Irish Christmas for generations. He smiled when I told him that he never came up with a stocking-filler – each was a Christmas cracker. When I asked him what was his favourite, he responded that this was too tough a question. However, he kindly shared one with me which, as it came from his own mouth as a Christmas gift to me, is the one I treasure above all others. The fact that his two main characters had such memorable names meant that the story is forever imprinted on my brain.

HAVE YOURSELVES A MERRY LITTLE CHRISTMAS STORY

Edgar Guff, if one was to believe the observations of his parish priest Canon Coodle, was the possessor of an enormous appetite for whiskey. His puce-coloured nose would also bear this out as would his bloodshot eyes and unsteady gait.

'He would drink whiskey,' the canon informed his housekeeper Hannie Hanlon, 'out of a senna saucepan.'

Hannie shook her head in disgust.

'Otherwise,' the canon continued, 'he's not a bad fellow at all and you could trust him in any enterprise that doesn't involve whiskey.'

The pair had adjourned to the presbytery kitchen after the evening meal and, as was their wont, would discuss minor parochial business until the evening confessions commenced in the parish church which stood impassively next door where it dwarfed every other building in the town square.

Hannie Hanlon had, a few moments before, completed the dusting of the four ornate confessionals. As she neatly folded her duster she heard the muted but unsteady footsteps approaching along the side aisle where she stood admiring the copper plaque which carried the name of Canon Cornelius Coodle and was affixed prominently to the central door of the canon's confessional. The canon's box, as it was called, was greatly favoured by penitents of both sexes and all ages and not merely because he was somewhat deaf but also because he was tolerant, discreet and sympathetic.

'Sure you couldn't shock the canon,' the more hardened sinners would assure themselves as they confidently made their way to his box.

Hannie did not have to look around to discover who the first arrival was. The creature's light footfall indicated that it could be none other than Edgar Guff who, despite his surname, rarely expressed himself in public. There was also the fact that he always arrived at the confessional well ahead of the prescribed time, often by as much as an hour on busy occasions such as Christmas and Easter. Seating himself on the innermost extremity of the long wooden stool, which led to the confessional, he nodded respectfully in the direction of the stern-faced housekeeper. She acknowledged the salute with a solemn nod, decidedly discouraging and not in the least bit conducive to further exchanges.

People of the parish would say that Edgar Guff was an exceptional listener and could hear most of what the penitents said especially when they were expected to raise their voices or provide clarification for transgressions at the confessor's behest. This was not often but when it occurred it was always interesting, not that Edgar would ever dream of betraying the confidences which his proximity to the confessional conferred on him.

Edgar was a professional sitter. That is to say, he was engaged by busy sinners such as lawyers, doctors and wealthy businessmen to hold places on their behalf next to the confessional. As soon as one of his clients arrived, always impatient and always in a hurry, he would hand over his seat near the confessional door and make his way to the far end of the wooden stool. For this service, he would be paid a half crown. From his lowly position at the end of the stool he would patiently wait as those who were seated nearer the confessional were shrived, thus allowing him to advance in the right direction. After a while he would find himself in the most prized position, right outside the confessional door. If his next client noted that Edgar was too far from the confessional the restless creature would exit to the town square and indulge in measured peregrinations until he judged that his sitter would be better placed.

THE MASTER STORYTELLER

During the busy seasons Edgar would spend nearly all of his waking hours on the stool. He was often asked by cronies if he was ever obliged to vacate his place due to a call of nature.

'Never!' he would answer firmly and then he would explain that he was always on the move so to speak in his earlier years when he was addicted to pints of stout. It was costing him too much in lost revenue so he changed over to whiskey which made hardly any demands because his bladder was never full.

When Hannie Hanlon returned to the presbytery kitchen she was asked by the canon if Edgar Guff had taken up his place.

'Just a few moments ago,' she answered.

'That gives me the best part of an hour,' the canon intoned happily as he settled himself comfortably in front of the gleaming Stanley. Later when the three curates arrived the canon was ready to lead his curates onward and outward against the forces of evil. From their confessionals they would keep the enemy at bay with forgiveness.

As the first penitents arrived, several at the same time, Edgar Guff, sitter-in-chief of the parish, fortified himself for the long hours ahead. He withdrew a voluminous handkerchief from his ample, inside pocket and gently blew on his purple proboscis after which he skilfully removed the cork from a noggin of whiskey, cleverly camouflaged by the handkerchief, and indulged in a modest swallow which instantly alerted him to his responsibilities.

Thereafter his clients began to arrive like clockwork. It was a boom time for sitters especially for Edgar who had a large clientele, most of them generous if the occasion deserved it. Their contributions were nearly always doubled at Christmas so that Edgar need not worry about the wherewithal required for the purchase of extra whiskey. He had already swallowed several half ones in the two public houses closest to the church and since these activities took place during intervals he wasn't in the least befuddled. To employ one of his own phrases he was just warming up and would be quite capable of swallowing the two noggins in his pockets before confessions ended for the night. He would, of course, feel a little groggy later but he would find his way home without difficulty and enjoy a good night's slumber before the noonday sittings of the morrow.

As the night wore on he started to grow drowsy, finding it difficult to keep his eyes open for long. The spirit of goodwill, luckily for him, was abroad and whenever he started to drop off he would be wakened by concerned penitents who sat near him. His clients came and went and not one neglected to pay his fee. He found his hands being opened wide on numerous occasions and almost always two half-crowns were pressed against his palm.

Only once in that long night was he jolted into wakefulness and that was when Canon Coodle raised his mighty voice in anger in the nearby confessional. Edgar sat upright at once. It must be some sin of outrageous proportions if the canon raised his voice to a shout. Edgar Guff nor indeed any of the other penitents had ever heard anything like it before.

Edgar deduced from the trembling, plaintive utterances that the penitent in the box was female. She was in the process at long last, after years of neglect and suffering, of acquainting her parish priest with the behaviour of the perfidious wretch to whom she had been chained for more than forty years. Edgar had missed the earlier part of the poor woman's disclosures but he gasped as he had never gasped before when she made the ultimate accusation. This was that she had not been in receipt of a single kiss from her husband for twenty agonising years. It was this that prompted Canon Coodle to shout 'What!' at the top of his voice. When she repeated the charge in broken tones he thundered the word 'What!' a second time.

Drunk as he was, Edgar Guff's heart went out to the victim of this disastrous marriage. He longed to lay his hands on the throat of the monster who had treated her so abominably for so long. But no! He must never reveal what he had heard or allow what he had heard to influence any future actions of his in relation to this confession or any other. The secrecy of the confessional was sacred and it dawned on a drunken Edgar, not for the first time, that he was an officer of the Church. He would agree that he was not a very high-up officer, that he was below the rank of assistant-to-the-sacristan or even a common altar boy but he was a Church officer no matter what.

He sat fully attentive as he heard the movements in the confessional. The penitent's door opened and there Edgar Guff beheld the dowdy clothes and tear-stained face of his wife, his one and only who had not qualified for a solitary kiss in twenty years. He sat stunned as she shuffled along the aisle and then she was gone.

Suddenly he sprang into action and dashed into the night. Outside she moved slowly and carefully, picking her steps in the darkness. Gently he forestalled her and placed an arm around her shoulder, his drunkenness totally dissipated by what he had heard. She turned to look into the face of the person who had come to her aid. Suddenly her sobs filled the night so that passers-by turned to stare. Overcome by grief he shepherded her into a laneway where he held her in his arms until her convulsive sobbing ended and she stood silent and limp, totally dependent on his support. He took her hand and led her homeward.

The days that followed were filled with silence and when she accepted silently his offer of a walk by the river on St Stephen's

Day he knew that if he played his cards right there was a chance, just a chance mind you, that things might work out in the course of time.

HEALING HURTS

The War of Independence ended with a Treaty. However, this in turn precipitated a bloody and bitter civil war in Ireland. Gaelic football and hurling were always about more than sport in rural Ireland and in Kerry in particular. My former teacher Professor Liam Ryan told me that the GAA played a greater part in healing the many rifts which have threatened to rupture families and communities throughout Irish history in the last century than the Catholic Church:

'Neighbours, for example, who had shot at one another in the Civil War displayed a greater desire to forgive and forget when gathered around the goalposts than when gathered around the altar. Nowhere was that more apparent than in Kerry.'

In 1914 there was a famous truce between British and German troops during the First World War. They met up in No Man's Land and played football. We had something similar in Ireland.

Gabriel Fitzmaurice's 'Munster Football Final 1924' recalls a game that led to a brief cessation in the ugly hostilities of the Civil War:

There's something more important here than war . . .
For what they love, they both put down the gun –

Nobody captured the power and historical importance of the GAA in Kerry better than John B. He also spoke to me about the power of the GAA to heal the wounds of the past:

'Football has also been part of our identity here. In Kerry, football was called "Caid" as it referred to the type of ball used. The ball was made from dried farm-animal skins with an inflated natural animal bladder inside. We take our football very seriously in Kerry but we also take politics very seriously. Sometimes our twin passions collide. This was probably most clearly illustrated in 1935 when Kerry refused to take part in the football Championship because of the ongoing detention of prisoners in the Curragh.

'The Civil War not alone cost a lot of lives. It split families down the middle and left intense bitterness. The one place in Kerry where the Civil War was put aside was on the GAA fields and it did bring old enemies together. Football united what politics divided. It was about our sense of Kerry. If we were playing Dublin in an All-Ireland final, politics was put to one side so we would win the match. So, in that way football helped clear the bad blood from the Civil War.

'A good example was Con Brosnan. He is one of the great legends of Kerry football and that is saying something. He reached out to his enemies from the Civil War on the football field. One of the things he did was to arrange safe passage for wanted IRA men so they could represent Kerry. Just a year after the Civil War ended, Kerry won the All-Ireland final with a team almost roughly divided between pro- and anti-Treaty players. When Con was nearing the end of his playing days "one of the other side", Joe Barrett, ensured that he was given the captaincy. It was proof that Con was Kerry's great peacemaker after the Civil War.'

FIERCESOME

John B. assured me that 'there are only two real kingdoms: the Kingdom of God and the Kingdom of Kerry.' He also told me a story about a Kerry County Junior football final. By the time the final was played, most of the better players had returned to college as it was delayed due to the usual quota of objections. Keane claimed he was drafted in to play at corner-forward, even though he was only about fifteen years of age. He gave a vivid description of his increasing trepidation as he went to take up his position and saw a 'seasoned' corner-back advancing to meet him. John B. was getting more intimidated with each step but was puzzled when the corner-back veered off at the last moment and went back towards his goalkeeper. He took out his false teeth and loudly told his keeper: 'Paddy mind these in case I forget myself and eat someone.'

John B. did not love all football pundits equally. When I quoted one to him, he shrugged his shoulders and said: 'Bigmouth strikes again.'

Despite the ongoing brilliance of David Clifford, John B. would have struggled with the reality that Kerry were underdogs facing Armagh in the 2025 All-Ireland quarter final. He would, though, have agreed with Joe Brolly's assessment: 'What's the definition of a Kerry inferiority complex? A man with two All-Irelands.'

John B. would have felt the natural order was restored when Kerry beat Donegal to win the 2025 All-Ireland and to the Kerry critics he would have said: 'O ye of little faith.'

29

SCHOOL OF THOUGHT

St Flannan's College

The mind is not a vessel to be filled but a fire to be ignited.
                                                            PLUTARCH

It was indeed right and fitting that earlier this year thirty-two Education Champion Scholarships were announced by the GPA (Gaelic Players Association) and the Irish American Partnership. The recipients – one from each of the thirty-two counties – are student teachers and those pursuing postgraduate studies to further their careers in education. More than 300 GPA members are in the teaching profession. Teachers, religious and lay, have been indispensable to the rich tapestry of the GAA.

Schools like St Kieran's Kilkenny, Coláiste Eoin Booterstown, St Mel's Longford, St Patrick's Maghera, St Patrick's Navan, St Patrick's College Armagh, St Jarlath's Tuam, St Colman's College Newry and St Eunan's College Letterkenny, to name just a handful, have played a pivotal role in the development of the GAA. To select one above all others seems odious but, in terms of their historical significance, one school has a pressing claim – because of their role in establishing the interschools games on the national consciousness.

Ger Loughnane had the good fortune to attend National School in Feakle. His teacher, Seán Harrington, was one of the old style teachers but he always got great results from his students. Loughnane was one of many students from the school to win a scholarship to St Flannan's. It was there that his hurling education really began:

'I was so lucky that when I went to Flannan's Willie Walsh and Seamus Gardiner, who were young priests at the time, decided to become involved in the hurling coaching.

'They started at under-15 level with a squad that included John Callinan, Colm Hohan and myself who later played for Clare. They had a new way of coaching: with a ball between three, developing skills and then playing games. Every fine evening we were out hurling. They really gave great encouragement.

'In second and third year we played for the junior team and in fourth and fifth year we played on the Harty Cup team. Getting on the Harty team in Flannan's gave you a huge profile and status within the college. Extra meals were provided, time off study and travel to exotic places like Limerick and Thurles were huge perks at the time.'

Bishop Willie Walsh, who went to his God in February a month after his ninetieth birthday, was an evangelist for the gospel but also for hurling in general and St Flannan's, where he attended as a student and taught maths and physics for twenty-five years, in particular. Anthony Daly said of him:

'Long after school was over you could pick up the phone to Willie and ask him for a bit of advice on anything. He married myself and Eilish. He was a Clare selector when Len Gaynor came. I often disagreed with him on a few decisions; you wouldn't say anything to Len, but you could have it out with

SCHOOL OF THOUGHT

Willie. You might meet him for a sneaky pint. He will be sadly missed. He lived in Ennis and was involved with Éire Óg a fair bit over the years. We had some great battles with them back in the day. He would be on the line and I'd be shouting out at him. "The lord save us, you are an awful man," he'd say. He was much loved by everyone in the community. He was the kindest, most genuine human being you could ever meet. Rest in peace.'

May he rest in the light and the love of his Boss. He wanted the church to continue to move forward rather than being dragged back to a place it took too long to rescue from. He believed that humanity, for all its wounds and wickedness, is still worth fighting for.

He spoke of love not as doctrine but as duty. His eyes didn't see denominations – they simply saw dignity. His voice, often soft but never weak, carried the weight of truth even when it unsettled the comfortable – perhaps especially when it unsettled the comfortable.

He reminds us that the better angels of our nature are still within reach. Goodness is still possible. We don't need to be perfect to do good – far from it – we just need to be brave. He was a man who chose compassion over judgement, who chose action over applause, who knelt beside the discarded and who challenged the powerful not with anger, but with moral courage. His way was to listen with tender ears and choose kindness over and over even when it hurt. His actions were a powerful, radical empathy. His humility was not weakness. It was a harnessed strength where his presence brought comfort and consolation.

One cannot but remember his faith in humanity and hope it will fuel our own. He would want us to keep making the right chess moves in this complicated, brutal, beautiful game of life.

He spoke truth with grace by protecting the vulnerable, questioning the powerful, and lifting others up.

Long before the word 'inclusive' was fashionable Willie Walsh lived it: reaching out to victims of clerical abuse, opening the lawn of his bishop's residence for members of the travelling community to set up home there and employing a traveller as his driver.

LORD OF THE BANNER

With the amiable openness of his nature, and an enthusiasm for hurling that remained dew-fresh, in conversation with this writer, he spoke about how he brought the lessons he learned in Flannan's to a wider stage and the cocktail of inspiration and luck that constitutes a good tactical change:

'One of the things that always struck me in hurling was about the strange ways positional switches were made in a match. Straight away I think of the 1990 All-Ireland hurling final between Cork and Galway. After about fifteen minutes I was wondering what the Cork selectors were going to do about Jim Cashman. Joe Cooney was destroying him and I couldn't understand why they left Jim there. They went in at half-time and I said, "Well, Jim Cashman won't be centre-back in the second half," but amazingly he was and he went on to win his battle with Joe Cooney in the second half and Cork won the All-Ireland.

'I went back to Clare and some people said to me, "Ah, you can't beat those Cork guys. Now if that was Clare we'd have panicked and taken Jim Cashman off but the Cork guys were wise and knew what was best." Of course, that was a bit hurtful to me as a Clare selector so I went down to Cork a month later and I went to Dr Con Murphy and I said, "Up front now, what happened with Jim Cashman and why didn't you change him?"

SCHOOL OF THOUGHT

So he replied, "Well, we all agreed that Jim was being beaten and we'd have to change him. The problem was that none of the selectors could agree on who we would replace him with. So we decided to do the usual thing and give him five minutes in the second half."

'I remember in 1994 we were playing Tipperary in the Munster Championship, when I was a selector on the county team, and we were being beaten in midfield and Ger Loughnane and myself had an argument on the sideline. Ger wanted to bring Jamesie O'Connor (himself a teacher in Flannan's – as is Tony Kelly) centre-field. I felt if we did that we would be robbing Peter to pay Paul because we had to get a few more points to beat Tipperary and Jamesie was the one forward who would do that for us. Eventually we called over Len Gaynor and both of us put our case to him and let him make the decision. Len favoured Ger's option and made the switch. Within a few moments Jamesie had scored two points and lifted the whole team and we won the match. Afterwards everybody said, "Ah that was a great change ye made" without knowing it was a toss of the coin. Often a match hangs on a thing like that. The day it works you're a hero. The day it doesn't you're useless.'

IT COULD HAPPEN TO A BISHOP

Bishop Willie spoke with an addict's passion about the fascinating people he had met through his love of hurling, particularly Paddy Duggan, 'the Duggie'. Duggie's whole life was hurling. He was a mentor to a host of teams in Clare. When he became ill Bishop Walsh went to see him in hospital. Duggan had got the news that day that he only had a short time to live. He said to the bishop, 'I'd like you to do the funeral Mass and make all the arrangements.' The bishop agreed. Then the Duggie said, 'That's fine, Willie. I still believe that we'd have won the county final last year if they'd listened to me at half-time.' As soon as the funeral was arranged, he was straight back to the most important thing in life – hurling!

The Duggie was not above misrepresenting Willie Walsh in his days when he was a humble priest. Both were mentors for a juvenile team in Ennis and in a club match Willie was stunned when, all of a sudden, he saw a young lad, Tomás Fogarty, being introduced as a sub on their team. He ran up the sideline to ask the secretary who had given the order to bring him on and he answered, 'Was it not you? The Duggie came up to me and said, "Father Willie wants him in"!'

THE MAN FROM CLARE

As a Clare minor Ger Loughnane's first introduction to inter-county hurling was under the 'Duggie'. Duggan gave a most amazing speech in the dressing room in Limerick. While whacking a hurley off a table and as his false teeth did three laps of his mouth he called on the team to kill and maim the opposition before saying an 'Our Father' and three 'Hail Marys'.

Despite all his achievements with Clare, Loughnane retains great affection for St Flannan's:

'All of us have such lovely memories of our time in the school.'

Not everybody can say the same.

THE BRADY BUNCH

An Irish legend turns seventy next year. Liam Brady's school-days were not completely happy.

He captained an under-15 Republic of Ireland side in Wales despite the threat of expulsion hanging over his head. He describes himself as a 'pretty good' Gaelic footballer during his time at St Aidan's CBS in Whitehall but his decision to choose soccer over a challenge game against Galway school St Jarlath's caused consternation in his school. I began our conversation by asking him about this incident and he said:

'The head Brother told me not to come to the school if I missed the match but I never considered missing the soccer game. I wasn't very pleased with my father who went to the newspapers with the story and my picture ended up on the front of *The Evening Herald*. Also, I had a very bad haircut at the time.

'Any other school would have been happy to have one of their students captaining his country. But I get on very well with the people there and we even have a soccer team in St Aidan's now.'

Brady always had an independent streak:

'It's a big move to go to England when you're fifteen. When I was fourteen I was supposed to go to Arsenal on trial and there was some frost on the roads. The Arsenal scout was supposed to pick me up on the road so I ran out onto the Santry road and got a bus up to the airport and made sure I was going to Arsenal.'

GOGGLEBOX

To the younger generation Liam Brady is best known for his punditry. Why did he turn his back on his punditry career?

'The time was right. I really enjoyed it. But I knew when to retire as a player, I knew when it was time to leave my work at the Arsenal academy, which I loved too, and I know the time was right now.

'I wouldn't say I have fallen out of love with football. But I feel now like I'd just like to watch the matches without all the hullaballoo that goes on around them. It isn't the game I knew. The enormity of the football business now – I do think the game is on a dangerous path to elitism driven by wealth.

'But I will be forever grateful to RTÉ for the opportunity. I had some fantastic times over twenty-five years – even though there was a sabbatical in there for a couple of years to work with Giovanni Trapattoni, which I loved too. I had a wonderful time with my great friends Eamon Dunphy, John Giles and Bill O'Herlihy. We had great fun together in between the arguments.'

For those of us lucky enough to have seen him play, Brady will always be remembered as one of our greatest and most skilful players. He won the first of his seventy-two Ireland caps against the Soviet Union at Dalymount Park in 1974:

'My first time at Dalymount was at seven years of age. My brother Ray was playing for Ireland with John Giles. They beat Austria 3-2 and I was dreaming I would get there and play. It happened in 1974. I was eighteen years of age and John Giles picked me to play against the Soviet Union. It was what dreams were made of to make a debut like that. It was unreal really. I have great memories of some big games at Lansdowne Road. We beat Brazil 1-0 in a friendly. To beat Brazil is good, but to get the goal was great. It made up for the time we got beat 7-0 in 1982, which was probably Ireland's worst defeat ever.'

Brady's career took him to huge European clubs like Arsenal and Juventus and Inter Milan. He had a seven-year spell with the Gunners, where he first joined as a schoolboy before signing his first professional contract at seventeen. In 1979 he was named Professional Football Association Players' Player of the Year.

His genius helped Arsenal emerge from their mid-seventies slump and reach three successive FA Cup finals between 1978 and 1980. It was the 1979 final that highlighted Brady's importance: he set up first-half goals for Brian Talbot and Frank Stapleton as Arsenal smashed Manchester United apart. The match has been labelled the 'Five Minute Final': United pulled back two very late goals to equalise by the eighty-eighth minute. Brady began the move which allowed Alan Sunderland to fire Arsenal to eighty-ninth-minute victory.

SCHOOL OF THOUGHT

But a year later he left Arsenal. Why did he move to Italy, as it was a very unusual step for an Irish footballer to take at the time?

'In 1980 Arsenal lost both the FA Cup and European Cup Winners' Cup finals. I wanted to win things. Arsenal had a level of ambition that wasn't matching the Liverpools and Man Uniteds. We had great cup runs but we were never going to win the league. I felt, and Frank Stapleton felt it too, that we were taken for granted as part of the furniture, because we'd grown up as kids there. A couple of years before our contracts expired, they should have been coming to us, but they never did.'

It was at Juventus that Brady first met the future Ireland manager, Giovanni Trapattoni, who was managing the top Italian side at the time. The Irish legend retains one vivid memory of 'Trap'.

Brady was keen to get settled into a new apartment in Turin. As a passionate music fan he had brought crates of his beloved LPs with him to Italy. Brady and his wife, Sarah, had found a place they liked in Turin, but one item was missing – a hi-fi system.

Liam could speak no Italian, Trap could speak no English, but the manager went along to help out his player. A suitable one was found but then there was another problem – setting it up:

'It's a story I like to tell because it shows how kind and professional he was. There was an instruction booklet but it looked like technical drawing to me. I couldn't make head nor tail of it. So Trap just gestured "leave it to me". I'll never forget it. There he was, down on his hands and knees, fiddling with knobs and leads. Wires everywhere.

'That was one of my first real introductions to Giovanni Trapattoni. He went through my records afterwards and was looking for classical music. He told me to get some and listen to it after training to relax. It was down to him that I started to buy classical records.'

Brady never got to represent Ireland at a major tournament, after injury robbed him of the opportunity of making an appearance at Euro 1988:

'We were going to qualify for Euro 1988, but unfortunately I went and did something stupid and got myself sent off. I got a four-game suspension, we appealed and it was reduced to three. Our manager Jack Charlton said he'd take me and I could be involved in the last game. I was delighted, but within three weeks I ruptured my cruciate ligament playing for West Ham and that was the end of that dream.'

There was considerable controversy about the way his career ended with Ireland and significant speculation that he had a bad relationship with the much-loved Irish manager Jack Charlton. He is delighted to have the opportunity to set the record straight.

'I didn't have a problem with Jack. I think I had a way I thought football should be played and he had his way. We differed and it was a shame the way it ended. When you read about the history of the Irish team, it's almost written that Liam Brady and Jack Charlton didn't see eye to eye right from the beginning. That wasn't the case. He picked me right from the off.

'In 1989, we had a friendly against West Germany. Thirty minutes into the game I saw my number going up. I wasn't happy. I knew walking across the pitch that this was the end. It was all over. Jack and I had words at half-time, a bit of a shouting match. So I decided there and then that was it. I retired.'

After retiring less than a year out from Ireland's first World Cup appearance at Italia '90, the former Arsenal legend received correspondence from Big Jack following his retirement:

SCHOOL OF THOUGHT

'I got this letter in the post from Jack. It stated':

Dear Liam. I'm sorry the way things worked out after the Germany game. I wish to thank you for what you did during my time with the Republic. I never intended to hurt you, believe that. You would be very welcome to come to Italy should we get there. In your testimonial I will do all I can to help.

I hope the next time we meet you will still have a little time for me and we might find time to repair some of the damage. This is just a quick note I felt I had to send you. All the best Liam, I hope things work out for you. Jack.

30

LION-HEARTED

Trillick

Courage isn't having the strength to go on – it is going on when you don't have strength.

NAPOLEON BONAPARTE

The phone call brought news that wrenched my soul.

All the rainbows in the sky started to weep and say goodbye.

Life can be so difficult to understand. Sometimes the only way forward is to surrender to what cannot be chosen and allow it to gracefully disturb what can often be taken for granted.

Fifty-three-year-old Tyrone footballer Jody Gormley had been diagnosed with stage four liver cancer, having suffered a stroke while on holiday earlier in the year.

He won two under-21 All-Irelands in 1991 and 1992, was midfield on the Tyrone team that lost to Dublin by a point in the 1995 All-Ireland football final and scored their only other point bar Peter Canavan's scores. He subsequently managed Antrim.

It is a curse of our time that the word 'Inspirational' is thrown around too easily – but Gormley really was an inspiration. Despite his serious illness he continued to manage his club team Trillick and they reached a Tyrone final in October, losing to Errigal Ciaran by a point. Errigal went on to win the Ulster title, beating Kilcoo in Armagh's Athletic Grounds. Gormley informed the Trillick players after the county final defeat of his illness and the prognosis he had been given. Before his death he melted hearts like sun-kissed snow when he gave a compelling interview. He told the BBC that he had 'no fear of dying. No fear of dying whatsoever. I've felt blessed my entire life. The sadness is the people you're leaving behind. That I'll not get to see my son – he's training hard with Trillick, he's come back after a couple of years – that I'll not get to see him play and I'll not get to see my family grow up and mature. That's not scary but sad really.'

He spoke of his priorities: 'I'd like to be remembered as a decent person, who helped people out as much as I could, who tried to find areas to help people improve their life and just give them a wee nudge in the right direction ... and obviously a Trillick man, and then Tyrone.'

Jody Gormley personified the adage that: It is not the strength of the body that counts, but the strength of the spirit.

Our grief for this giant of the game will take years to condense – but will remain for decades.

In the words of the thrilling, terrifically talented writer Sorcha Woods he is now, 'A fast-moving cloud, unobstructed and gallant across the sky.'

He is a huge loss to Irish life that leaves a tiny, pitched hole in the sky at night.

But the sun will shine in Trillick again with the dazzling brilliance of radiant light and its sweet melodic chants.

Good night and God guard you forever.

· Light shines in the darkness, and the darkness cannot overcome it.

31

GIANT OF THE ASH

The Limerick Leader

The founder of the GAA, Michael Cusack, said of hurling: 'When I reflect on the sublime simplicity of the game, the strength, the swiftness of the players, their apparently angelic impetuosity, the apparent recklessness of life and limb, their magic skill, their marvellous escapes and the overwhelming pleasure they give their friends, I have no hesitation in saying that the game of hurling is in the front rank of the fine arts.'

Hurling is a parable of life at its innocent best, the world as it ought to be, the ideal for a moment realised. Our national sport is an expression of optimism: enshrouding sports lovers with a redemptive feeling, melting away depression, pain and bitter disappointment, hinting at a bygone age of innocence and values that no longer obtain.

Hurling is drama's first cousin. It is theatre without the script. It has the capacity to stop your heart and leave the indelible memory of a magic moment. A great hurling match is something thrilling to watch, a miracle of speed, balance and intense athleticism, a thoroughbred leaving a trail of mesmerised opponents in his slipstream, who have been as transfixed in wonder as the crowd by his silken skills.

Hurling is like a gift wrapped up in deliciously pretty paper, to be given, with discretion, to the faithful. It transcends mere sport. It is about identity and how we feel about ourselves, individually and collectively. Hurling produces a defining moment, an experience that redirects, the revealed truth by whose light all previous conclusions must be rethought.

In the words of Cork great Justin McCarthy: 'Hurling identifies my Irishness. I'm not an Irish speaker, so the game portrays my national spirit – it's so Irish, so unique.'

Despite its vast history and our radically different cultural, social and economic context, hurling has in many ways changed very little – the changeless is what it's been about since the beginning. Hurling takes us, at heart, into a mythic place, an ageless space alight with Celtic warriors – not men but giants – who know who they were, are and will be. It's not just part of who we are – it could be argued it *is* who we are. The great hurling teams and the great hurlers make that possible. Sometimes the two seem synonymous, notably Mick Mackey's Limerick. The team won three All-Irelands in 1934, 1936 and 1940.

EXPERT GUIDANCE

When I spoke to Jack Lynch, I was keen to get his opinion of Mick Mackey:

'Christy Ring was the greatest hurler that I knew. I know there are some who will contend that others were better – Mick Mackey, for example. Mackey was great, but in my opinion, Ring's hurling repertoire was greater. He was totally committed to hurling, perhaps more so than any player I have ever met. He analysed games in prospect and in retrospect. In essence, he thought and lived hurling.

WHERE HEROES ARE MADE

'I think Mick Mackey was the most effective hurler that I played against. If there was one game which proved that, it was when he scored no less than five goals and three points in the 1936 Munster final against Tipperary. His fifth goal in particular was a thing of beauty. It came on the end of a solo run. He mightn't have pioneered the solo run, but he turned it into an art form, and his presence brought a golden age for Limerick hurling. To me, Mackey personifies Limerick.'

32

KING OF THE KINGDOM

Waterville

It is not so much that they broke the mould when they made Mick O'Dwyer; it's that he broke the mould himself, again and again.

PAUL ROUSE

'Sure, we'll turn up anyway.'

This was Mick O'Dwyer's response on being asked what shape his Kerry team was in ahead of their next challenge. It was a revealing insight into a legend of Gaelic football.

As this book was being finished the sad news broke that the eighty-eight-year-old was gone to his eternal reward. His achievements were phenomenal. As a player he won four Senior All Ireland medals in 1959, 1962, 1969 (the year he was chosen as Footballer of the Year) and 1970. The GAA Hall of Famer will best be remembered as the architect of the Kerry golden years of the 1970s and 1980s. He guided a thrilling young Kerry team to an insurgent All Ireland title in 1975 as manager and went on to coach the Kingdom to seven further All-Ireland titles over an eleven-year period, including the famous four-in-a-row between 1978 and 1981.

Later he enjoyed further success as a manager, leading Kildare and Laois (remember the famous 'UnLaoised by Micko' banner?) to Leinster titles and guiding Wicklow to a Tommy Murphy Cup win. As a small tribute to a great man I am including his native Waterville in this collection – particularly because his love for Kerry was matched only by his great love for Waterville. He proved that by coaching local underage teams in Waterville up to the age of seventy-nine.

AN UNFORGETTABLE OCCASION

The morning after the news broke about Micko's death I spoke to Irish rugby legend Ollie Campbell:

'Although my father played for Louth Minors I only ever managed to play one game of Gaelic football in my entire life and that was for the Jimmy Magee's All Stars. I lined out at full-forward but unfortunately my opposite number was the enormous Martin Quinn of Meath, who sadly passed away. It was like being marked by Cú Chulainn!'

Ollie got to see Mick O'Dwyer's team up close and personal:

'Back in the halcyon days of the Micko era, I was in Killarney one early summer's evening and heard the Kerry team would be training that night at Fitzgerald Stadium, so naturally I went along and quietly made my way into the stand to observe the session.

'What followed frightened me. I had never seen a training session like it. They ran and they ran and they ran seemingly non-stop for nearly two hours, sometimes with the ball, sometimes without one. I was in very good shape myself at the time but would not have survived this Micko session and left before the end feeling quite disillusioned.

'Years later I was at the annual Renault Sports Awards in the Burlington Hotel in Dublin as were that great Kerry team, including their iconic manager Mick O'Dwyer. At the drinks reception beforehand Mikey Sheehy invited me over to join them and introduced me to Micko and the team. Teasingly, Mikey asked me, "Ollie, do you remember attending a training session of ours in Killarney in the early eighties?"

'"Of course, I do, I'll never forget it as long as I live," I replied.

'"Do you know what happened that night?" he said with a glint in his eye.

'"No idea," I said honestly and intrigued.

'"Well, Micko spotted you in the stand before the session began and enthusiastically addressed us in a huddle saying 'Lads, let's show him what a Kerry football training session is really like".'

'Everyone laughed heartily being reminded of this, particularly Micko himself as I did too, before Mikey went on to say, "Ollie, none of us shared Micko's enthusiasm that night so for the sake of every future Kerry Gaelic football team, if you are ever in Killarney again on an evening when a Kerry team are training, will you please find something else to do?"

'I did think of that story when I heard of Micko passing yesterday. He got great fun out of it; not sure the players enjoyed it quite so much!'

GAMECHANGERS

O'Dwyer's team came to prominence at a time when the most exotic thing on Irish television was an ad for a drink, which featured an Irishman overseas reminiscing on everything he missed about home. Chief among the things he missed was Sally O'Brien 'and the way she might look at you'. Her knowing smile sent pulses racing. At a time when we hadn't yet heard the term 'va-va-voom', we knew we craved it. A football team gave us a taste of it as we longed to end the era of recession, repression, and rejection – with moments of ephemeral grace. They left us with memories that linger like the delicious fragrance of flowers.

In American basketball they use the phrase 'ride the ref'. Most people like to be liked. So if you scream at the referee every time, even when they've blown you up legitimately, they're more likely to give a marginal call in your favour. While it's difficult to imagine Mick O'Dwyer using the phrase 'riding the ref', he was familiar with the concept. Pat Spillane contends that nobody was more adept at getting into the heads of referees than him before Kerry played in big matches, particularly in the era when the hand pass reigned supreme. It was one of his many talents.

The mid-1970s witnessed the thrilling rivalry between Dublin and Kerry. While the Dubs won in 1974, '76 and '77, Kerry in contrast only won in 1975. By 1978 and '79, Kerry reigned supreme. They thrashed Dublin in both finals, winning by seventeen and eleven-point margins respectively. In the 1980 All-Ireland semi-final, they would play out a high-scoring classic, with Kerry beating Offaly 4-15 to 4-10.

Roscommon awaited them in the final, with the Kingdom winning a bruising encounter by three points. The Roscommon side were both puzzled and bewildered by many of the decisions of the referee, and after thirty-three minutes the Roscommon fans started chanting: 'We want a ref; we want a ref.' This might seem like sour grapes, but it is worth noting Micheál O'Hehir's words at half-time to the television audience: 'It can only be described as unsatisfactory, and I must say contributing to the unsatisfactory nature was the referee who appeared to lose control of the game and whose decisions were more than mysterious.'

The following year, Kerry and Offaly clashed once again, this time in the final, and a brilliant Jack O'Shea goal would ensure that Sam Maguire would again return to Kerry. In 1982, Kerry were confident of achieving something that had never been managed before in either code: win five All-Irelands in a row. Séamus Darby's sensational late goal denied Kerry by a solitary point. Offaly completed the greatest upset in football history.

That defeat was the biggest regret of O'Dwyer's career but he had one other major one:

'I was very disappointed that Waterville did not win one of our three county finals. We worked so hard to win. We were well out of it in 1968 but ran a powerful East Kerry team very close in 1969 and 1970.'

THE EARLEY YEARS

One man who had a unique insight into O'Dwyer was Dermot Earley who managed Kildare in between Micko's terms as Kildare manager:

'I was flattered to be asked to take on the Kildare job. I wouldn't have taken on any other managerial job at the time, except some kind of role in Sarsfields. The fact that I lived in Newbridge and the job was on my doorstep was the deciding factor.'

An initial problem was that he had big shoes to fill when he took the helm:

'Without Kevin Heffernan and Mick O'Dwyer, who knows what Gaelic football management would have been? Micko, the greatest manager of all time, had come into Kildare three or four years earlier and reawakened Kildare as a serious force in football. They were incredibly fit and he re-energised not just the team but the fans and there was a sudden upsurge of interest in the county. There was a buzz I had never experienced in all my years living in Kildare. There were great performances but no trophies and the county board got rid of him with unseemly haste in the eyes of many.

'When he left it was like a cloud of gloom fell on the fans, especially among those who saw him as the Messiah – the only one who could deliver an All-Ireland to Kildare. It was like watching a bicycle getting a puncture and seeing the air drifting out of it.'

In a job in which your reputation is your currency, Earley's recent history did not help matters much:

'There were some older fans who saw me as the man who had played so long for Roscommon but there were others who saw me as someone who had failed as a manager in Roscommon. Worse still in the eyes of some my biggest crime was that I wasn't Mick O'Dwyer. The mood music was never right.'

Seasons came and seasons went. Dermot's two-year term was not a success:

'The lads tried hard. I tried hard. We had some good performances in the league but we weren't consistent enough. It was frustrating because we had some great players and I knew there was great potential in the squad. These were a group of lads who could go somewhere if we all brought our A game to the big matches. The cold, harsh reality is that I won not a single Leinster Championship match with Kildare.'

As things started to unravel his family had to get used to this absorption of his: he would sometimes sit through a meal without speaking, not noticing what he ate, sometimes laying down his knife and fork before his plate was empty, thinking about the problem, his brow heavy with worry:

'When we lost the second year I was in the position no GAA manager wants to be in: standing on the sideline after losing a big match with disappointed players, fans and a county board to be faced, and Marty Morrissey effectively asking me on live television if I was going to consider my position.

'We were beaten and the story could only end one way. Again. Oscar Wilde would have had a field day. To lose one job was bad enough. To lose two in a row in such a short time seemed like carelessness.'

The shadow Kildare cast was broadened and darkened by their long years in the wilderness and had the fierce commitment of their people pressing at their backs like a forest fire. It was time for the Lilywhites to revive an old friendship. Sometimes old flames are better not rekindled. Not in this case for Dermot Earley:

'In 1964 Joe Lennon published a book called *Coaching Gaelic Football for Champions*. Mick O'Dwyer made a point of not reading it. It didn't seem to do him any harm. The great leader is the one who enthuses others to rally to the cause. He had that gift. Kerry would have won All-Irelands without him because they had so many talented players but they would not have won eight. He kept them wanting to come back for more.

'Micko was brought back to Kildare and I have to take my hat off to him and give him great credit because he turned the team around and made them one of the best sides in the country, winning two Leinster titles, which was a fantastic achievement.

'How can I put this tactfully? He was very imaginative in his recruitment of players from "outside"! There were some players coming through within the county, like my own son Dermot, and the new injection of talent combined with the experience of the older lads made them a force to be reckoned with.'

Dermot Earley Jnr would help the Kildare team managed by O'Dwyer to beat Kerry in the All-Ireland semi-final in 1998. He saw his manager's genius up close and personal in his half-time talk in the 2000 Leinster final replay against Dublin, which saw Kildare overturn a six-point deficit at the interval to win by five:

'I think one of the things Micko was very good at was calming the situation. Micko said, "We're not playing well. These are the things we're not doing good. This is what I want you to do, and now just go out and do it."'

GALLING

The love of football legends is evident throughout Kerry. In Waterville Mick O'Dwyer is cast in bronze in his prime, selling a dummy. Legend has it that Micko waved at it every time he passed it.

When I asked Dwyer about it, he recalled: 'On the day of the unveiling, a number of fellas who went to school with me said: "This fella will be here and we'll be long gone."'

Close by is a monument to Charlie Chaplin, who loved visiting Waterville from his first appearance there in 1959. That was the year Micko won his first All-Ireland Senior football medal.

Another case in point is the beautiful town of Sneem which has a life-size bronze monument to one of the star forwards of Mick O'Dwyer's famous team of the 1970s and 1980s, John Egan.

More surprising, though, is that a few hundred yards further down the town is a large limestone boulder which marks the commemoration of Charles de Gaulle's 1969 visit to Sneem.

Shortly after resigning the presidency of France, de Gaulle and his wife Yvonne sought sanctuary from the political fallout and came to Ireland. In pursuit of a haven of peace and tranquillity for some quiet contemplation, they spent two weeks on vacation. Apparently, de Gaulle felt a great kinship with the Irish Liberator Daniel O'Connell, and knowing O'Connell was from the region, chose to spend time there to regain perspective on his political career.

His visit was not without incident. He was so tall that the hotel had to procure a new bed to accommodate him. The Kerry wit is evident in the name locals give the monument: 'The Gallstone'.

33

WITH A LITTLE HELP FROM OUR FRIENDS

Bansha

Courage is being scared to death but saddling up anyway.
JOHN WAYNE

The Tipperary village of Bansha was famous seventy years ago because Canon Hayes, a founder of Muintir na Tíre, lived there. He was not actually from Tipperary, he was from Limerick, but as the locals said that was not his fault.

John Hayes was born in a Land League hut. The family had been evicted from Lord Cloncurry's estate in 1872 for non-payment of rent and spent twelve years there.

After the eviction of the Hayes family from their farm in Moher, Murroe, Co Limerick, the local Land League moved quickly into action, erecting a wooden hut on the side of the road at Ballyvoreen for them. They were to live in this temporary accommodation for nearly thirteen years until they returned to Moher in 1894. During their time in the hut, four more children were born to Michael and Hanora Hayes, including their son

John Martin, who was born in 1887. Seven of the Hayes children died during their time in the hut.

The fact that John Martin was born in such dire circumstances, 'on the side of the road' as he put it, undoubtedly fuelled his determination to improve the lot of rural inhabitants.

After deciding he had a vocation for the priesthood, in 1905 he went to St Patrick's ecclesiastical college in Thurles, Co Tipperary, where he remained for three years. He then received a free place at the Irish College in Paris. There he developed a great love of Paris, where one of the highlights of his stay was the beatification of St Joan of Arc (1909).

After he was ordained in 1913 Fr Hayes quickly immersed himself in community activities. This led him to establish the first unit of Muintir na Tíre in Tipperary town in November 1937 to nurture the development of communities in rural Ireland. It was to act as a rural self-help group based on collective parish organisation with a strong emphasis on the teaching of the Church. It quickly became part of the fabric of national life.

In 1946, Canon Hayes left Tipperary Town to become Parish Priest of Bansha and Kilmoyler. He lobbied the Department of Agriculture over the lack of agricultural industry in the Tipperary region and began organising rural weekends where activists and educators debated rural issues, based on the French semaines rurales (weekend in the countryside).

The canon had great charisma and was way ahead of his time with his emphasis on community co-operation and community integration. He was a major advocate for sharing and voluntarism. His philosophy was that you start building a society brick by brick from the bottom up. You would put up with a lot if you have a community – a balanced community he used to call it with young and old, rich and poor. To be a member of that community was to be in touch with the poor and those in need – but he was worried that we were not in touch any more. It was taken for granted that the old were treated with respect and that the strong took care of the weak, regardless of age or social status. Those who marched to a different drum and to an outsider might be considered eccentric were neither ridiculed nor feared but were accepted as just one other face of the varied community.

Hayes quickly became a national figure, using newspapers and radio to spread the gospel of rural self-help. Insisting on a non-sectarian association, he memorably reminded those who advocated an exclusive Catholic membership that 'this country is becoming so Catholic it forgets to be Christian', and he began relentlessly to organise social weeks, vocational education, and summer schools.

One of the highlights of the canon's career was his address to the Pioneer Association in Croke Park in June 1949 on the occasion of the Pioneers' golden jubilee – the largest Catholic gathering seen in Dublin since the Eucharistic Congress in 1932. His mantra was that 'real Ireland is rural Ireland, and rural Ireland is Ireland true to Christ'.

The canon died in 1957. He dominated the parish, a colossus in a small area. His funeral was a national media event. Not alone was news of his death covered on Radio Éireann, but they announced a few days previously that he was critically ill.

Canon Hayes' true epitaph is written in the memory of his people because community is about people. His philosophy is as relevant now as it was seventy years ago because it was about encouraging people to ask: How can we help? This ethos lives on today in the GAA in Tipperary and beyond.

Matt Nugent was typical of the old ways – a man who was totally committed to the GAA. He died watching a Munster under-21 final in Thurles. He could not have died in a more appropriate way. Of course, he read attentively about Babs Keating's awe-inspiring feats as both a hurler and footballer in the local Bible, *The Clonmel Nationalist*.

Despite the intensity of the rivalries in hurling Jimmy Doyle was particularly proud of hurling's tradition of sporstmanship. One parable which illustrates this came in the 1958 All-Ireland semi-final between Tipperary and Kilkenny when he scored eight points off Paddy Buggy. After the match a Kilkenny supporter asked Paddy, 'What happened – why didn't you hit him?'

Buggy replied, 'Why should I? He didn't hit me.'

The late John Moloney was one of the all-time great inter-county referees. However, he personified the ethos of Tipperary hurling. His philosophy was best summed up in the old Irish adage Mol an óige agus tiocfaidh siad (encourage the young and they will flourish). He was very active in organising juvenile hurling and football and was very influential in developing and conditioning young players for future life. He was a native of Bansha and his club was Galtee Rovers/St Pecaun's. The latter part of the name came from the fact that within the townland of Toureen there was the ruins of a monastery associated with St Pecaun and every year there was a pattern on 1 August – which was a mix of a religious and social event and was a huge occasion in the area. There was also a sports day on the first Sunday of August.

Moloney embodied the ethos of Canon Hayes. He would cram twelve or fourteen lads into his car to take them to matches. It was an awfully big adventure for them because going on a trip from Bansha to Golden, Cashel, Tipperary Town, Emly and Lisvernane then was as big a deal as going to New York.

An essential element of the appeal of Gaelic games, that extra quality that distinguishes them from all other sports in Ireland, is the tribalism on which the structures are based. No other sports enjoy the intense rivalry that exists in the GAA between clubs and counties. From time to time this creates problems, but in the main it generates a sense of community which has been all but lost in contemporary Irish society.

THE FINAL WHISTLE

Home, is where I want to be
But I guess I'm already there.

TALKING HEADS

I gave up being a perfectionist when I attended the wedding of a prominent camogie player. In truth I was surprised that she got married. A few years earlier she had defined a bachelor for me: 'A man so selfish he cheats a good woman out of a divorce.'

As would be expected, with her attention to detail everything ran like clockwork during the wedding ceremony. Well, almost everything. She was so concerned that the pageboy would let the wedding ring fall as he headed to the altar to present it to the happy couple that she had stitched it with surgical precision to the ceremonial cushion. The problem was that she forgot that scissors would be needed to release the ring. After a few moments of chaos and confusion the blushing bride (literally) ripped away the stitch with her teeth. It made for an unforgettable wedding especially when she told me that she was bringing her wool and knitting needles on her honeymoon.

When I asked her why, she told me that she was going to be: Weaving on a Jet Plane.

Th experience of that day has cured me of any temptation to cover every significant location in the history of the GAA in this book.

Time is the moving image of eternity. Our creative activities participate in the cosmic story which sees us simultaneously continuing and extending that process, while also from time to time returning to its source.

There are still the odd bumps on the road. In May, Kilkenny and Dublin faced off in the Leinster Senior camogie semi-final; however, before the match could get going, both teams initially came onto the pitch wearing shorts instead of the regulatory 'skorts', and almost saw the match being completely called off as a result. This is because under rule 6(b) of the sport's code, playing gear must include a skirt/skort/divided skirt.

Dublin star Aisling Maher described the 'skortgate' episode:

'Career low for me today when sixty plus players ready to play a championship game in shorts are told their match will be abandoned if every player doesn't change into skorts. I love this game but I am sick of being forced to wear a skort that is uncomfortable and unfit for purpose. How are female players still having to push for permission to wear shorts while they compete at the highest level of their sport? In no other facet of my life does someone dictate that I have to wear something resembling a skirt because I am a girl. Why is it happening in my sport?'

It is a case of a lot done but more to do when it comes to the integration of women in the GAA. There are lessons to be learned from other Irish sports like rugby. To take one example, in 2023 Roscommon native Su Carty was elected to the prestigious Executive Board of World Rugby. She has a long history with Irish rugby, having played for twelve years with St Mary's

College RFC and UL Bohemians. She has been a referee for a number of years and won the Alain Rolland Award for Referee Performance in 2017. She was the last president of the Ireland Women's Rugby Football Union, which was dissolved in June 2008. She is also a member of the IRFU committee. She is one of the IRFU representatives to World Rugby. She was appointed Women's Development Manager with World Rugby in 2009 and served in the role for seven years. In 2018, she was voted Irish Woman of the Year for her work in advancing women's rugby on a global scale. Her comments have a powerful contemporary resonance for the GAA:

'Inclusivity is essential in cultivating a warm and welcoming atmosphere for clubs. It is not just about the players on the pitch, we need more females in coaching and leadership roles in our clubs. Sport can play such a vital role in a young girl's life, making it easy to access and engaging more female voices is vital to drive women's sports to new levels in Ireland.'

However, there are also advances. The new football rules are a good illustration of this. In the words of Joe Brolly: 'The robot era is over, long live Gaelic football. The game that was dead has risen again along with all the emotions that used to go with it.' Evidence to support this claim was provided by Donegal's Ulster title win over All-Ireland champions Armagh in a pulsating provincial decider played out in glorious sunshine in front of 28,788 fans in Clones.

Since 1884 the GAA have kept the home fires burning.

It has been a beacon of light in the darkness of night.

It glows like a fire and shines like a star.

To this day one of my favourite TV ads is the one for Aer Lingus with the powerful caption 'You're home', and the accompanying air of 'Gabriel's Oboe'; back in the days when most of us lived in two-channel land.

THE FINAL WHISTLE

The places we have considered speak to us beyond our limited words, definitions and language. They speak on behalf of others and are the medium for a myriad of voices and stories. They serve as symbols of hope. They have paths marked with traces of love, the scent of memory and the enchantment of the games. The best journeys take you to hearth and home.

These are the locations that hint that if you can't give your heart to the GAA you have no heart to give. They kindle our imagination and transport us to a realm where emotions harmonise. They are a reminder that Gaelic games wield an unparalleled storytelling power, capable of weaving tales as captivating as any cinematic script, leaving an enduring impact on our hearts and thoughts – sometimes so fine as to be invisible to the naked eye.

Like a single candle burning in an empty church, a bad day in the GAA is perhaps better than a good day anywhere else.

With Gaelic games life is beautiful.

An áit ina bhfuil t'anam is ann a thógas do chosa tú.
Your feet will always take you to the place of your soul.

ACKNOWLEDGEMENTS

I am profoundly honoured that the legendary Michael Lyster wrote the foreword for this book.

Special thanks to Danielle Caldwell, Brendan Coffey, Bernard Flynn, Brendan Graham, Dave McGreevy, Paul McKiernan, Leo Moran, Ailish O'Reilly and Jason Sherlock.

I am profoundly grateful to David Hickey for teaching me that success is not final, failure is not fatal: it is the courage to continue that counts.

Special thanks to Emma Dennis whose story made me want to laugh and cry simultaneously.

Thanks to all at Black & White for backing this book so enthusiastically. My thanks also to Simon Hess and Declan Heeney for their great support.

Gareth O'Callaghan knows that true compassion means not only feeling another's pain but also being moved to help relieve it. I am greatly enriched by his friendship.

Brian D'Arcy has been a constant supporter of my books. He always displays the ability and desire to have a positive impact on others.

ACKNOWLEDGEMENTS

Thanks to the best of the West, Dave O'Connell, for his enduring promotion of my books.

Thanks too to Shannonside's Kevin McDermott for his practical support.

Thanks to the wonderful Dee O'Donnell for her ongoing support of my books.

January saw the passing of Noel Daly, a proud Clare man from Sixmilebridge, who held a county hurling medal for Cloughduv from 1956. More importantly, he is remembered by his daughter Susan as 'my lovely Da'. This soul needs to be honoured.

We also lost Hugh Gerard O'Neill (everyone called him 'Gerry'). An avid GAA supporter who enjoyed watching club and county matches. He was thrilled when local club Errigal Ciaran secured their eleventh Tyrone Senior Football Championship in 2024. He will be much missed by his son Darren and a wide circle of family and friends.

During Holy Week Wilfrid Harrington O.P. went to his God. He was a formidable intellect, a distinguished scholar and a good and kind man.

He will be much missed by his Dominican family and the community of the Priory Institute.

After thirty-three remarkable years of service, sincerity and selflessness Patricia Seery has reached the stage where she has decided it is time to say goodbye to her teaching career. She leaves the pitch having made an incalculable contribution to so many young people, mentoring them with humour, patience and kindness. May the road rise to meet her and may the wind be at her back in the next exciting chapter in the game of life. May all her skies be blue.

Beannachtaí.

ALSO BY JOHN SCALLY

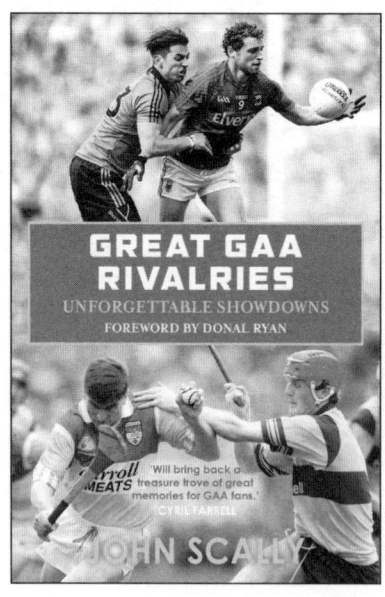

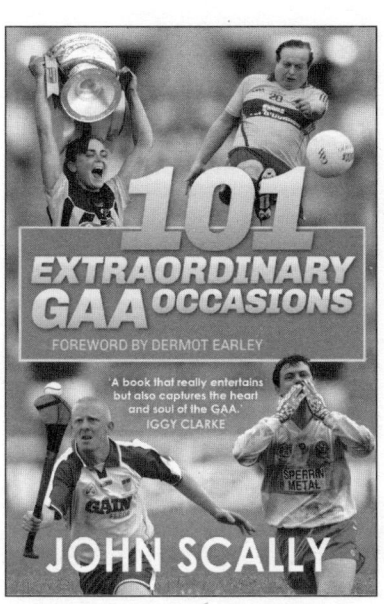

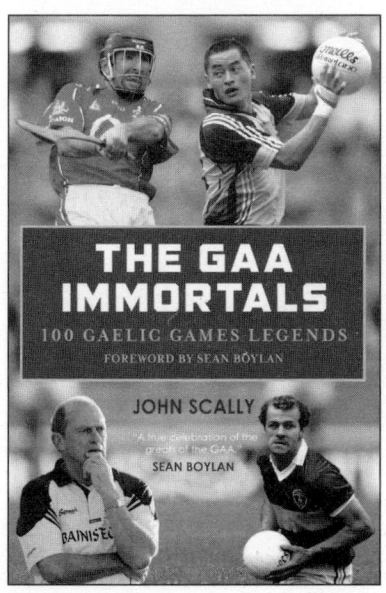
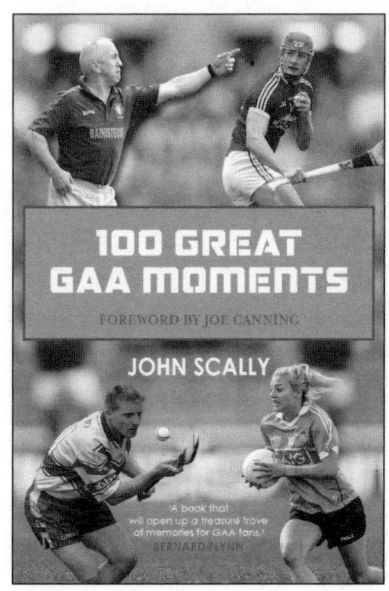

ABOUT JOHN SCALLY

A native of Roscommon John Scally is the author of over 50 books. These include the bestselling *Great GAA Rivalries*; *101 Great GAA Teams* and *101 Great GAA Controversies*. He is a two time winner of the McNamee Award for best programme on national radio on a GAA theme.